The
Silent Past
and the
Invisible Present

RELATIONAL PERSPECTIVES BOOK SERIES

Volume 54

RELATIONAL PERSPECTIVES BOOK SERIES

LEWIS ARON & ADRIENNE HARRIS
Series Editors

The Relational Perspectives Book Series (RPBS) publishes books that grow out of or contribute to the relational tradition in contemporary psychoanalysis. The term *relational psychoanalysis* was first used by Greenberg and Mitchell (1983) to bridge the traditions of interpersonal relations, as developed within interpersonal psychoanalysis and object relations, as developed within contemporary British theory. But, under the seminal work of the late Stephen Mitchell, the term *relational psychoanalysis* grew and began to accrue to itself many other influences and developments. Various tributaries—interpersonal psychoanalysis, object relations theory, self psychology, empirical infancy research, and elements of contemporary Freudian and Kleinian thought—flow into this tradition, which understands relational configurations between self and others, both real and fantasied, as the primary subject of psychoanalytic investigation.

We refer to the relational tradition, rather than to a relational school, to highlight that we are identifying a trend, a tendency within contemporary psychoanalysis, not a more formally organized or coherent school or system of beliefs. Our use of the term *relational* signifies a dimension of theory and practice that has become salient across the wide spectrum of contemporary psychoanalysis. Now under the editorial supervision of Lewis Aron and Adrienne Harris, the Relational Perspectives Book Series originated in 1990 under the editorial eye of the late Stephen A. Mitchell. Mitchell was the most prolific and influential of the originators of the relational tradition. He was committed to dialogue among psychoanalysts and he abhorred the authoritarianism that dictated adherence to a rigid set of beliefs or technical restrictions. He championed open discussion, comparative and integrative approaches, and he promoted new voices across the generations.

Included in the Relational Perspectives Book Series are authors and works that come from within the relational tradition, extend and develop the tradition, as well as works that critique relational approaches or compare and contrast it with alternative points of view. The series includes our most distinguished senior psychoanalysts along with younger contributors who bring fresh vision.

RELATIONAL PERSPECTIVES BOOK SERIES

LEWIS ARON & ADRIENNE HARRIS
Series Editors

The
Silent Past
and the
Invisible Present

—————

Memory, Trauma, and Representation
in Psychotherapy

Paul Renn

Foreword by Judith Guss Teicholz

Routledge
Taylor & Francis Group

New York   London

Routledge
Taylor & Francis Group
711 Third Avenue
New York, NY 10017

Routledge
Taylor & Francis Group
27 Church Road
Hove, East Sussex BN3 2FA

© 2012 by Taylor & Francis Group, LLC

Routledge is an imprint of the Taylor & Francis Group, an informa business

International Standard Book Number: 978-0-415-89858-4 (Hardback) 978-0-415-89859-1 (Paperback)

Library of Congress Cataloging-in-Publication Data

Renn, Paul.
 The silent past and the invisible present : memory, trauma, and representation in psychotherapy / Paul Renn.
  p. cm. -- (The relational perspectives book series ; vol. 54)
 Includes bibliographical references and index.
 ISBN 978-0-415-89858-4 (hardcover : alk. paper) -- ISBN 978-0-415-89859-1 (pbk. : alk. paper) -- ISBN 978-0-203-12686-8 (alk. paper)
 1. Memory. 2. Psychic trauma. 3. Psychotherapy. I. Title.

BF371.R383 2012
150.19'5--dc23   2011035106

Visit the Taylor & Francis Web site at
http://www.taylorandfrancis.com

and the Routledge Web site at
http://www.routledgementalhealth.com

To Anne, Nic, Claire, and Rosa

Contents

Foreword

Judith Guss Teicholz

This book may signal the latest in a near-century of revolutions roiling psycho-analysis. Renn's, however, is a dignified, respectful, and peaceful revolution.

He both describes and contributes to profound changes in theory and practice that have emerged largely in response to findings from new empirical research conducted across diverse academic disciplines and presented here in lucid and measured prose.

Not so long ago, postmodern attitudes led us to question the value of seeking objective "truths" through scientific study as a basis for understanding and diminishing the suffering of our patients. Now, Renn goes a long way toward restoring our belief in the value of such seeking while at the same time highlighting the cocreated, elusive, and hard-won "truths" that can only emerge from intersubjective experience. With his integrative approach Renn in no way suggests that these two approaches to reality might contradict each other. Rather, he takes as a given that the different ways of thinking about the clinical situation are mutually enhancing, and he seems to make them so.

Renn's project also dissolves much of the tension that until recently divided analysts adhering to different theories coexisting under a broad relational umbrella. These theories have included American relational and interpersonal psychoanalysis as well as a contemporary self psychology largely coinciding with intersubjective nonlinear dynamic systems theory. Renn downplays any distinctions among these theories by focusing on the latest findings from cognitive and developmental psychology, from attachment and trauma studies, from infant–caregiver research, and from neuroscience—in particular, a new understanding of the implicit and explicit memory systems and their functioning. In these findings there is affirmation to be found for the basic tenets of all relational theories, an affirmation that enables Renn to sustain a beautifully balanced approach to his topic while also seeming to embody something close to passion in his commitment to the central concepts and clinical recommendations of all the (formerly) competing theories.

In addition to these achievements, Renn has developed his own clinical model based on an integration of the research findings he describes. He explains and demonstrates his model by reviewing the relevant research while also interweaving the life history, the therapeutic exchanges, and the treatment trajectory for each patient whose psychotherapy he presents. Because his patient population consists largely of men imprisoned for violent crimes, the seeming ease with which Renn is able to facilitate significant changes in their minds and lives would ordinarily defy belief on the part of his readers and fellow psychotherapists. But Renn earns our trust with his step-by-step report of the research, followed with his step-by-step report of the treatments. His case studies are all the more persuasive because they include the disappointments and setbacks as well as the forward and more hope-filled movements in his patients' lives.

From a conceptual viewpoint, Renn gives no hint that he actually set out with the intent of resolving earlier areas of disagreement among the different relational theories, and perhaps some of these disagreements have been more salient in North American psychoanalysis than in Great Britain or other parts of the world. But the recent convergence of findings from neuroscience, attachment studies, and infant–caregiver research may eventually serve to bring into closer alignment diverse theories that have historically divided psychoanalytic communities not only within, but also across, national boundaries. It is not terribly difficult to see how British object relations theories might be included in such alignment, but it is admittedly more of a stretch to imagine a unified theory that could meld some of the central ideas from such communities as the French Lacanian or Latin American Kleinian/Bionian. Even so, the research findings reported by Renn have already begun to blur some of the previously drawn lines among the different relational theories within North America (Teicholz, 2009).

This blurring of prior theoretical boundaries, as well as the inclusive scientific affirmation for our several versions of relational theory, is of particular interest because until recently these theories have been seen as alternative ways to conceptualize human development and psychic change. Now, based on the work Renn presents here, it would seem that all three of these relational theories have gotten most things right (albeit with differing emphases) and that together they provide our most comprehensive understanding of human development to date, as well as an effective approach to psychic change through psychoanalytically oriented psychotherapy—even when such treatment is offered in abbreviated form to an unaccustomed (forensic) population as it is in Renn's ample clinical material.

In reaching as he does for synthesis, Renn understandably does not deconstruct his clinical model to identify which research findings might coincide most closely with which of the diverse but overlapping relational theories. But in order to appreciate better the cosmic shifts currently affecting the multifaceted field of relational psychoanalysis, I shall transiently "undo" Renn's magnificent synthesis by trying to identify some of the specific earlier theoretical and clinical controversies that now seem to be disappearing in the face of the research findings that Renn describes. If the diminishment of difference among formerly more distinct theories continues to evolve, then my endeavor in these pages may represent a "last gasp" of comparative psychoanalysis, before such a project becomes no longer necessary or even meaningful.

I shall organize my comments primarily around the concepts of self and relationship, which have been a major focus of contemporary theorists in recent years, though at times seen differently from one relational theory to the next. As will soon become evident, even these two concepts turn out to be difficult to address independently of one another because in all theories under discussion and in lived experience as well, self and relationship seem to constitute something of an endless feedback loop between them.

SELF-IN-RELATIONSHIP

As founder of the late-20th century psychoanalytic self psychology movement, Kohut (1971, 1977, 1984) used a language that straddled modern and postmodern thinking (Teicholz, 1999) and thereby left his concept of *self* open to (mis)interpretation, in which it was sometimes understood to signify a singular and bounded entity. However, Kohut's closely related and equally important concept of *selfobject* left no doubt that his self was a complexly organized, fluid, permeable, ever-changing, and multifaceted process that from the start could evolve only in interaction with others in the human environment. In Kohut's view the self–selfobject system or milieu was in constant flux and shifting always among multiple self-states under the influence of relational engagement. This Kohutian understanding of the self fits well with a postmodern characterization of the concept and is compatible with how it has been seen by American relational psychoanalysts (Mitchell, 1997) as well as by others outside self psychology (Barratt, 1993; Ogden, 1992).

In Kohut's concept of selfobject, the self and the other engage from the start in a constant exchange of psychic "content" or influence and are, therefore, mutually constituted. In all relational theories, the self is originally constituted and then constantly revised through intersubjective processes, from birth until death. This view of the self has now been confirmed by all facets of the research presented by Renn with an emphasis on the relational context of individual development and the constant exchange of unintended and often unregistered influence between interacting partners at all levels of experience (Beebe, 2005; Beebe & Lachmann, 1988a, 1988b) as well as brain function (Bucci, 2011; Schore, 2011; Siegel, 1991).

In all relational theories today, the self and self-in-relationship are two sides of the same coin (Shane, 2006) and *affect* is the predominant organizing (or disorganizing) experience in their development (Demos, 1988; Socarides & Stolorow, 1984; Stern, 1985). As Bucci (2011) has written, "Emotion schemas are types of memory structures that constitute the organization of the self in the interpersonal world. They are formed on the basis of repeated interactions with caretakers and others from the beginning of life" (p. 49). In other words, the organization of the self is constituted through the affective experiences evoked by (and contributing to) the individual's repeated interactions with caregivers and others, from birth onward. As previously mentioned, this is the neuroscientist's view, but it is also the view of Kohut (1971, 1977, 1984) in his notion of self–self-object relationship, and of Stolorow, Brandchaft, and Atwood (1987) in their notion of intersubjectivity. It is probably something close to what Winnicott (1960) meant when he wrote that "there is no such thing as an infant... without maternal care" (p. 39, fn); it is compatible as well with Mitchell's (1997) and others' relational thinking in which the sense of self is seen to develop only in and through the individual's intimate relationships with important others.

Working from a biological model, there is current consensus among researchers and psychoanalysts that the self is an open system continuously forming larger and more complex systems in interaction with others (Coburn, 2006; Lyons-Ruth, 1999; Trevarthen, 2005; Tronick, 2007). It is exactly because the individual sense of self develops only in intimate exchange with another—and because minds are permeable, fluid, and ever-changing—that psychotherapy, involving as it does a psychologically intimate relationship between patient and therapist, can provide an opportunity for change in new directions. When things go well enough in this uniquely structured relationship, "positive" psychic growth can emerge. Nevertheless Renn rightly acknowledges that this potential for change can move toward either constructive or destructive ends.

INTEGRATION AND RELATEDNESS

One of self psychology's primary treatment goals is to strengthen the (sense of) self by integrating previously split-off or dissociated experience. Such integration is understood by self psychologists to be facilitated by attuned engagement in the therapeutic relationship. In presenting his clinical material, Renn spells out specific kinds of interactions that can foster processes of integration in the patient, such as repeatedly focusing on the details of the patient's dissociated traumatic experience and thereby bringing it into the therapeutic exchange.

In self psychology, there is an additional treatment goal seen as equal in importance to integration, namely enhancement of the patient's capacity to (co)create sustaining relationships outside of the clinical situation—relationships in which mutual empathy will be a significant feature. Similar to self psychology in the matter of treatment goals, relational psychoanalysis also privileges the expansion of self through relationship (Mitchell, 1988, 1993, 1997) and the development of intersubjective relatedness (Benjamin, 1988, 1990; Ogden, 1992; Stern, 1985), a relatedness which has much in common with mutual attunement or empathy (Teicholz, 2001). Thus each of these two relational theories centers its treatment goals on the development, integration, and enhancement of self toward an increasing capacity for intimacy in sustaining relationships. Renn's clinical material makes clear how the failure of such integration, caused by the dissociative response to early trauma, contributes to his patients' unbearable sense of isolation by interfering with their later capacity to negotiate satisfying relationships. Their failure of integration also leaves them vulnerable to enacting, in the form of violent and criminal behaviors, aspects of their past and painful affective experiences.

TWO KINDS OF INTERSUBJECTIVITY: MUTUAL REGULATION AND MUTUAL RECOGNITION

Thus far, I have for the most part highlighted historical areas of agreement among the differing relational theories. But there have been areas of disagreement as well, and one way to look at these is in terms of their (until now) differential focus on two conceptually distinct but overlapping kinds of intersubjectivity. Self psychology has usually emphasized the intersubjectivity (or mutuality) of *regulation* (Lachmann & Beebe, 1996a), while relational and interpersonal psychoanalysts have placed greater emphasis on the intersubjectivity (or mutuality) of *recognition* (Benjamin, 1988, 1990). In American relational psychoanalysis, recognition refers to the appreciation of unique mind (or of individual psychic life) in both self and other.

The recognition of unique mind in self and other is called "intersubjective relatedness" in the work of both Stern (1985) and Ogden (1992). It is an achievement close in meaning to Kohut's ultimate goal of treatment: the exchange of mutual empathy in which both individuals appreciate the minds of self and others as unique, but also as capable of mutual sharing, understanding, and resonance (Stern, 1985; Teicholz, 2001). By comparison, American relational and interpersonal theorists—in privileging mutual recognition of mind—have placed a higher value on the experience of interpersonal difference and the negotiation of conflict than have traditional self psychologists.

These different theoretical emphases—on regulation and attunement in self psychology versus on recognition and difference in relational psychoanalysis—have had important consequences for the clinical approaches advocated by adherents to the two theories. Self psychologists see affective resonance and empathic understanding as likely to enhance the patient's capacities for self- and mutual-affect regulation as well as to increase the patient's access to previously disavowed and split-off experience, which can then be integrated and interactively engaged. By comparison, the greater emphasis by relational and interpersonal theorists on the analyst's expression of her unique and disjunctive subjectivity not only necessitates the negotiation of difference and conflict between patient and analyst, but also highlights the analyst's inevitable participation in enactments as an ongoing aspect of the treatment relationship (Bromberg, 1996; Davies, 1997; Levenkron, 2006; Renik, 1998). The subsequent analysis of these enactments in relational psychoanalysis is seen as an enhanced opportunity for opening up windows to the unconscious (Davies, 2007).

When self psychologists analyze enactments in the treatment relationship they tend initially to search for and acknowledge their own unintended hurtful behavior toward their patients. Usually only *after* such acknowledgement do they seek to link these unwittingly hurtful behaviors on their parts to their patients' similar early experiences of hurt in the primary relationships of their childhoods. By contrast, relational and interpersonal analysts are more likely to explore the *patient's* experience and contribution to the enactment without first searching for and acknowledging unintended hurtful behavior on the therapist's part. All relational theories have been evolving, however—perhaps under the influence of each other as well as under the influence of the cumulating research findings reported in this book. And some relational psychoanalysts have more recently begun to argue for what was earlier a uniquely self-psychological approach, such as insisting that the analyst explicitly take responsibility for the ways that she has unintentionally hurt the patient (Benjamin, 2004).

In fact, advocates for all the relational theories have almost always acknowledged *both* kinds of intersubjectivity—regulation and recognition—in their views of human experience, even while tending to lead clinically with one kind of mutuality over the other. There have also been psychoanalytic authors who from the start have argued for the centrality of *both* regulation and recognition in human experience, an argument that provides support for both affective attunement *and* a fuller authentic self-expression on the part of the analyst in the treatment situation (Stern, 1985; Ogden, 1992; Stolorow, Brandchaft, & Atwood, 1987; Teicholz, 2000, 2001, 2006). For instance, based on his own and others' infant–caregiver observation research, Stern (1985) saw affective regulation as developmentally preceding recognition; but once both were initially established (late in the first year of life), he saw the two kinds of experiences as coexisting in fluctuation with each other throughout the life cycle. Based on his work with adults in psychoanalysis, Ogden (1992) arrived at an understanding of regulation and recognition very similar to Stern's research-based view. In particular, Ogden argued for a lifelong dialectic between recognition and nonrecognition, once the initial establishment of recognition was achieved in later infancy. Both Stern and Ogden saw recognition as a complex psychological achievement whose initial emergence could easily be derailed by less than optimal developmental conditions. Among those requisite conditions, in the view of these authors, was an adequate quality of affective attunement and regulation in the relationships of infancy and early childhood.

Meanwhile the phrase *mutual regulation* in all cases refers to mutual *affect* regulation, an experience central to much of the research Renn describes in this book. In the view of contemporary self psychologists but now also supported by decades of infant–caregiver observation research, affect regulation plays a major role in human development. All three of Lachmann and Beebe's (1996b) principles of salience in patient/analyst interaction include at least implicit reference to affective experience and its regulation. Lachmann and Beebe's principles include: (a) "ongoing regulation," referring to everyday interactions that accumulate to create an ongoing affect-regulating holding environment; (b) "heightened affective moments," referring to points of more intense emotional engagement between patient and analyst, either positive or negative, which serve to heighten (or diminish) affective arousal; and (c) disruption and repair, in which the mutual affective attunement between patient and analyst is inevitably and repeatedly ruptured, but in good-enough treatment those ruptures are reliably followed by relational exchanges in which there is open mutual exploration of the disruption with eventual restoration of the relationship to its previous (or improved) levels of mutual affective attunement.

In self psychology, it is through mutual affective *attunement* in relationship that affective *regulation* is achieved. But researchers have found that the optimal degree of attunement does *not* coincide with total resonance or with "perfect" affective tracking; rather, it coincides with something in the middle zone. The most secure children turn out to have enjoyed moderate or "good-enough" developmental attunement in their primary relationships, something less than constant and perfectly accurate emotional tracking, the latter of which—to the extent it is even possible—is associated with *inse*cure attachment in later childhood (Beebe et al., 2010; Beebe, Lachmann, & Jaffe, 1997). Also suggesting the benefits of moderate rather than perfect attunement is the notion of "marking" (Fonagy, Gergely, Jurist, & Target, 2002), in which the caregiver responds to the infant's facial expressions, sounds, and gestures with only approximate or slightly exaggerated mimicry, rather than with exact imitations of the young child's expressive productions. Such interactions "mark" the caregiver as affectively attuned, but also as distinct from the infant, a multifaceted experience that aligns both with the self-psychological emphasis on attunement and regulation and the relational/interpersonal emphasis on difference (Teicholz, 2009).

In keeping with this "both–and" approach to attunement and difference, Lachmann and Beebe's (1996a) initial focus on affect regulation has now been well-matched by their additional emphasis on such qualities of inter-action as spontaneity, surprise, and humor in the treatment relationship, qualities that Lachmann (2000) sees as no less facilitative of human development than attunement. Still, whereas for relational analysts these latter qualities of interaction are valued primarily as pathways to differentiation and mutual recognition, in Lachmann's (2000) work they are also valued because they can foster a sense of intimacy that necessarily involves recognition, but can also contribute to affect regulation. In particular, Lachmann sees these qualities of relationship—spontaneity, surprise, and humor—as holding the potential to increase or decrease arousal, or to enhance mood and self-esteem in the patient's experience, effects more closely related to affect regulation.

With affect regulation having been highlighted as it was in the late 20th century by all these psychoanalytic authors, it is not surprising that it has now become a central focus of infant–caregiver research as well as an essential feature in the findings from the neuroscientific study of brain development such as in the work of Schore (2003a, 2003b, 2011) and Bucci (1997, 2001, 2011), also reported in this book.

TRAUMA AND DISSOCIATION

In fact, given the importance attributed to affect regulation from so many different viewpoints, it makes sense that an abiding interest in trauma—defined as the experience of overwhelming and unprocessed affect—cuts across all three relational theories under discussion. Trauma is also a central focus of the way in which Renn understands his patients' painful experiences and violent behaviors. By definition, the affect accompanying trauma cannot in anyway be processed, contained, or regulated because of its surfeit of intensity in relation to the strength and complexity of the individual psyche under assault. Trauma, in other words, is any emotional experience that cannot be processed or regulated.

The human psyche has a built-in capacity to split off or dissociate from conscious awareness the indigestible experience of trauma in an attempt to preserve at least a modicum of psychic functioning in realms of living not directly associated with the traumatic devastation. Kohut (1971), Tolpin (2003), Bucci (2011), and others have highlighted the adaptive aspects of this psychic phenomenon even while acknowledging the extent to which it can seriously interfere with the individual's psychic life and relationships. Kohut's (1971) initial emphasis on psychic integration and cohesion emerged from his observation that psychic dissociation and fragmentation were ubiquitous in human functioning, mostly to detrimental effect. He came to see disavowal, splitting, and fragmentation as universal responses to inescapable childhood trauma both acute and cumulative. In his view, cumulative trauma was endemic to the human condition and the dissociative response to it a near-universal phenomenon. His privileging of relational attunement and empathy was intended to facilitate the healing of these traumatically induced splits in the personality.

Writing from an interpersonal tradition, Bromberg has also contributed an important body of work on dissociation suggesting a dialectic between empathy and anxiety (Bromberg, 1980, 1996). Bromberg's ideas are surprisingly compatible with Kohut's self psychology on these points in which he acknowledged a potentially facilitative dialectic between empathy and "optimal frustration" (Kohut, 1971, p. 50) or repeated cycles of relational disruption and repair. Davies and Frawley (1992) brought their own concern with trauma and dissociation to the relational literature with their groundbreaking work on the psychic ramifications of childhood sexual abuse and its impact on transference/countertransference in the treatment relationship. All these authors have recognized multiple dissociated self-states and have addressed the processes through which psychoanalytic treatment might bring rigidly dissociated and split-off states back into mutual exchange with the individual's more fluid, ever-changing, and yet also somewhat more abiding and predominant sense of self.

Renn's model of treatment builds on all these models, firmly supported by the latest research. In presenting his model he provides his readers with a clearly delineated guide to interacting with traumatized patients. The primary goal of these interactions is to move his patients toward better integration of painful experiences that had been previously split-off or dissociated. Such integration is expected to enable his patients to go forward in life with greater access to, and therefore better guided by, the feelings that constitute their affective worlds as these are increasingly linked through the therapeutic dialogue to their origins in the actual events and experiences of their personal histories.

Today, analysts adhering to all three psychoanalytic relational theories recognize the desirability of integration for emotional health, while at the same time highlighting the necessity for openness and flexibility of mind, brain, and psychic functioning. Neurobiologists give credence to this viewpoint that privileges both integration and openness—both stability and flexibility. They see the human brain (and mind) as an open biological system that, like all other biological systems, inherently moves toward both greater complexity/multiplicity *and* greater cohesion (Tronick, 2007).

ATTUNEMENT AND DIFFERENCE

As noted earlier, many of the distinctions previously drawn among our different relational theories centered on how much the analyst understands herself to be struggling for emotional attunement, understanding, and resonance with her patients toward the goal of greater mutual affect regulation and enhanced self-organization/integration, which in turn can expand the possibilities for greater mutuality and satisfaction in the relationship, versus how much the analyst undertakes to express her distinctive subjectivity in order to offer her patients growth-promoting experiences of "alterity" or difference also believed to foster integration and intersubjective relatedness. The research findings presented by Renn in this book seem to render these emphases more mutually compatible and inextricably intertwined than previously perceived in the eyes of some analysts.

One more reason for a diminishment in tension among the differing relational viewpoints (even beyond the accumulating empirical evidence) might be that all relational analysts now share a view of the therapist as an optimally engaged partner responding to the patient with an admixture of attunement and authentic self-expression (Teicholz, 2000). The therapist will sometimes amplify one of these modes of engagement over the other based on a conscious understanding of the patient's momentary needs and capacities, but also on the basis of nonconsciously communicated and nonconsciously perceived psychic states in both patient and analyst. These implicit as well as explicit exchanges between patient and analyst inevitably include the incessant back-and-forth of mutual influence at emotional, procedural, presymbolic, or right-brain levels of experience in which much of psychic growth and healing occurs—importantly including the development, disruption, and repeated repair of the self (Beebe, 2005; Lachmann & Beebe, 1996; Lyons-Ruth, 1999; Schore, 2011).

EMPATHY AND COLLABORATIVE COMMUNICATION

Today, most relational analysts accept that the ongoing experience of mutual attunement (centrally including its inevitable and repeated ruptures and repairs) is a fundamental building block of personhood *along with* repeated opportunities for authentic relational engagement in which difference is experienced and negotiated. In these interactions, mutually expressed exchanges of unique psychic experiences between dyadic partners influence one another back-and-forth to the extent that each partner to the relationship contributes to the very "substance" of the other's mind, always to some degree open to expansion and revision.

In regard to the first of these kinds of experiences—namely affective attunement, resonance, or empathic understanding—neuroscientists have recently discovered mirror neurons that are activated very soon after birth, denoting an inborn capacity to register even at the level of neurological firing, the feelings and intentions of others (Decety & Jackson, 2006). Within days of birth, this "empathy" in the neurological domain is matched at the behavioral level as infants engage in mutual mimicry with their caregivers, readily exchanging imitative gestural, postural, and facial expressions (Trevarthen, 2005). Trevarthen sees these active mimicking behaviors in newborns as forerunners to empathy and playfulness, as well as to the later exploration of psychic worlds in self and other. All of these findings suggest that empathy is operative almost from the start of life and that for optimal development it must be met by a matching empathy from the human environment.

With each developmental step forward the infant may feel exhilarated by his or her newfound capacities, but also rendered psychically more vulnerable during these transitional periods. A transient increase in empathy from caregivers at such times can enable the infant to consolidate the new and still-shaky developmental achievements as the infant moves forward to the next set of challenges (Kohut & Seitz, 1978; Stern, 1985). These findings are surprisingly relevant to Renn's clinical material even though his patients have all become prisoners of Britain's adult penal system by the time he introduces them to us. The relevance to the research can be found in the fact that his patients were all once also "child prisoners" of families in which an essential attunement was chronically absent, sometimes in the presence of extreme neglect and abuse as well. Not just Renn but also Lachmann (2000) has written of the frequency with which violent criminals are found to have suffered extremes of childhood neglect, abuse, and trauma, presumably contributing to their later criminally destructive behaviors.

Adding to the expanding research on affect attunement and regulation, developmental scientists have recently identified a certain kind of interchange between infants and their caregivers shown to be essential for later secure attachment in children. The researchers have labeled these kinds of exchanges as "collaborative communication" (Beebe et al., 2010; Lyons-Ruth, 1999; Tronick, 2007), by which they mean a communication process marked by openness, flexibility, and inclusion. More specifically, collaborative communication encourages the mutual expression in relationship of the full range of human emotions both positive and negative. This inclusive dialogue encompasses the empathic responsiveness and mutual attunement of self psychology as well as the authenticity particularly valued by relational and interpersonal analysts. Such authenticity is understood to entail an alignment or resonance between an individual's internal affective experience and its interpersonal expression (Teicholz, 2000).

Thus, we see that the research findings reported in this book implicitly affirm the human need for experiences in which the partners to a relationship can provide each other with a mutual exchange of affective resonance and understanding as well as opportunities for the expression of interpersonal differences and negotiation of conflict. We have apparent consensus concerning the centrality of mutual attunement in early development, but we also have Stern (1985), Benjamin (1988), and Ogden's (1992) "recognition of mind"; Lichtenberg's (1989) "adversive" motivation; Lachmann & Beebe's (1996a) "heightened affective moments"; Stern et al.'s (1998) "now moments"; Lachmann's (2000) "perturbations" and "violations of expectations" (Lachmann, 2008); or Bromberg's (2009) "safe surprises," all of these notions suggesting a rationale—now confirmed by diverse scientific studies—for the judicious but authentic expression of the analyst's disjunctive subjectivity in the treatment relationship as originally recommended by interpersonal and relational psychoanalysts. Still, in all relational theories it is either (explicitly) stated or (implicitly) assumed that in order to promote psychic growth, these important experiences of engagement must emerge in dyads where empathic understanding and affective resonance have already been established and will be re-established again and again, after their inevitably repeated losses.

In fact—whether we look at the formerly competing theories in terms of their different stances on empathy versus authenticity, in terms of their different stances on attunement versus conflict negotiation, or in terms of their different stances on cohesion versus multiplicity—none of these contrasting emphases was ever really seen as mutually exclusive in any of the theories. Analysts committed to each of the differing theories have always fully expected the clinical emphasis to shift flexibly among these various approaches from patient to patient, as well during the course of any given analysis (Benjamin, 1988, 1990; 2008; Mitchell, 1991, 1993, 1997; Teicholz, 1995, 1996, 1998, 1999, 2000, 2001, 2006a, 2006b, 2009).

RENN'S CLINICAL MODEL, MOVING TOWARD A MORE UNIFIED PSYCHOANALYTIC THEORY

As Renn's presentation makes evident, much of the new research has helped us to break down our more general and abstract psychoanalytic concepts via a microanalysis of relational interaction (Beebe, 2005), or has helped us to understand—at the level of interacting biochemical, hormonal, and neuronal functions and processes (Schore, 2003a, 2003b)—what, in the past, we were conceptualizing primarily in psychological terms. Renn spells out for us the links among these diverse realms of abstraction and the related scientific research. He then translates and integrates all of these elements into a model of psychotherapy we can effectively use to ease the suffering of our patients.

I am suggesting that because of what Renn has been able to bring together in this book, many of the earlier psychoanalytic points of debate among our competing relational theories will soon fade from our discourse. As one further example that touches on the need for an integrated sense of self in the face of our otherwise overwhelming multiplicity, Rotenberg (2004) writes of the right brain as the locus of "the highest human mental function, responsible for creativity and integration of past, present, and future experience" (p. 864; cited in Schore, 2011, p. 93). By linking together the notions of creativity and integration, Rotenberg seems to nudge us away from an earlier postmodern attitude in which openness, chaos, and creativity were valued *over* integration or cohesion. Additionally, both Schore (2004) and Siegel (1999) write of the importance of forging an autobiographical narrative for a cohesive sense of self, the latter being a marker of mental health in the views of both these authors.

As yet another example of dissolving theoretical divisions, Renn reports on attachment research, suggesting that the capacity in *prospective parents* to create a cohesive autobiographical narrative is predictive of their *future child's* later security of attachment. By comparison, prospective parents whose autobiographical narratives are less cohesive have later been found to have infants who are disorganized in their attachment modalities. Research findings such as these once again underscore the relational asymmetry (Aron, 1996; Lachmann & Beebe, 1996) that prevails even in spite of the striking mutuality of infant–parent and patient–analyst influence. The asymmetry is demonstrated by the power of the prospective parents' modes of communicating about their own life histories to predict how their future children will experience and enact their basic attachment needs in later infancy.

While we now recognize that the mutuality of influence in infant–caregiver interaction is immediate and constant (Beebe, 2005), we also know that the influence does not necessarily move equally nor with the same potency in each direction. Rather the caregiver—presumably the partner with the more fully developed (and usually the less fragile) psyche—has a greater influence on the development of the infant's brain structure and on the infant's psychic functioning than the infant has on those same structures and functioning in the caregiver whose brain and psyche, while changing and changeable, are of course already to some degree formed prior to the start of the infant–caregiver relationship.

This acknowledgement of a power and influence differential is perhaps best expressed in Lyons-Ruth's (1999) concept of "scaffolding," in which (what she calls) the "developmentally advantaged" partner lends his or her strength and varieties of functioning to the "developmentally less advantaged." While the parallels between the infant–caregiver and the patient–analyst dyads are not exact, today's researchers are seemingly united in emphasizing the *similarities* more than the differences between initial development and later change processes in psychotherapy (Bucci, 2011; Lachmann & Beebe, 1996; Lyons-Ruth, 1999; Schore, 2011; Tronick, 2007).

Mitchell (1988) long ago questioned "the developmental tilt" (p. 151) in Winnicott's writings as well as in self psychology. But attitudes have changed across theories in large part due to the research Renn describes in this book. Today's neuroscientists (Schore, 2003a, 2003b, 2011) and infant–caregiver observation researchers (Beebe & Lachmann, 1997; Stern et al., 1998; Tronick, 2007) argue that the interactive processes—their sensory and affective registration, their influences on the brain as well as on psychic development—are similar (even though not equal) regardless of age or developmental level in the interacting partners. The processes of exchange in other words are similar and mutual, even though asymmetrical (Aron, 1996; Beebe & Lachmann, 1996), whether in initial development or in later changes occurring through psychotherapy.

In this impressive project, Renn has provided us with a new integration of a wide range and variety of research relevant to our field while highlighting the best of what we have already absorbed into our theories. Postmodern theorists initially rejected the kind of scientific empiricism that character-izes Renn's book, in part because the "authority" of scientific findings had in the past sometimes led us to perceive categories and universalities that too quickly became constricting of human growth and freedom or destruc-tively prescriptive for sub-groups who did not fit well within parameters of the research findings (Teicholz, 1999, 2001). But the very findings from scientific research that quite recently might have been rejected by postmod-ern purists now present us with a view of "reality" that turns out to coin-cide closely with what postmodern theory itself would lead us to expect (Teicholz, 2009); namely, we find a psychological world in which nothing is fixed or bounded and in which any relational "truth" we arrive at can be cocreated only through our mutual participation in the intersubjective contexts constituted by our interactions with others, including the interac-tions between patients and analysts (Hoffman, 1999; Lachmann & Beebe, 1996; and many others).

Given this postmodern "bent" in the picture of relational "realities" emerging from the latest scientific research, it is all the more impressive that Renn has been able to bring us a pragmatic, down-to-earth, and effec-tive model of how to proceed with individual traumatized patients. We now also realize that the experience of at least *cumulative* trauma has to some degree touched *every* patient and every analyst as well.

Renn's treatment model is firmly rooted in findings from the far-ranging empirical research on which he reports. And yet his therapeutic efforts seem to embody an open-ended, creative, and emergent spirit, one that welcomes the necessary chaos of its own richness while in its rigor inspires us to bring both an essential self-discipline and a liberating creativity to our own clinical endeavors.

REFERENCES

Aron, L. (1996). *A meeting of minds: Mutuality in psychoanalysis*. Hillsdale, NJ: Analytic Press.

Barratt, B. (1993). *Psychoanalysis and the postmodern impulse: Knowing and being since Freud's psychology*. Baltimore, MD: Johns Hopkins University Press.

Beebe, B. (2005). Mother–infant research informs mother–infant treatment. *Psychoanalytic Study of the Child, 60,* 7–46.

Beebe, B., Jaffe, J., Markese, S., Buck, K., Chen, H., Cohen, P., Bahrick, L., Andrews, H., & Feldstein, S. (2010). The origins of 12-month attachment: A microanalysis of 4-month mother–infant interaction. *Attachment & Human Development, 12,* 1, 3–141.

Beebe, B., & Lachmann, F. M. (1988a). The contribution of mother–infant mutual influence to the origins of self and object representations. *Psychoanalytic Psychology, 5,* 305–337.

Beebe, B., & Lachmann, F. M. (1988b). Mother–infant mutual influence and precursors of psychic structure. In A. Goldberg (Ed.), *Frontiers in self psychology: Progress in self psychology* (Vol. 3, pp. 3–26). Hillsdale, NJ: Analytic Press.

Beebe, B., & Lachmann, F. M. (1994). Representation and internalization in infancy: Three principles of salience. *Psychoanalytic Psychology, 11,* 127–165.

Beebe, B., Lachmann, F. M., & Jaffe, J. (1997). Mother–infant interaction structures and pre-symbolic self and object-representations. *Psychoanalytic Dialogues, 7,* 133–182.

Benjamin, J. (1988). *The bonds of love: Psychoanalysis, feminism, and the problem of domination*. New York: Pantheon.

Benjamin, J. (1990). An outline of intersubjectivity: The development of recognition. *Psychoanalytic Psychology, 7*(Suppl.), 33–46.

Benjamin, J. (1995). *Like subjects, love objects: Essays on recognition and sexual difference*. New Haven, CT: Yale University Press.

Benjamin, J. (2004). Beyond doer and done to: An intersubjective view of thirdness. *Psychoanalytic Quarterly, 73,* 5–46.

Boston Change Process Study Group. (1998). Noninterpretive mechanisms in psychoanalytic therapy: The "something more" than interpretation. *International Journal of Psychoanalysis, 79,* 903–922.

Boston Change Process Study Group. (2002). Explicating the implicit: The local level and the microprocess of change in the analytic situation. *International Journal of Psychoanalysis, 83,* 1051–1062.

Bromberg, P. M. (1980). Empathy, anxiety, and reality: A view from the bridge. *Contemporary Psychoanalysis, 16,* 223–236.

Bromberg, P. M. (1996). Standing in the spaces: The multiplicity of self and the psychoanalytic relationship. *Contemporary Psychoanalysis, 32,* 509–535.

Bromberg, P. M. (2009). Truth, human relatedness, and the analytic process: An interpersonal/relational perspective. *International Journal of Psychoanalysis, 90,* 347–361.

Bucci, W. (1997). Psychoanalysis and cognitive science: A multiple code theory. New York: Guilford Press.

Bucci, W. (2001). Pathways of emotional communication. *Psychoanalytic Inquiry*, *21*, 40–70.

Bucci, W. (2007). Dissociation from the perspective of multiple code theory. *Contemporary Psychoanalysis*, *43*, 165–184.

Bucci, W. (2011). The interplay of subsymbolic and symbolic processes in psychoanalytic treatment: It takes two to tango—but who knows the steps, who's the leader? The choreography of the psychoanalytic interchange. *Psychoanalytic Dialogues*, *21*, 45–54.

Coburn, W. J. (2006). Self psychology after Kohut: One theory or too many? *International Journal of Psychoanalytic Self Psychology*, *1*, 1–4.

Davies, J. M. (1997). Dissociation, therapeutic enactment, and transference–countertransference processes: A discussion of papers on childhood sexual abuse. *Gender & Psychoanalysis*, *2*, 241–257.

Davies, J. M. (1998). Multiple perspectives on multiplicity. *Psychoanalytic Dialogues*, *8*, 195–206.

Davies, J. M. (2006, October 27). *On the nature of the self: Multiplicity, unconscious conflict and fantasy in relational psychoanalysis.* Paper presented at the 28th Annual International Conference on the Psychology of the Self, Chicago, IL.

Davies, J. M., & Frawley, M. G. (1992). Dissociative processes and transference-countertransference paradigms in the psychoanalytically oriented treatment of adult survivors of childhood sexual abuse. *Psychoanalytic Dialogues*, *2*, 5–36.

Decety, J., & Jackson, P. (2006). A social-neuroscience perspective on empathy. *Current Directions in Psychological Science*, *15*, 54–58.

Demos, V. (1988). Affect and the development of the self: A new frontier. In A. Goldberg (Ed.), *Frontiers of self psychology: Progress in self psychology* (Vol. 3, pp. 27–54). Hillsdale, NJ: Analytic Press.

Fonagy, P., Gergely, G., Jurist, E., & Target, M. (2002). *Affect regulation, mentalization, and the development of the self.* New York: Other Press.

Hoffman, I. Z. (1991). Discussion: Toward a social-constructivist view of the psychoanalytic situation. *Psychoanalytic Dialogues*, *1*, 74–105.

Hoffman, I. Z. (1992). Some practical implications of a social-constructivist view of the psychoanalytic situation. *Psychoanalytic Dialogues*, *2*, 287–304.

Hoffman, I. Z. (1996). The intimate and ironic authority of the psychoanalyst's presence. *Psychoanalytic Quarterly*, *65*, 102–136.

Hoffman, I. Z. (1998). *Ritual and spontaneity in the psychoanalytic process: A dialectical-constructivist view.* Hillsdale, NJ: Analytic Press.

Kohut, H. (1959). Introspection, empathy, and psychoanalysis. *Journal of the American Psychoanalytic Association*, *7*, 459–483.

Kohut, H. (1971). *The analysis of the self.* New York: International Universities Press.

Kohut, H. (1977). *The restoration of the self.* New York: International Universities Press.

Kohut, H. (1984). *How does analysis cure?* (A. Goldberg & P. Stepansky, Eds.). Chicago: University of Chicago Press.

Kohut, H., & Seitz, P. (1963). Concepts and theories of psychoanalysis. In P. Ornstein (Ed.), *The search for the self* (Vol. 1, pp. 337–374). New York: International Universities Press, 1978.

Lachmann, F. M. (2000). *Transforming aggression.* Northvale, NJ: Jason Aronson.

Lachmann, F. M. (2001). Some contributions of empirical infant research to adult psychoanalysis: What have we learned? How can we apply it? *Psychoanalytic Dialogues, 11*, 167–185.

Lachmann, F. M. (2008). *Transforming narcissism: Reflections on empathy, humor, and expectations.* New York: Analytic Press.

Lachmann, F. M., & Beebe, B. (1996a). The contribution of self- and mutual regulation to therapeutic action: A case illustration. In A. Goldberg (Ed.), *Basic ideas reconsidered: Progress in self psychology* (Vol. 12, pp. 123–140). Hillsdale, NJ: Analytic Press.

Lachmann, F. M., & Beebe, B. (1996b). Three principles of salience in the organization of the patient-analyst interaction. *Psychoanalytic Psychology, 13*, 1–22.

Levenkron, H. (2006). Love (and) hate with the proper stranger: Affective honesty and enactment. *Psychoanalytic Inquiry, 26*, 157–181.

Lichtenberg, J. D. (1989). *Psychoanalysis and motivation.* Hillsdale, NJ: Analytic Press.

Lichtenberg, J. D., Lachmann, F. M., & Fosshage, J. L. (1996). *The clinical exchange: Techniques derived from self and motivational systems.* Hillsdale, NJ: Analytic Press.

Lyons-Ruth, K. (1999). Two-person unconscious: Intersubjective dialogue, enactive relational representation, and the emergence of new forms of relational organization. *Psychoanalytic Quarterly, 19*, 576–617.

Mitchell, S. A. (1988). *Relational concepts in psychoanalysis: An integration.* Cambridge, MA: Harvard University Press.

Mitchell, S. A. (1991). Wishes, needs, and personal negotiations. *Psychoanalytic Inquiry, 11*, 147–170.

Mitchell, S. A. (1993). *Hope and dread in psychoanalysis.* New York: Basic Books.

Mitchell, S. A. (1997). *Influence and autonomy in psychoanalysis.* Hillsdale, NJ: Analytic Press.

Ogden, T. H. (1992). The dialectically constituted/decentered subject of psychoanalysis, II: The contributions of Klein and Winnicott. *International Journal of Psychoanalysis, 73*, 613–626.

Renik, O. (1998). Getting real in analysis. *Psychoanalytic Quarterly, 67*, 566–593.

Rotenberg, V. S. (2004). The ontogeny and symmetry of the highest brain skills and the pathogenesis of schizophrenia. *Behavioral and Brain Sciences, 27*, 864–865.

Sander, L. (2002). Thinking differently: Principles of process in living systems and the specificity of being known. *Psychoanalytic Dialogues, 12*, 11–42.

Schore, A. N. (2003a). *Affect dysregulation and disorders of the self.* New York: W. W. Norton.

Schore, A. N. (2003b). *Affect regulation and the repair of the self.* New York: W. W. Norton.

Schore, A. N. (2011). The right brain implicit self lies at the core of psychoanalysis. *Psychoanalytic Dialogues, 21*, 75–100.

Shane, E. (2006). Developmental systems self psychology. *International Journal of Psychoanalytic Self Psychology, 1*, 23–46.

Siegel, D. J. (1999). *The developing mind: How relationships and the brain interact to shape who we are.* New York: Guilford Press.

Siegel, D. J. (2003). An interpersonal neurobiology of psychotherapy: The developing mind and the resolution of trauma. In M. F. Solomon & D. J. Siegel (Eds.), *Healing trauma: Attachment, mind, body, and brain* (pp. 1–56). New York: W. W. Norton.

Socarides, D., & Stolorow, R. D. (1985). Affects and selfobjects. *Annual of Psychoanalysis, 12/13*, 105–120.

Stern, D. N. (1985). *The interpersonal world of the infant.* New York: Basic Books.

Stolorow, R. D., Brandchaft, B., & Atwood, G. E (1987). *Psychoanalytic treatment: An intersubjective approach.* Hillsdale, NJ: Analytic Press.

Teicholz, J. G. (1995). Loewald's "positive neutrality" and the affirmative potential of psychoanalytic interventions. *Psychoanalytic Study of the Child, 50*, 48–75.

Teicholz, J. G. (1996). Optimal responsiveness: Its role in psychic growth and change. In L. Lifson (Ed.), *Understanding therapeutic action: Psychodynamic aspects of cure* (pp. 139–161). Hillsdale, NJ: Analytic Press.

Teicholz, J. G. (1998). Self and relationship: Kohut, Loewald, and the postmoderns. In A. Goldberg (Ed.), *The world of self psychology: Progress in self psychology* (Vol. 14, pp. 267–292). Hillsdale, NJ: Analytic Press.

Teicholz, J. G. (1999). *Kohut, Loewald, and the postmoderns: A comparative study of self and relationship.* Hillsdale, NJ: Analytic Press.

Teicholz, J. G. (2000). The analyst's empathy, subjectivity, and authenticity: Affect as the common denominator. In A. Goldberg (Ed.), *How responsive should we be? Progress in self psychology* (Vol. 16, pp. 33–53). Hillsdale, NJ: Analytic Press.

Teicholz, J. G. (2001). The many meanings of intersubjectivity and their implications for analyst self-expression and self-disclosure. In A. Goldberg (Ed.), *The narcissistic patient revisited: Progress in self psychology* (Vol. 17, pp. 9–42). Hillsdale, NJ: Analytic Press.

Teicholz, J. G. (2006a). Enactment as therapeutic hand-grenade: Discussion of Holly Levenkron's "Love (and hate) with the proper stranger." *Psychoanalytic Inquiry, 26*, 263–278.

Teicholz, J. G. (2006b). Qualities of engagement and the analyst's theory. *International Journal of Psychoanalytic Self Psychology, 1*, 7–77.

Teicholz, J. G. (2009). A strange convergence: Postmodern theory, infant research, and psychoanalysis. In R. A. Frie & D. M. Orange (Eds.), *Beyond postmodernism: New dimensions in clinical theory and practice* (pp. 69–91). London: Routledge.

Tolpin, M. (2003). Doing psychoanalysis of normal development: Forward edge transferences. In M. J. Gehrie (Ed.), *Explorations in self psychology: Progress in self psychology* (Vol. 19, pp. 167–190). Hillsdale, NJ: Analytic Press.

Trevarthen, C. (2005). First things first: Infants make good use of the sympathetic rhythm of imitation, without reason or language. *Journal of Child Psychotherapy, 31*, 91–113.

Tronick, E. Z. (2007). The neurobehavioral and social-emotional development of infants and children. New York: W. W. Norton.

Winnicott, D. W. (1960). The theory of the parent-infant relationship. In *The maturational process and the facilitating environment* (pp. 37–55). New York: International Universities Press, 1965.

Acknowledgments

First and foremost I would like to acknowledge my gratitude to my patients, both forensic and private, as the theoretical ideas that I explore and discuss in this book could only become meaningful in my clinical work with them. This, in turn, has helped me to better understand the therapeutic process which, I hope, has been of benefit to them.

In the Introduction, I acknowledge that the idea for this book emanated from Dr. Lewis Aron. Not only do I have him to thank for encouraging me to write the book in the first place, but also for his many erudite suggestions on how to improve the manuscript during the writing process in his role as co-editor of the Relational Perspectives book series. I would also like to acknowledge the encouragement to write a book that has been forthcoming at various times from Dr. Gwen Adshead, Dr. Gwyneth Boswell, Dr. Donna Orange, and Dr. Joseph Schwartz. While I delayed doing so for a number of years, the time seemed ripe and the topic conducive to proceed with Dr. Aron's idea for a book.

I am grateful to friends and colleagues who commented on the original paper on memory, trauma, and representation that forms the core of this book. They include Michael Eigen, Viviane Green, Celia Harding, Jeremy Holmes, Bernice Laschinger, Joseph Lichtenberg, Lynda Morgan, Annie Power, Bruce Reis, and Judith Guss Teicholz. Additional thanks are due to Bernice Laschinger for her insightful comments on theoretical and clinical matters as the writing progressed, and to Lynda Morgan for commenting on each chapter and undertaking the laborious task of proofreading the finalized text. I am also indebted to Kristopher Spring of Routledge, for his always timely help and support in bringing this book to fruition.

More generally, I would like to acknowledge the International Association for Relational Psychoanalysis and Psychotherapy (IARPP), whose regular online colloquia and seminars provide a stimulating forum from which to engage with participants from all over the world. Sharing and exchanging ideas of common interest to relational psychoanalysis with such a wide and well-informed group of people has been of enormous help in shaping my theoretical thinking and informing my clinical practice, as reflected in this book.

Finally, I would like to acknowledge Dr. Ronald Britton, albeit indirectly, for his thought-provoking chapter "Making the Private Public" in *The Presentation of Case Material in Clinical Discourse* published by Karnac Books in 1997. On commenting on the issue of "publication anxiety," Dr. Britton writes

> The manifest problems that I have found are that some people are afraid to publish, some are too ready to publish, and that in some others the conflicts inherent in publication lead to deviation, distraction, or distortion of their texts. I believe that *publication anxiety* is natural unless it is denied as part of a manic defense which may lead to over-readiness to publish. . . . I think publication anxiety is ubiquitous and has two sources. One is fear of rejection by the primary intended audience. The other is fear of recrimination by affiliated colleagues and possible exile from them. I think that a profound *fear of rejection by the primary intended listener* in its most serious form leads to an inability to conceptualize or, in lesser states of inhibition, produces an inability to write. (p. 14, emphasis in original)

I would agree with the central thrust of Dr. Britton's argument, but trust that the aforementioned support provided by friends, colleagues, and the IARPP community has sufficiently contained my own publication anxiety, and, therefore, that the text I have produced does not suffer too greatly from an over-readiness to publish, a fear of rejection and exile by colleagues, or a state of inhibition!

Introduction

The idea for this book came from Dr. Lewis Aron, who suggested expanding a paper that I had written on memory, trauma, and therapeutic action into a text for use by clinicians and graduate students. Further encouragement came from Dr. Judith Guss Teicholz, whose enthusiasm for my thinking about the implications of neuroscience and infant research findings for psychotherapeutic treatment was infectious. Although written primarily for clinicians and psychotherapy trainees, I believe that this book will be of interest to clinical psychologists, child psychotherapists, couples counselors, social workers, mental health professionals, forensic psychotherapists, probation officers, domestic violence professionals, specialist teachers, and attachment theorists.

The title of the book, *The Silent Past and the Invisible Present*, derives from Daniel Stern's view that the past is "phenomenologically silent," and from Daniel Schacter's description of implicit memory as being "invisible." Thus, although the silent past may, under certain conditions, become an active, alive past, its functioning and influence on our thoughts, feelings and behavior in the present are largely invisible.

Some of the contents of this book are based on previously published papers and book chapters, on presentations to colleagues, on contributions to online colloquia and web seminars, and on material for teaching seminars and continuing professional development workshops. Given this, there is inevitably a degree of overlap of ideas between some chapters, but repetition within a chapter has been kept to a minimum during editing.

Recent advances in research in the fields of attachment, traumatology, and neuroscience are helping to deepen our understanding of the process of change in psychotherapy. In this book, I draw on this research, as well as on a wide range of clinical approaches to inform a new model of clinical practice. The themes that unify the book reflect my interests in memory, child development, neuroscience, attachment theory, traumatology, affect regulation, intimate violence, the continuity of experience across the life cycle, and the process of therapeutic change. As the title of the book suggests, I am particularly interested in the silent, invisible processes deriving from the past that maintain non-optimal ways of experiencing and relating in the present, as these strike me as posing eminently pertinent questions for psychoanalysis and psychotherapy. I would argue that a neuroscientific understanding of the dynamic nature of memory processes and of the way in which the two main memory systems operate and interact is salient to a concomitant understanding of personality development and therapeutic action. These interests have emerged during some 20 years of clinical practice and reflect a paradigmatic shift in psychoanalytic thinking about clinical work and the process of change. Whereas earlier clinical models emphasized a largely verbal, interpretative technique in the explicit domain, newer models focus on a nonverbal, affective understanding of communication in the implicit/enactive domain. I argue that therapeutic change consists of a dual process and needs to proceed in both of these domains.

This new understanding of therapeutic action is informed by advances in the empirical sciences, specifically in the fields of cognitive and developmental psychology and cognitive neuroscience, but also by the findings from attachment research with children and adults. Although there is concern and resistance in some quarters about integrating the ideas and language of scientific disciplines into psychoanalytic discourse, the gap between these diverse disciplines is gradually being narrowed by a dialogue on matters of common interest. Indeed, I detect a thirst for knowledge among my colleagues about the findings from related disciplines, and a keen interest in understanding how such data may inform clinical work. In my view, relational psychoanalysis is well-placed to incorporate the findings emerging from related disciplines into a clinical model that integrates such data with the current emphasis on intersubjectivity, trauma, dissociation, mentalization, nonlinear dynamic systems theory, and mutual enactments. In this context, I would like to stress that integrating the findings from cognitive science, developmental psychology, and attachment theory into an overarching relational model need not diminish the psychoanalytic focus on a hermeneutic understanding of the individual's subjective meaning. Rather, I would argue that the process of interdisciplinary integration enhances our clinical work in this very endeavor. Indeed, as is well-documented, Freud developed his metapsychology in the context of the then state of scientific knowledge, but his clinical emphasis remained firmly embedded in the hermeneutic tradition.

THE STRUCTURE OF THE BOOK

Chapter 1 explores the role of memory and repression in Freudian psychoanalysis. It shows that in many ways Freud's thinking was ahead of his time, anticipating and influencing subsequent developments. For example, his observation that nonverbal motor phenomena, as expressed in bodily and affective symptoms, is an unconscious form of memory repeated in action predated current psychosomatic–somatization theories. Also, in phenomenological terms, Freud's theorizing about primal repression, screen memories, and the repetition compulsion may be seen as a description of the operation of implicit/procedural memory. Moreover, his concept of *Nachträglichkeit* or deferred action, whereby memories undergo a process of retroactive reworking, with old events being newly translated and taking on a different significance, may be equated with contemporary views of the dynamic nature of memories, and of therapeutic action deriving from the modification of archaic representational models and accompanying sets of implicitly encoded predictions and expectations.

Freud considered that every event deposited in memory structures the individual's unconscious. However, whereas he originally believed that repressed memories of sexual trauma were the sole cause of hysteria, he partially renounced his seduction theory in 1897, emphasizing instead the interpretation of dreams, fantasies, and parapraxes, that is, the fulfillment of unconscious wishes manifested in such behavior as forgetting, mislaying, and slips of the tongue. Thus, although Freud retained an interest in trauma throughout his working life, his apparent repudiation of the theory of sexual seduction has led to an ongoing debate about the complex relationship between memory, fantasy, and reality, and about how to distinguish between true and false memories of childhood sexual abuse. In this context, I briefly allude to the dispute that arose between Freud and Pierre Janet at the turn of the 20th century. The chapter concludes with an examination of the hotly debated controversy surrounding recovered memories of childhood sexual abuse and the so called "false memory syndrome" that erupted in the 1980s. The dispute focuses on the issue of whether abuse that occurred in childhood can be entirely forgotten, only to reemerge in adulthood, or whether such memories are simply false, in that they are the product either of the person's own imagination or of a psychotherapist's implanted suggestion.

Chapter 2 summarizes the findings from neuroscience on the two major memory systems, explicit or declarative memory and implicit or nondeclarative memory, which are relevant to the focus of this book. The operation of implicit memory is emphasized as research findings show that it influences our thoughts, feelings, and behavior in invisible, nonconscious ways and thus functions to maintain personality traits and non-optimal ways of experiencing self with other. I compare the nonconscious world of implicit memory with the Freudian dynamic unconscious, and suggest that Winnicott's theorizing about unremembered "primitive agonies," Christopher Bollas' theory of the "unthought known," and Donnel Stern's concept of "unformulated experience" may, in phenomenological terms, be seen as examples of implicit/procedural memory.

Contemporary perspectives on psychological trauma and affect regulation are discussed in Chapter 3. I stress the importance of cumulative developmental trauma in understanding the manifestation of psychopathology in adulthood. I provide a clinical vignette to illustrate theoretical issues. I suggest that in the absence of an appreciation of the subtle nature and silent impact of cumulative developmental trauma, and of the way in which the implicit/procedural memory system operates, there is a danger of assuming that the subject's present difficulties in living must derive from an unremembered dramatic trauma, such as childhood sexual abuse, when this may not necessarily be the case.

Trauma and pathological forms of dissociation tend to be strongly, though not inevitably, associated. From a neurobiological perspective, Chapter 4 explores these links and the disabling impact that trauma has on the explicit and implicit memory systems. I suspect that most clinicians have experienced the reemergence of trauma-related childhood memories in their clinical work. I summarize research findings that link this phenomenon to the way in which stress in later life suppresses the explicit memory system, allowing long latent trauma-related implicit memories to resurface. I illustrate theoretical points with a clinical vignette.

In Chapter 5, I outline the way in which the paradigmatic shift from drive theory to a relational model has been paralleled by a new understanding of the nature of the representational world. Starting with Freud and moving through object relations theory to a relational perspective, I summarize some of the major ways that the mind or internal world has been conceptualized. I also examine the polemical argument surrounding hermeneutics and empiricism, and briefly discuss the problem of integrating neuroscience and psychoanalysis. The chapter concludes with an example of my own attempt at such integration.

Chapter 6 is divided into three parts. The first part centers on attachment theory, setting out the two main research methodologies used with infants and adults, namely, the Strange Situation procedure and the Adult Attachment Interview. I also summarize research employing the doll-play story completion task. Findings illustrate the intergenerational transmission of attachment organization and the way in which these research methods tap into implicit–procedural memory at the representational level. The doll-play story completion research paradigm builds on the Strange Situation procedure and shows that disorganization at the representational level is consistent with a system of representation that is dissociated from consciousness, but which may suddenly become activated under the stress of separation. In young children, this is manifested in controlling behavior, and in the inversion of their relationships with caregivers. Accepting that implicit–procedural memory creates a bridge between childhood and adulthood, I suggest that disorganized–controlling 6-year-olds may develop into adults who use violence to control their intimate partners.

The development of the psychological concept of mentalization by Peter Fonagy and his colleagues is discussed, as this is inextricably linked to attachment dynamics, specifically to the level of the parent's reflective functioning in relation to his or her child. Mentalization not only helps us to appraise our own and other people's intentions and behavior by reference to underlying mental states, but also sheds light on the processes involved in the interpersonal transmission of attachment states of mind between parent and child. Findings by Howard and Miriam Steele indicate that attachment is "relationship specific," with representational models of mother and father developing separately, rather than as one overarching model of attachment. Thus, a child may be disorganized with one parent but not with the other. These findings would seem to confirm the relational concept of multiple self-states.

The second part of Chapter 6 examines Daniel Stern's form of intersubjectivity and also his theory of the development of self. Stern argues that repeated patterns of interaction constitute the basic building blocks of psychic formation and structures the infant's representational world. His concept of "representations of interactions that have been generalized" parallels Bowlby's concept of "internal working models" and Bucci's "emotion schemas." Neuroscience research suggests that these nonconscious psychic structures are encoded and stored in the systems of implicit–procedural memory and guide and direct behavior, thoughts, and feelings in powerful but nonconscious ways. I illuminate the process of interactive regulation with a mother–infant observation. The third part of this chapter concludes with a description of the therapeutic process using a model that integrates theories and data from attachment, relational, intersubjective, and neuroscience perspectives.

Chapter 7 brings a specific focus to bear on relational psychoanalysis. Using a clinical vignette by Stephen Mitchell and one from my own practice, I illustrate the way in which findings emanating from attachment, traumatology, and neuroscience may be integrated into an overarching relational model. This chapter also draws attention to the clinical usefulness of Giovanni Liotti's theory of competing motivational systems. Liotti posits that the subject may consciously or unconsciously "choose" a motivational system other than the attachment system in order to avoid re-experiencing attachment trauma and dissociation associated with loss, abandonment, and abuse. The main alternative motivational systems are the "agonistic system," which is characterized by violence and aggression, the "caregiving system," which is characterized by a compulsive, controlling form of caregiving, and the "sexual system." The latter is used to sexualize relationships, and its "choice" may reflect a history of childhood sexual abuse.

Employing a relational model may raise certain clinical concerns and ethical dilemmas about such issues as disclosure of the countertransference, acknowledgement of the "real" relationship, the asymmetry of power in the therapeutic relationship, working with enactments, self-disclosure, and the risk of retraumatizing the patient. Chapter 7 discusses aspects of these various concerns from a relational perspective.

Chapter 8 discusses the intersubjective motivational system and the development of self–other representational models from an intersubjective–attachment perspective. These concepts are linked to a discussion of the mirror neuron and implicit memory systems. I summarize the key ideas of the Boston Change Process Study Group, connecting these ideas to the form of intersubjectivity developed by Beatrice Beebe and her colleagues. The intersubjective and interpersonal processes that lead to the development of enduring character and personality traits are illustrated, and the mechanisms that maintain non-optimal representational models, making them resistant to change, are outlined. The chapter concludes with a clinical vignette that illustrates these various ideas, as well as the dialectic between the verbal, explicit domain and the nonverbal, implicit domain.

Chapters 9 and 10 draw on my clinical experience of working with violent people in a forensic setting. In Chapter 9, I further explicate the role that implicit memory, trauma, dissociation, and representational models play in the development of personality and adult psychopathology. I present a relational perspective, informed by attachment theory and traumatology, on affective violence. I argue that aggression and destructiveness are secondary, arising in response to a perceived threat to the self in an intersubjective–attachment matrix characterized by trauma and abuse, rather than as an expression of an innate "death instinct." I contend that situations involving loss, betrayal, and abandonment activate an implicitly encoded disorganized representational model, which may culminate in the violent reenactment of dissociated personal trauma in a context of separation and loss. I outline gender differences and similarities in violent behavior, explore the attachment dynamics that maintain violence in same-sex and opposite-sex intimate relationships, and suggest that working with the violent couple may, in certain circumstances, be more clinically effective than working with the partners separately. In Chapter 10, I present an extensive case study using a brief, time-limited psychodynamic model with a violent man to illustrate theoretical points, and the way in which research findings from attachment theory, developmental psychology, affect regulation, traumatology, and cognitive neuroscience can be integrated into an overarching relational model.

Chapter 11 concludes the book with a discussion of the implications of implicit memory for therapeutic action in contemporary psychoanalysis and psychotherapy. Following John Bowlby and Peter Fonagy, I emphasize the view that representational models are the psychic structures that organize behavior and experience. Given this, the modification of these structures needs to be the focus of treatment rather than the events that might have contributed to their development. I illustrate how to recognize the activation of archaic representational models and, somewhat controversially, suggest that such models may be modified not only via enactments in the transference–countertransference matrix, but also by working with enactments in the patient's extra-therapeutic relationships. While acknowledging that psychoanalysis and psychotherapy can help to bring about profound change in the lives of our patients, I suggest that we need to be realistic about the limits of therapeutic action. Neuroscience research indicates that the traumas our patients have experienced do not disappear as a result of treatment, and thus may reemerge in stressful situations that cue the retrieval of traumatic implicit memories and activate maladaptive representational models.

Chapter 1

Memory and Freudian Psychoanalysis

INTRODUCTION

The way in which traumatic memories of childhood sexuality influence experience and behavior in later life has been a concern of psychoanalysis since its inception by Freud in the 1890s. This chapter explores the genesis of Freud's thinking about the repression and recovery of traumatic memories of childhood sexual trauma and sets the scene for the discussion that follows on a contemporary understanding of memory, trauma, and representation.

Freud first conceptualized repression as a form of voluntary dissociation from consciousness of memories associated with emotions that were threatening to the person's values and ideals. According to Freud's theory, such memories became dynamically unconscious. His original therapeutic model was one of lifting repression and recovering memories into consciousness. In this context, Freud assumed that the conscious and pre-conscious representation in the internal mental space of an object, person, or event in the external world might become subject to repression. He further assumed that some trace of the external reality would be retained in memory; that a "memory trace" preserves its relation to the object represented through its resemblance to it (1894). By the turn of the century Freud (1900) was drawing a distinction between a pathogenic form of repression aimed at protecting consciousness from disturbing thoughts and feelings, and a normal form of repression that characterized everyday life. Moreover, in a broad sense, he also used the concept to describe the way in which the patient separates conscious awareness from aspects of his or her behavior, rather than as solely relating to the loss of specific memories (Laplanche & Pontalis, 1988). Indeed, contemporary Freudians have widened the concept of repression to include both conscious and unconscious dimensions (Erdelyi, 1994).

Freud, then, used the term *memory-trace* to denote how real events in early life are inscribed in memory and reappear during the "return of the repressed" in the form of a symptom. Moreover, he viewed nonverbal motor phenomena, as expressed in bodily and affective symptoms, as an unconscious form of memory that is repeated in action (1914). The attempt to overcome repression that has produced a failure of memory and the associated symptoms is one of the major themes in Freudian psychoanalysis. The therapeutic model to which Freud remained attached to the end of his life consisted of trauma/repression/forgetting/symptom/remembering/healing. This model may be seen in "Analysis Terminable and Interminable" (1937) in which Freud argued that, like hysterics, psychotics also suffer from reminiscences, implying that delusional representations were, in fact, the reappearance in consciousness of past experiences that were disguised or unrecognized as such. However, in a now famous letter to Wilhelm Fliess in 1897, Freud apparently repudiated his early belief that traumatic sexual experiences were the sole basis for hysteria.

By 1907 Freud largely took for granted the idea that sexual seduction was often a fantasy-based recollection representing the fulfillment of sexual wishes (Laplanche & Pontalis, 1988). Indeed, commenting on this topic in his "Autobiographical Study" (Freud, 1925, in Gay, 1995), he states: "the neurotic symptoms were not related to actual events but to wishful fantasies and that as far as the neurosis was concerned psychical reality was of more importance than material reality" (p. 111). In this same work, he also questioned whether he had perhaps "forced" the scenes of seduction onto his patients. The shift in Freud's thinking from a belief in real events was paralleled by an emphasis on the interpretation of dreams, fantasies, and parapraxes (Schwartz, 1999).

Among the various reasons put forward to account for Freud's repudiation of his seduction theory is the suggestion that he found it more congenial to work with the repression of fantasized sexual abuse rather than with the dissociation of real sexual trauma (Schwartz, 1999). While such motivations must remain in the realm of conjecture, Freud's later writings reveal that he never fully abandoned his belief in the existence of real childhood experiences of seduction and abuse, nor in the role these experiences played in the aetiology of neuroses (Gay, 1995; Sandler & Sandler, 1997). This notwithstanding, in the wake of the partial renunciation of his seduction theory, it became unfashionable in psychoanalytic circles to attribute psychopathology to real-life experiences (Bowlby, 1984). This has led to an ongoing debate about the complex relationship between memory, fantasy, and reality, and about how to distinguish between true and false memories of childhood sexual abuse. I discuss the disputes surrounding these controversial issues in the concluding part of this chapter.

BREUER AND FREUD'S *STUDIES IN HYSTERIA*

Freud studied under Jean-Martin Charcot in Paris for four months in 1885–1886. Charcot was working with patients who had unexplained physical symptoms. He concluded that the symptoms were the result of a form of hysteria which had been induced by the patient's emotional response to a traumatic event. Freud was impressed by Charcot's work on traumatic hysteria and was also influenced by the thinking of Pierre Janet, who also studied under Charcot. On his return to Vienna and in collaboration with Joseph Breuer, Freud developed the theory that neurosis came about when a traumatic experience led to a process of symptom-formation.

Breuer and Freud acknowledged the influence of Charcot and Janet in their *Studies in Hysteria* (1895). Indeed, they refer to Janet's concept of "dissociation" in their "Preliminary Statement" on the origins of hysterical phenomena, stating that the "tendency to dissociation and thereby to the emergence of abnormal states of consciousness . . . is the fundamental phenomenon of this neurosis" (p. 14). However, whereas Breuer found "dual consciousness" and "hypnoid states" to be compelling explanations of hysteria, Freud favored his concept of repression (Schwartz, 1999). Indeed, in the concluding pages of his case study of Frau Emmy von N., Freud states: "Janet has, I think, wrongly elevated those states resulting from changes in consciousness due to hysteria to the rank of primary conditions of hysteria" (p. 96). Thus, it would seem that the seeds for the more serious dispute that arose between the two men were already being sown.

Breuer and Freud's original belief in the profound influence of traumatic childhood memories is reflected in their statement that "hysterics suffer for the most part from reminiscences" (p. 11). The first edition of their classic case studies of hysteria was published in 1893 and described five female patients whose conscious memories included experiences of grief and longing for lost or unrequited love, and, in one case, the sexual advances of an uncle/father in adolescence. The patients' symptoms included tic-like movements, phobias, anorexia, stuttering, disabling fears, intrusive thoughts, and disturbing images.

Freud assumed that sexuality, as the "most powerful of all drives" (p. 95), was the likely source of the patients' psychical trauma. He also assumed that the repression from consciousness of childhood sexual ideas and experiences was "more liable than any other to give rise to traumas" (p. 94) and therefore likely to play a major role in the pathogenesis of hysteria. Thus, despite the absence of any conscious memories of a traumatic sexual element as, for example, in the case of Freud's patient, Frau Emmy von N., Freud assumed that such an experience undoubtedly must have occurred and had then been subject to repression. For Freud, the fact that Frau Emmy von N. could not remember the origin of her symptoms of hysteria meant that she had no sense of the causal connections between the precipitating event (sexual seduction) and the pathological phenomenon.

The therapeutic process, as described in *Studies*, consisted of the patient telling or reliving, retrospectively, her recovered history in conversation. Freud assumed that it was possible, through a process of consciously remembering, to reinterpret a past traumatic event and, thereby, to rid it of its pain and symptomatology. Breuer and Freud then considered that hysterical symptoms represented a mental conflict that could only be resolved through an active process of thinking and talking. Indeed, Breuer's patient, "Anna O." (Bertha Pappenheim), labeled this process the "talking cure," a conversational process resulting in the modification of repressed memories.

Freud referred to this aspect of therapeutic action in a letter to Wilhelm Fliess in 1896, a year after the publication of the second edition of *Studies*. He used the term *Nachträglichkeit* to describe a form of deferred action by which the patient's clinical material, in the form of memory traces, may be revised and rearranged at a later date to fit in with new experiences and thus be endowed with a new meaning and psychic efficiency. Indeed, Freud eventually came to acknowledge that every perception, every memory trace, and, therefore, every representation is "constructed" by the dynamics of the psyche itself and undergoes a constant process of retroactive reworking (Laplanche & Pontalis, 1988).

Freud's thinking with regard to *Nachträglichkeit* may be seen in *Studies* in which he speaks of old events being newly translated and taking on a different significance at a later point. However, while initially Breuer and Freud considered that a disturbing reminiscence would vanish and not return if it had been talked away, the second edition of *Studies* concluded with the more modest promise that all analysis could do was try to transform "hysterical misery into common unhappiness" (p. 306). Freud subsequently developed his theories independently of Breuer. Indeed, the relationship between the two men grew increasingly strained because of their differences in style. Whereas Freud considered Breuer too cautious in developing theoretical formulations, Breuer, for his part, saw Freud as a man of fixed ideas and huge, presumptuous generalizations (Schwartz, 1999).

With respect to Freud's theory of "infantile amnesia," he did not consider this to be the result of any functional inability of the young child to record his or her impressions; instead, he attributed the absence of memories of early childhood to the repression of infantile sexuality (1905a). Similarly, he argued that "screen memories" are recollections that conceal repressed memories of sexual experiences or fantasies, viewing such memories as representing the forgotten years of childhood. Indeed, in "Remembering, Repeating, and Working-Through" (1914), Freud contends that all of what is essential, but which has been forgotten from childhood, has been retained in screen memories. However, he found it paradoxical that, whereas important events from childhood are not remembered, apparently insignificant memories, in the form of screen memories, sometimes are. Reflecting on childhood memories in particular, and on the origins of conscious memories in general, Freud (1899, in Gay, 1995) suggests that perhaps we do not have "memories at all *from* our childhood," but rather that what we possess are "memories *relating to* our childhood" (p. 126, emphasis in original).

He conceptualized the defensive process involved in screen memories as a "compromise-formation," seeing this process as condensing a large number of real or fantasy childhood elements which became subject to repression and displacement.

Freud, then, argued that screen memories, infantile amnesia, and hysterical amnesia are formations produced by a compromise between repressed elements and defense against them, suggesting that the interpretation of screen memories leads back to indelible childhood experiences of a sexual nature (Laplanche & Pontalis, 1988). However, in "Inhibitions, Symptoms and Anxiety" (1926), Freud refers to "primal repression," conceptualizing this as a fixation that exerts a continuous after-pressure on repression proper or secondary repression. He considered it unlikely that primal repression is derived from the superego, as this psychical agency develops subsequent to primal repression. Rather, primal repression should probably be sought in very intense archaic experiences, which, by their very nature, have broken through the protective shield against stimuli. Lacan (1993) subsequently theorized primal repression as a form of memory that remains inaccessible to the person. In this sense, primal repression and the theory that repetitive actions are a form of unconscious memory (Freud, 1914, 1926) may be seen as having certain phenomenological features in common with the performative and enactive features of implicit memory (Reis, 2009a). Moreover, Fonagy and Target (1997) argue that screen memories may be conceptualized as a manifestation of the implicit–procedural memory system "which can achieve no other phenomenal representation" (p. 215).

As noted above, Freud's patient, Frau Emmy von N., had no conscious memories of sexual seduction to account for her symptoms of hysteria, but Freud assumed that such an experience must have occurred (Freud & Breuer, 1895). In so doing, he appears to have minimized the significance of her experience of multiple bereavements, which he describes in great detail in the case study. The clinical material in the case of "Dora" (Ida Bauer), who commenced an analysis with Freud in 1900, was quite different from that of Frau Emmy von N. in that she reported conscious memories of sexual seduction by Herr K., who was a neighbor and friend of the family (1905b). Freud accepted Dora's story and seems to have been fully aware that her father had handed her over to Herr K., using her as currency in his sexual barter with the latter so that his liaison with Frau K. could continue undisturbed (Mitchell, 1993). Freud was also of the opinion that Herr K.'s seductive behavior towards Dora had caused the psychical trauma prerequisite for the production of hysterical symptoms.

However, despite knowing and accepting the details of Dora's sexual trauma, Freud's theoretical frame led him to focus on intrapsychic neurotic conflict. Thus, the root of the problem for Freud was Dora's unconscious infantile sexual fantasies and impulses towards her father. He concluded that these repressed instinctual wishes had returned and that Dora was defending against the knowledge that she loved and desired her father and Herr K. For Freud (1905b), Dora's cure was dependent on her awareness and acceptance of her repressed infantile sexual and aggressive fantasies and impulses. Once these childhood amnesias had become conscious, they could be made subject to rational, realistic control.

Mitchell (1993), on looking at the study from the vantage point of relational psychoanalysis, articulates our surprise at the lack of acknowledgement that Freud accorded Dora's subjective experience of sexual abuse. However, he observes that it is easy to criticize the case study when taken out of its own conceptual and historical context. Given this, he argues that Freud's model of the analytic process and set of theoretical premises concerning human knowledge and subjectivity made sense in his day. Indeed, as we have seen, Freud was well aware of the fact that Dora had been mistreated and seduced by Herr K., but, as Mitchell emphasizes, he (Freud) did not think this mattered as far as the analytic process was concerned. It may be thought that Mitchell's apologia of Freud's theory and practice from an historical perspective would be more compelling were it not for a contemporary critique of Freud's theory and methodology by Janet, as discussed below.

MEMORY DISPUTES IN PSYCHOANALYSIS

Janet made a public critique of Freud and psychoanalysis in a paper given at the 17th International Congress of Medicine in London in 1913. In a similar vein to Breuer, Janet criticized Freud for making unrestricted generalizations about sexuality, and for what he saw as Freud's tendency to select evidence to support his theories. He suggested that Freud's eagerness to link hysterical trauma to repressed sexual wishes led to a subordination of obvious grief trauma. Thus, the symptoms deriving from the trauma of loss were instead interpreted in terms of frustrated unconscious sexuality (Janet, 1913, in Brown & van der Hart, 1998). This would appear to describe precisely Freud's thinking and approach in his work with Frau Emmy von N. (Freud & Breuer, 1895). Indeed, Janet's critique of Freud is supported by Israels and Schatzman (1993), whose close reading of *The Aetiology of Hysteria* (Freud, 1896) led them to conclude that his patients had not actually reported scenes of sexual seduction to him, but that Freud had imposed such stories onto them.

More specifically, Janet (1913, in Brown & van der Hart, 1998) argued that in most cases involving sexual trauma, the trauma is readily reported by the patient and thus does not need interpreting. It may be accepted that this was the clinical situation in the case of Dora. However, Janet conceded that in other cases the trauma may need to be uncovered, but he emphasized that in some instances the patient would be unable to recall memories of sexual trauma of any kind. Furthermore, as noted above, Janet held the view that hysteria may derive from nonsexual trauma, a position espoused by Charcot as well. Janet also criticized Freud for substituting repression for dissociation, arguing that repression is an active, independent process that results in dissociation, and that dissociation provides a more powerful explanation of the subconscious character of traumatic memories.

In Chapters 3 and 4, I elaborate on the way in which dissociated traumatic memories encoded in implicit memory may be expressed as sensory perceptions and affect states, and be reactivated and reenacted under state-specific trigger conditions. The concluding section of this chapter, however, examines the competing claims regarding the truth or falsity of childhood sexual abuse (CSA).

The dispute that arose between Freud and Janet at the beginning of the 20th century led to the two men going their separate ways. In the decades following Freud's partial recantation of his seduction theory in 1897, interest in sexual abuse and sexual trauma waned and became something of a taboo subject (Bowlby, 1988). A notable exception to this trend was Ferenczi (1933), who complained about the neglect in psychoanalysis of such traumatic factors. In a paper given in Wiesbaden in 1932, he stated: "The sexual trauma, as the pathogenic factor cannot be valued highly enough. Even children of very respectable, sincerely puritanical families, fall victim to real violence or rape much more often than one had dared to suppose" (p. 161). However, it was not until the mid-1980s that the issue of sexual trauma erupted with full force. This was in a context of mounting evidence showing widespread sexual abuse of children in the domestic arena, and for the partial or complete amnesia of such abuse (Herman, 1981). Entrenched positions regarding the truth or falsity of such memories evolved with, on the one side, the recovered memory movement and on the other, those who regarded "recovered memories" as constituting a "false memory syndrome."

As Webster (1995) points out, a crucial factor in the rise of the recovered memory movement was the extensive denial of the reality of CSA among lawyers and mental health professionals throughout most of the twentieth century. This made it extremely difficult for women and children to gain a hearing for accusations of sexual assault by men. This situation began to change with the rise of the second wave of feminism in the 1980s, as a result of which women felt more able to disclose their histories of sexual abuse in the knowledge that therapists were prepared to listen to their stories and believe them.

While critiquing Freud's phallocentric theory of the Oedipus complex, the recovered memory movement embraced his pre-1897 affect-trauma model (Herman, 1981). As we have seen, this model has at its core the concept of repression of actual sexual abuse. Thus, as matters developed, it was not solely the case of believing the spontaneous disclosure of consciously remembered CSA, but also of recovering and reconstructing previously repressed memories of sexual trauma. Webster (1995) suggests that an unintended consequence of adopting the concept of repression and employing a form of therapy with the explicit goal of recovering memories of CSA is that there is likely to be a reaction against recovered memory therapy. This, in turn, may endanger the progress made in acknowledging the widespread incidence of sexual abuse and, moreover, risk bringing the entire concept of psychotherapy into disrepute.

Indeed, commentators such as Kihlstrom (1995) and Crews (1995) mounted attacks on psychoanalysis in this context, asserting that claims of CSA were largely false and the result of suggestion and that such claims had reached epidemic proportions. Indeed, Crews traced the recovered memory movement back to Freud's abandonment of the seduction theory, seeing the movement as feeding on what he regarded as the most essential but spurious and pseudoscientific assumptions of psychoanalysis. Crews described the recovered memory movement as pernicious and as having deluded countless patients into launching false charges of sexual abuse against bemused and mortified members of their families.

There is a certain irony to Crews' (1995) critique of Freud. This centers on Freud's pre-1897 practice of interpreting sexual abuse to patients who had no conscious memory of such abuse, and who resisted believing him, as in the case of Frau Emmy von N. Given this, the sexual trauma that Freud subsequently came to disbelieve was, it would appear, the abuse that he himself had suggested to his patients (Israels & Schatzman, 1993). In repudiating his seduction theory, Freud was, in effect, not only accusing his patients of having lied to him, but also abandoning the practice of recovered memory therapy. These important aspects of this complex and controversial topic seem to have eluded Crews in his less than nuanced critique of Freud and psychoanalysis. Furthermore, for most ego psychologists in the United States, the goal of therapy for many decades was not the recovery of memory, but rather the analysis of defenses in order to form more adaptive compromise formations. This shift in clinical work was implicit in the development of Freud's (1923) structural model, comprising id, ego, and superego, which, in ego psychology, replaced the topographical model of unconscious, preconscious, and conscious (Arlow & Brenner, 1964).

The argument about recovered memories, then, focuses on the issue of whether sexual abuse that occurred in childhood can be entirely forgotten only to reemerge as an accurate memory in adulthood, or whether such memories are simply false; that is, the product either of the person's own imagination or of a psychotherapist's implanted suggestion. The controversy surrounding this issue not only involves complex social, legal, and moral dimensions, but also ones of a philosophical and psychological nature (Fonagy & Target, 1997; Pally, 2000). From a philosophical perspective, setting up truth against falsehood, history against fantasy, fact against desire is an error, as these pairs of opposites do not exist independently and, thus, cannot be separated into individual components. Similarly, in psychological terms there is an interplay between memory, reality, and fantasy, between what is subjective and what is objective, that is extremely hard to disentangle (Fonagy & Target, 1997).

Knox (2003) suggests that therapists who are unaware of the complexity of memory processes may put considerable pressure on their patients to recover memories of CSA. She argues that "the constant focus on finding such material may lead the patient to imagine such events and perhaps eventually come to believe that these imaginative representations are accurate representations of real past events" (pp. 4–5). On the other hand, therapists "may be unaware that memories can be forgotten for long periods of time and then recovered and may cause their patients distress if they fail to believe them" (p. 5).

The significance of a neuroscientific understanding of the function and structure of memory is emphasized by Solms (2000, cited in Pally, 2000). He observes: "Few topics are of more importance for psychoanalytic practice than an understanding of the varieties and vagaries of human memory" (p. iii). Similarly, Fonagy and Target (1997) note: "It is very likely that clinicians would profit from a more detailed knowledge of the nature of memory processes, and most particularly of the properties of procedural memories" (pp. 208–209). Indeed, informed by empirical research, Fonagy (1999b) argues that, "Any pressure from the psychoanalyst to find the roots of implicit memory traces...is doomed to failure" (p. 219). Making his position on this issue abundantly clear, he states: "The recovery of memory is an inappropriate goal," adding for good measure, "Therapies focusing on the recovery of memory pursue a false god" (p. 219). In Chapter 2, I summarize research data pertaining to the two main memory systems, explicit or declarative memory and implicit or nondeclarative memory, as these findings may helpfully inform the controversial issue of recovered memory.

Although I would wholeheartedly agree with Solms (2000, cited in Pally, 2000) and Fonagy and Target (1997) that a neuroscientific understanding of memory processes is helpful to the clinician, the current state of knowledge is not sufficient to ascertain whether recovered memories are true or false. This notwithstanding, and as I note in the following chapter, findings from cognitive neuroscience show that the explicit memory system may be damaged by trauma and result in dissociative defenses, altered states of consciousness, and the disconnection between memory systems. Although amnesia for the trauma may thus occur, implicit memory of the abuse may be expressed in emotional and somatic terms. Explicit memories of the trauma may, however, subsequently reemerge on being activated by a current retrieval cue (Schacter, 1996).

This argument is countered by research showing that memories are highly dynamic and unstable records. From a neurobiological perspective,

Rose (2005) speculates that this may help to explain the controversy about recovered memory of CSA. Because of the dynamism of memory and the active nature of remembering, such apparent memories may be biologically real for the person, in that they correspond to neurochemical traces in the brain, even though those traces may have been induced not by a real event, but by the later unwitting implanting of a false memory. In this sense, historical "reality" and biological "reality" are not one and the same thing.

Rose's (2005) supposition is consonant with research into the "illusion-of-truth" effect of implicit memory. This found that children and adults are susceptible to "remembering" false information about an event as true and are also more likely to believe a familiar statement than an unfamiliar one. Thus, the statements that participants rated as true were the ones they had previously heard (even though they did not consciously remember having heard them), regardless of whether the statements were true or false (Hasher, Goldstein, & Toppino, 1977).

More generally, research has shown that young children often have great difficulty remembering the source of information, which, in turn, renders them vulnerable to false recollections. Also, suggestive questioning can have devastating and distorting effects on the accuracy of some preschool children's memories. This reflects the fact that the hippocampus and temporal lobes are especially slow to develop and are immature in preschool children (Schacter, 1996).

CONCLUSION

What is clear from this debate, and from memory research in general, is the complex relationship between memory, fantasy, and reality. Indeed, it may be argued that memories do not exist in either a true or false state. Given this, as therapists we need to be aware of the importance of subjective experience in memory and strive to balance respect for historical truth with affirmation of the patient's narrative truth (Schacter, 1996). In accomplishing this, we need to be able to contain within the therapeutic relationship both our own and our patients' anxiety about uncertainty and "not knowing." As Bucci (2011) observes, traditional guides to theory and technique are no longer sufficient to help the therapist negotiate unpredictable interaction in the therapeutic encounter. Given this, the therapist "can no longer assume that there is a particular repressed scenario that is guiding the patient's experience, that he or she is avoiding, and that can be uncovered" (p. 50).

More specifically, and in agreement with Fonagy and his colleagues, I would argue that a neuroscientific understanding of the process and structure of implicit/procedural memory suggests that the therapeutic goal in classical psychoanalysis of lifting repression in order to recover previously unavailable memories needs to be reconceptualized as a process that facilitates change in the way the patient understands and feels in relation to a childhood experience (Fonagy et al., 2004; Fonagy & Target, 1997). This contemporary aspect of therapeutic action may be seen as being consonant with Freud's (1899) early thinking in respect to screen memories, which, as noted above, he viewed in terms of memories *relating to* childhood rather than memories *from* childhood. I discuss the role of implicit/procedural memory in therapeutic action in more detail in Chapter 11.

Chapter 2

The Two Main Memory Systems
A Neuroscience Perspective

INTRODUCTION

Recent findings from neuroscience suggest that memory is composed of a variety of distinct and dissociable processes and systems. Each system depends on a particular constellation of networks in the brain that involve different neural structures, each of which plays a highly specialized role within the system. It is generally accepted that brains deal in meaning rather than merely processing information and that emotion is as important as cognition in encoding and storing experience in memory. Moreover, cognitive-affective memories are subjective records of how we have experienced events and not replicas or facsimiles of the events themselves. The experiences we have are encoded by brain networks whose connections have already been shaped by previous encounters with the world. Thus, this preexisting knowledge powerfully influences how we encode and store new memories (Mancia, 2006; Schacter, 1987, 1996). However, memory is not only about learning, but also about subsequently recalling or retrieving what has been encoded and committed to memory. As part of this process, human beings classify what they see and experience as ways of discriminating between various possibilities. Without the ability to discriminate, predict, and classify we would experience the world as chaotic and confusing and thus would not survive (Rose, 2003). Indeed, neuroscience research emphasizes that prediction is one of the brain's most fundamental functions (Pally, 2005).

Linked to processes of classification, prediction, and discrimination, memory researchers have found that we possess an elaborate mechanism called "perceptual filtering." This ensures that we select and commit to memory salient information from the outside world and that we block information not deemed salient. Such filtering processes are largely nonconscious, but the information is, nonetheless, classified in accordance to its importance to us. These classifications about how we perceive and what we remember are based on experience and permeate our adult lives (Rose, 2003).

THE EXPLICIT AND IMPLICIT MEMORY SYSTEMS

Following Tulving (1983), psychologists and cognitive neuroscientists who specialize in memory research broadly agree that there are two main forms of memory: explicit or declarative memory, and implicit or non-declarative memory. Declarative memory has two aspects, being comprised of episodic memory, that is memory of autobiographical events in our own life history, and semantic memory, which refers to conceptual and factual knowledge of the world. Autobiographical memory allows us explicitly to recall personal events that uniquely define our lives (Damasio, 2003; Schacter, 1996). Indeed, Damasio (2003) views autobiographical memory, consciousness, and a sense of self as being interlinked:

> With the help of autobiographical memory, consciousness provides us with a self, enriched by the records of our own individual experience. When we face each new moment of life as conscious beings, we bring to bear on that moment the circumstances surrounding our past joys and sorrows, along with the imaginary circumstances of our anticipated future.... (p. 270)

However, he asserts that certain contents of declarative memory remain submerged for long periods of time and may always remain so. Furthermore, memories undergo a complex process of reconstruction or recontextualization during retrieval. Therefore, memories of some autobiographical events may be reconstructed in ways that differ from the original, or may never again see the light of consciousness. Instead, such memories may promote the retrieval of other memories, which then become conscious in the form of other facts or emotional states (Damasio, 1999; Mancia, 2006).

Implicit memory includes a type of memory in which previous experiences aid in the performance of a skill or task, such as learning to play a musical instrument or to ride a bicycle, and emotional memory, which influences current thoughts, feelings, and behavior in a relational context without conscious awareness of those previous experiences. Research into implicit memory indicates that it operates through a different mental process from explicit memory and is automatic in operation and not accessible to verbal report. Indeed, studies of brain-damaged patients have shown that implicit memory involves emotion-laden action and can be recontextualized in the absence of any capacity for explicit memory (Damasio, 1999; Mancia, 2006; Rose, 2005; Schacter, 1996). Implicit memory, then, is principally perceptual, nonconscious, and nonreflective, and allows us to learn new skills and acquire habitual ways of acting outside of conscious awareness. In daily life, we rely on implicit memory in the form of procedural memory (Schacter, 1987, 1996; Mancia, 2006; Pally, 2000, 2005). Research findings confirm that implicit, nonconscious, emotionally laden learning occurs and is available to reconstruction in the light of new experience (Boston Change Process Study Group [BCPSG], 2008). Moreover, a person's "character" and ways of interacting with others may be mediated and supported by procedural memory systems (Grigsby & Hartlaub, 1994; Schacter, 1996).

The brain structures that support implicit memory are in place before the systems needed for explicit memory and are used by pre-linguistic infants to learn from experience (Schacter, 1987, 1996; Pally, 2000, 2005). For example, face recognition occurs within hours of birth, with even day-old babies being able to distinguish between their mother's and another woman's face. Similarly, olfactory recognition, based on pheromone chemical signaling, contributes to the mother–infant attachment, with babies being able to discriminate between, and showing a preference for, the mother's smell to that of a stranger (Rose, 2005).

Unlike explicit memories, implicit memories do not seem to become forgotten, but persist, even in the face of brain damage and disease (Rose, 2003; Schacter, 1996). Indeed, while our sense of self and identity is highly dependent on explicit memory for past episodes and autobiographical facts, our personalities may be more closely tied to implicit memory processes. Appreciating the pervasive and invisible influence of implicit memory on our thoughts, feelings, and behavior provides an essential insight into the fragile nature of human memory, as well as its powerful effect on our mental life (Grigsby & Hartlaub, 1994; Schacter, 1996).

IMPLICIT MEMORY, REPRESSION, AND THE DYNAMIC UNCONSCIOUS

The nonconscious world of implicit memory revealed by cognitive neuroscience differs markedly from Freud's conceptualization of the dynamic unconscious (BCPSG, 2008). The dynamic unconscious consists of what was once consciously known and has since then been subject to repression. Given this, repression can only act on events experienced at a developmental-neurobiological stage that allows encoding into autobiographical memory (Fonagy, 1999b; Mancia, 2006; Schacter, 1996). By contrast, implicit memories arise in early development as a natural consequence of such everyday repetitive and habitual experiences as perceiving, relating, and acting. Implicit memories of a traumatic or nontraumatic nature may then be enacted in behavioral terms in the form of emotional procedural memories in contexts that cue the retrieval of such memories. From the vantage point of neuroscience, primal repression, as conceptualized by Freud (1926), and theorized by Lacan (1993) as an inaccessible form of memory, may, in phenomenological terms, be seen as having certain features in common with implicit memory. This may also be the case with Bollas' (1987) formulation of the "unthought known," and D. B. Stern's (1997) concept of "unformulated experience."

As I discuss more fully in Chapter 5, Bollas (1987) connects Winnicott's concept of the "true self" and Freud's concept of the ego to the notion of primal repression. Bollas argues that the primal repressed must be the inherited disposition that constitutes the core of the personality. However, he avers that "The concept of primal repression does not address early intersubjective contributions to the infant's knowledge of being and relating" (p. 280). Given this, Bollas suggests that the term *primal repression* should be replaced by the concept of the "unthought known," a term he uses to stand for everything that on some deep level is known, such as moods, somatic experiences, and personal idiom, but which has not yet been thought, in that the phenomena have remained unavailable for mental processing.

In a way somewhat similar to Bollas' thinking, D. B. Stern (1997) contends that "unformulated experience" is composed of vague, ambiguous tendencies and is "content without definite shape" (p. 39); it is the "uninterpreted form of those raw materials of conscious, reflective experience that may eventually be assigned interpretations and thereby be brought into articulate form" (p. 37). Stern suggests that "The way in which each of us shapes moment-to-moment experience is the outcome of our characteristic patterns of formulation interacting with the exigencies of the moment" (p. 38). Moreover, he contends that "the resolution of the ambiguity of unformulated experience is an interpersonal event" (p. 38).

The Boston Change Process Study Group (BCPSG, 2008) posit that D. B. Stern's (1997) concept of unformulated experience is a form of "implicit relational knowing" (IRK), that is, a nonsymbolic, nonconscious form of "knowledge" that operates outside of focal attention and conscious experience. IRK is not necessarily dynamically repressed into the Freudian unconscious; rather, it is a form of "knowing" that "has never been put into words, has never had to be, or never could be" (p. 129). The BCPSG point out that non-language-based knowing "is the only form of knowing in infancy by developmental default" (p. 129). The ideas of the BCPSG are discussed in more detail in Chapter 8.

I would suggest that the phenomenological description of implicit/procedural memory may also be seen in Winnicott's (1974) final paper, "Fear of Breakdown." Here, Winnicott speaks of "primitive agonies" and of "a fear of a breakdown that has already happened" but which has not been "experienced" and is thus prone to being repeated at an unconscious level of mental functioning (p. 107). His thinking in this regard is clearly influenced by Freud's (1920) notion of the "compulsion to repeat," whereby the subject repeats old, unconscious experiences under the strong impression that his or her actions are fully determined by the circumstances of the present moment (Freud). However, Winnicott makes it clear that he is not referring to Freud's dynamically repressed unconscious, but rather to unconscious phenomena that the ego was too immature to encompass and gather "into the area of personal omnipotence" (p. 104). He contends that "the original experience of primitive agony cannot get into the past tense unless the ego can first gather it into its own present time experience and into omnipotent control" (p. 105). In the absence of such a resolution, the patient must "go on looking for the past detail which is *not yet experienced*. This search takes the form of looking for this detail in the future" (p. 105, emphasis in original). If the patient can accept this "queer kind of truth, that what is not yet experienced did nevertheless happen in the past, then the way is open for the agony to be experienced in the transference, in reaction to the analyst's failures and mistakes" (p. 105). Via the transference, "the past and future thing then becomes a matter of the here and now, and becomes experienced by the patient for the first time" (p. 105). Significantly, Winnicott (1974) argues that the transference experience "is the equivalent of remembering, and this outcome is the equivalent of lifting of repression that occurs in the analysis of the psychoneurotic patient (classical Freudian analysis)" (p. 105).

Winnicott (1974), then, is drawing a distinction between the repressed unconscious on the one hand and unremembered unconscious phenomena from early childhood on the other hand. From the vantage point of neuroscience research, I am suggesting that the fear of breakdown, the unthought known, unformulated experience, and the compulsion to repeat, may all be understood, at least in part, as phenomenological descriptions of the functioning of implicit/procedural memory. As noted in Chapter 1, Fonagy and Target (1997) hold a similar view in respect of Freud's (1914) concept of "screen memories." I would also see Bion's (1984) concept of untransformed, split off "beta elements," and the subjective experience of "nameless dread," in similar terms. By extension, I would argue that this distinction may be found in the writings of those influenced by Bion, for example, Ferro (2011) and Ogden (2009). I discuss Bion's "elements" theory in more detail in Chapter 5.

Certain aspects of Winnicott's thinking may be seen in Sandler and Sandler's (1998) integration of ego psychology and object relations theory. The authors differentiate the "past unconscious" and the "present unconscious." Consonant with neuroscience research and an attachment theory perspective, the Sandlers (1997) regard the past unconscious as a system of implicit procedures embodied in dynamic templates or "rules of functioning" (p. 177). These rules derive from the internalization of significant self- and object representations and shape the form of unconscious fantasies, thoughts, wishes, and memories as they arise in the present unconscious. The Sandlers argue that repression occurs in the present unconscious, being used defensively to protect consciousness from unpleasant or traumatic affective experiences. Procedural rules are expressed in repetitive behavior patterns and in the reactivation of object relations in the transference. The transference is understood in terms of the patient attempting to get the therapist to play a particular role in the present which accords with the rules laid down in the patient's past. This perspective may also be seen in the respective writings of Eagle (2003) and Wachtel (2008).

Implicit/procedural memory, then, becomes an integral part of the transferential experience. Indeed, Clyman (1991) contends that procedural memories formed in early childhood underline the transference. In this context, Mancia (1993) argues that transference enactments are not so much a reactivation of historically definable experiences as a "facilitation of the comparison and integration of present and past experience, as reactivated *by* the transference" (p. 164, emphasis in original).

THE DYNAMIC NATURE OF MEMORY

More generally, memory is seen as an emergent property of the brain which, as an open, dynamic system, is continually in interaction with the natural and social worlds outside, both changing them and being changed in their turn (Rose, 2003). Indeed, Edelman (1987) critiques a computer model of mind, arguing that the developing neural system has the capacity to change its properties as part of a process of continuous selection of preexisting groups of neurons and their synaptic connections in response to environmental challenges and demands. Edelman (1987) calls this process "neural Darwinism." From this perspective, explicit memory is viewed as a dialectical and highly dynamic phenomenon. Each time we remember, we work on and transform our memories; they are not simply called up from store and, once consulted, replaced unmodified. Rather, our conscious memories are recreated each time we remember. Thus, when we remember an event, we are actually not remembering the event itself, but the last time we remembered it (Rose, 2003, 2005).

The dynamic nature of memory is an example of brain plasticity. Respecting the brain as an open learning system avoids reductionist thinking and helps to create order out of chaos (Damasio, 1999, 2003; Edelman, 1989; Rose, 2003; Schacter, 1996). From a neurobiological perspective and consonant with the concept of brain plasticity, Rose (2003) contends that learning evokes a biochemical cascade that permanently alters the brain. A similar biochemical process occurs when a memory is reactivated. However, Tulving (1983) suggests that although the brain has been lastingly changed, the resulting engram of the encoded experience only exists when it is activated and the memory is retrieved.

Chapter 3

Contemporary Perspectives on Psychological Trauma and Affect Regulation

INTRODUCTION

As noted in Chapter 1, Pierre Janet was a contemporary of Freud and, like him, was influenced by Charcot's idea that hysteria was a phenomenon linked to a traumatic event. Indeed, Janet studied under Charcot at the Pitié-Saltpêtrière Hospital in Paris and wrote extensively about trauma and memory, coining the terms dissociation and subconscious. He became renowned during his lifetime as a psychologist, philosopher, and psychotherapist, and his theory of the psyche was seen as competing with that of Freud's. While psychoanalysis prevailed over Janet's psychological analysis, in recent years there has been renewed interest in his thinking, fuelled, in part, by the debate about recovered memories of childhood sexual abuse (Brown & van der Hart, 1998), as discussed in Chapter 1.

Janet undertook a systematic study of dissociation in the 1890s, seeing this concept as the crucial psychological process with which the person reacts to traumatic experiences. He also showed that traumatic memories may be expressed as sensory perceptions, affect states, and behavioral reenactments (van der Kolk & van der Hart, 1989). In the intervening decades, psychological trauma and dissociation have dropped in and out of fashion, predominantly in a context of war (Herman, 1992). Certainly, during the past five decades there has been renewed interest in trauma fuelled by the experience of American veterans of the Vietnam War, but also by an acknowledgment of the widespread incidence of emotional, physical, and sexual abuse in Western culture. These factors have, in turn, generated a renewal of interest in the mental defense of dissociation and contributed to a debate about multiple personality disorder or dissociative identity disorder (MPD/DID).

The word *trauma* derives from the Greek meaning "penetration" and "wounding." Psychological trauma results in feelings of intense fear, helplessness, loss of control, and threat of annihilation. Such feelings overwhelm the adaptations that ordinarily provide people with a sense of self-agency, emotional connection, and meaning (Herman, 1992). Traumatic affect is therefore viewed as having a disorganizing effect on mental functioning and as being a significant motivating factor in the manifestation of psychopathology (de Zulueta, 1993; Schore, 1994; Tyson & Tyson, 1990; Wilkinson, 2010). Given optimal development, affects come to serve a signal function, enabling the child to master and regulate his or her own affects instead of being overwhelmed by their disorganizing effects (Freud, 1926; Tyson & Tyson, 1990). However, where there is a failure of parental empathy or traumatic interference of one form or another, this process is disrupted. Hence, the development of a coherent sense of self is compromised, leading to fragmentation of experience and personality and to the manifestation of psychopathology in later life (Kohut, 1971; Tyson, 2002; Tyson & Tyson, 1990).

CUMULATIVE DEVELOPMENTAL TRAUMA

From an intersubjective/attachment perspective, the child's experience of self becomes meaningful in the context of the caregiver's capacity to reflect on the current mental state of the child and upon her own mental states as these pertain to her relationship with her child (Fonagy et al., 2004; Slade, 2008). Parental mentalization is especially critical during early childhood because nonverbal behavioral cues are the child's primary means for communicating his or her mental states to the parent. Indeed, it is generally agreed that the capacity to mentalize one's own and the other's emotional and intentional states crucially depends on the infant's earliest affective exchanges with the primary caregiver (Target, 2008). When this context is characterized by dramatic or cumulative developmental trauma, the attachment system is hyperactivated and the capacity to mentalize is compromised (Fonagy, 2008). As a consequence, the child relives the traumatic experience in the mode of psychic equivalence, characterized by a frightening correspondence between internal reality and external reality, instead of in the pretend mode characterized by play, imagination and metaphor, and thence the ability to differentiate inner reality from outer reality (Fonagy et al., 2004; Fonagy & Target, 1996). A compromised capacity for mentalization, then, has implications for self-organization, self-agency, impulse control, and affect regulation. Defensive strategies and implicit procedures developed in infancy in response to cumulative trauma consequent on repeated non-contingent interactions with low-mentalizing caregivers become aspects of character and relating that persist precisely because they are automatic and outside awareness. Stressful interpersonal contexts in later life may activate representational models developed in such an early relational context and again compromise the capacity to mentalize (Fonagy, 2008; Renn, 2006).

Affects, then, are seen as organizers of self-experience throughout development, and the significance of the caregiving environment as a potentially traumatic influence on the development of psychopathology is emphasized (Bowlby, 1973; Fonagy et al., 2004; Fonagy & Target, 1996; Holmes, 1993; Lyons-Ruth & Block, 1996; Orange, 1995; Schore, 1994; Stolorow, 1995; Teicholz, 2009; Tyson & Tyson, 1990; Wilkinson, 2010). Indeed, findings show that it is often not the traumatic event in and of itself that is salient in personality development and adult psychopathology, but rather the characteristic intersubjective/attachment system within which the child experiences the trauma (Lyons-Ruth & Block, 1996; Lyons-Ruth, Bronfman & Atwood, 1999; Lyons-Ruth & Jacobvitz, 1999; Lyons-Ruth et al., 2005; Renn, 2003; Rutter, 1997; Settlage et al., 1990). For example, Lyons-Ruth and Block (1996) and Lyons-Ruth et al. (2005) found that women who had been exposed to childhood violence were at elevated risk for hostile or emotionally withdrawn caregiving on becoming mothers and for establishing disorganized attachment relationships with their infants. Of relevance to the link between cumulative developmental trauma and disorganized attachment, the authors found that subtle aspects of the relationship seemed to be involved, rather than gross abuse, neglect, or abandonment. This was manifested as profound disruption in patterns of mother–infant verbal and nonverbal affective communication, with repeated infant communication of distress, anger, or contact-seeking being entirely overridden by repetitive nonresponsive behaviors by the mothers. Moreover, there was little or no attempt by the mothers to repair the derailed interaction.

Lyons-Ruth and Block (1996) conclude that mothers who were severely traumatized in childhood by their attachment figures may use unresponsive withdrawal and unresponsive hostile intrusiveness in the service of minimizing their own responsive emotional contact with the infant as a means of self-protection and to avoid activating their own unintegrated traumatic memories. Such indirect displays of fear by the mother evoke fear in the infant, whose felt security is directly tied to the communicative adequacy of the maternal relationship. In essence, the attachment behavioral system becomes nonfunctional, with no protective function at the level of infant experience. These findings reflect Schore's (2011) contention that preverbal communication, consisting of implicit relational knowing, is transmitted intergenerationally by means of the psychobiological exchanges embedded in the cocreated attachment bond. Schore (1994, 2011) argues that relational trauma deriving from dysregulated attachment experiences, as described by Lyons-Ruth and Block (1996), is imprinted in the right brain and associated with the child's use of dissociation. He cites findings showing that an impaired ability to regulate the intensity of affect is the most enduring consequence of early relational trauma and, moreover, is strongly associated with psychopathology in adulthood.

These circumspect views suggest that a consideration of trauma needs to address the effects derived from family dysfunction, parenting practices, parental psychopathology, and the transmission of trauma across generations, as well as those stemming from the traumatic event itself (Fonagy, 1999a; Holmes, 1999a; Lyons-Ruth & Block, 1996). These views reflect, in part, findings which reveal that child abuse rarely occurs in isolation and that its traumatic effects can often be accounted for by coexisting family dysfunction (Benjamin & Pugh, 2001; Lyons-Ruth & Jacobvitz, 1999; Rutter, 1981, 1997). Moreover, research has found that emotional abuse is far more common than physical or sexual abuse, yet just as significant in the development of psychopathology because the child has to employ defensive strategies to deal with negative affect; for example, suppressing hate, anger, and sadness by being either good or inappropriately happy (Bradley, 2003).

The child's adaptive response to emotional abuse may be seen in terms of Winnicott's (1960) formulation of the "false self." This defensive structure comprises a compliant, acquiescent way of organizing self-experience and is constructed in reaction to conflict and cumulative trauma in the infant–caregiver relationship. As a result of this, the child withdraws from self-generated spontaneity and, instead, conforms to the imposed images and narcissistic needs of the caregiver upon whom he or she depends for love and protection. In suppressing vital aspects of self-experience, the child adopts an alien reality and inauthentic mode of being and relating (Fonagy et al., 2004; Fonagy & Target, 1996). In a phenomenological sense, the child ceases to exist in those moments when the parent fails to greet his or her spontaneous gesture (Winnicott, 1987). Moreover, the failure to mirror the child's current state leads to an internalization of the caregiver's actual state, which becomes an alien part of the child's nascent self-structure (Fonagy et al., 2004; Winnicott, 1967).

The false self, then, reflects a lack of recognition and validation by the caregiver of the child's subjective experience and authentic sense of self. It operates defensively as a means of splitting off separation anxiety, fear of abandonment, and dread of self-annihilation, and is maintained at an unconscious level of mental functioning (Mills, 2003). Such splitting is not simply a defense, but may become a characteristic mode of organizing self-experience (Ogden, 1986). The prevalence of false self phenomena in contemporary society, in the form of an obdurate attachment to inauthentic and constricted internalized relational configurations, has led Mitchell (1993) to assert that pseudo-normality is the clinical problem of our time. Mitchell's thinking in this respect resonates with Bollas' (1994) concept of the "normotic" personality and description of "normopathic" characterological traits, and also with McDougall's (1990) "plea for a measure of abnormality." McDougall argues that a measure of abnormality may help to preclude us from developing a stultifying "normopathic" personality, the function of which is to maintain a well-compensated psychotic state. McDougall is clearly influenced by Winnicott who, in a self-reference, asserted that through analysis and self-analysis he had achieved some measure of insanity.

Although not discussing madness, Schore (1991, 1994, 2001) emphasizes the impact that family dysfunction has on the developing infant, seeing the primary caregiver as the source of the infant's stress regulation and sense of safety and security. Indeed, Panksepp (2001) found that early emotional experiences can profoundly influence the development of the brain, since it causes a change in the child's mental economy, as described by Edelman (1987) in terms of "neural Darwinism." Findings confirm that the infant's attachment to the caregiver is promoted by the interactive regulation of emotion (Sroufe, 1996). During this intersubjective process, characteristic strategies of affect regulation and "distance regulation" are cocreated during attachment transactions (Sroufe & Waters, 1977). As noted above, the process involves the recognition and labeling of specific emotions in the self and in others and, optimally, the development of flexible strategies to control uncomfortable levels of arousal and mediate interpersonal conflict (Bradley, 2003; Fonagy & Target, 1996). Early trauma, such as abandonment, and physical, sexual and emotional abuse, can create the conditions for a lifelong tendency to sadness, depression, anger, and resentment (Mancia, 2006; Wilkinson, 2010).

It is not always appreciated that affect regulation involves both an appropriate dampening of negative emotions, such as shame, guilt, anger, and sadness, and an intensification of positive emotions, such as pride, joy, and interest-excitement (Schore, 1994). The caregiver's capacity to reflect on and regulate his or her own affect plays a key role in the interactive regulation of the child's emotional states. This, in turn, facilitates the child's ability to recognize and self-regulate a wide range of emotions. Significant disruptions in caregiver–infant affective communications are associated with disorganized and ambivalent-resistant forms of child attachment. Such disruptions may consist of clearly dramatic trauma—sexual or physical abuse—or be correlated with more subtle parental behavior, for example, withdrawal, dissociation, role-reversal, frightened and/or frightening behavior, and hostile, critical, and intrusive attitudes (Lyons-Ruth & Block, 1996; Lyons-Ruth et al., 2005). These kinds of caregiver orientations thwart the child's psychological integration and are characteristics of cumulative developmental trauma. An emerging body of evidence suggests that affect regulation constitutes an important part of the relationship between cumulative relational trauma and psychopathology in adulthood (Bradley, 2003; Schore, 1994).

CLINICAL ILLUSTRATION

"Peter" is the oldest of four children, having a younger brother and two younger half siblings. His mother had immigrated to Britain from the West Indies when she was 17. Peter has only a skimpy recollection of his biological father, who deserted the family when he was just 3 years of age leaving the mother to cope as best she could with little social or emotional support in a new country. Shortly after this, she sent the two brothers to Barbados to be raised by her parents. Some 5 years later, when she had established herself in a career and a new relationship, she arranged for the children to be returned to her.

Peter had developed a close, loving relationship with his grandmother during his 5-year stay in Barbados and had felt intense distress at having to leave her to return to England. This transition was particularly fraught because of the mother's routine emotional and physical abuse of Peter and his brother on their reunion.

Peter responded to this traumatic situation by manifesting emotional and behavioral problems at home and at school, where he was bullied and subjected to racist taunts, a situation not helped by his being separated from his brother, who was educated at a different school. Peter became confused, withdrawn, and socially isolated, and took to carrying a knife because he feared for his personal safety. At the age of 12, he began to refuse to attend school and was referred to a child psychologist. He refused to talk with her, and so the therapy was discontinued. In his teens he developed a serious alcohol problem and was soon appearing before the courts. Peter's relationships with women were short-lived and often violent. He has numerous criminal convictions for assaulting his female partners, which have resulted in his being imprisoned on several occasions.

From a relational perspective, informed by the literature on attachment and trauma, I see the roots of Peter's violence as residing in his unresolved traumatic experience of separation, loss, and abuse within a disorganized caregiving/attachment system. Despite the early loss of the father and separation from the mother, had he received appropriate help to securely reattach to his mother, and thus to use her as a secure base to mourn the separation from the grandmother, his development may well have taken a different pathway. As it was, his sadness, fear, and distress were cruelly dealt with, and he was forced to adapt to a harsh reality and alien culture as best he could.

This fraught situation was further complicated by his experience of the mother as being not only powerful, dominant, and abusive, but also loving, caring, and concerned that he should make a success of his life. Thus, Peter both loved her and feared and hated her. These ambivalent, conflicting feelings led to the development of a multiple, incoherent representational model in respect of his mother, and to a concomitant disorganized pattern of attachment. As a consequence, his capacity to regulate negative feeling states and to reflect on and organize traumatic experiences was seriously compromised. As it was, Peter displayed a pronounced tendency to react violently to even relatively insignificant personal slights, losses, and rejections. Such minor injuries to the sense of self seemed to activate the original trauma, together with unintegrated affective states of shame, hate, and rage associated with racism and physical and emotional abuse, and thus to elicit a response that was disproportionate to the current narcissistic mortification.

Moreover, because of persisting states of insecurity and lack of trust Peter was unable to enter into a committed, emotionally mature relationship. It would seem that the prospect of becoming attached to another person elicited expectations that oscillated between fear of engulfment and fear of abandonment, as expressed in his catastrophic narrative. As a result, emotionally meaningful relationships were avoided and intimacy was defended against.

From a neuroscience perspective, Peter's incapacity to modulate negative affect is seen as deriving from the caregiver's failure to interactively regulate states of fear, shame, hate, and rage during critical phases in the development of emotional systems in the right brain in the second year of life (Schore, 1991, 1994, 2011). Early unregulated shame-exchanges, in particular, create a rupture to the attachment bond and are an important source of developmental trauma. Such states are bypassed or dissociated by the child, and later by the adult. This defensive maneuver inhibits exploration of the external environment and knowledge of internal emotional states, leading to an impaired ability to recognize, label, and articulate discrete feelings, a condition known as alexithymia (Krystal, 1988; McDougall, 1985, 1989; Schore, 1994; Sifneos, 1973). Knowing that we have feelings is the stepping stone in the process of planning a specific response (Damasio, 1999). Similarly, having access to, and the capacity to reflect on, affective states is critical to effective self-agency (Aron, 1998, 2000; Fonagy et al., 2004; Fonagy & Target, 1996; Slade, 2008).

Research indicates that developmental trauma is typically embedded in the child's family situation and so is not merely a single event phenomenon but cumulative (Khan, 1979; McDougall, 1985, 1989; Rutter, 1981, 1997; Schore, 1994; Wilkinson, 2010). In such an interpersonal context, the caregiver either wittingly or unwittingly dysregulates the infant's affective state and, crucially, either withholds any interactive repair or is inconsistent and ineffective in this endeavor (Lyons-Ruth & Block, 1996; Lyons-Ruth et al., 2005). As a result of such severe misattunement, the infant is left for long periods in an intensely disorganized psychobiological state that is beyond his or her coping strategies. The infant's response to such a fear-inducing environment consists of hyper-vigilance and hyper-arousal, followed by hypo-arousal or dissociation, which involves numbing, avoidance, compliance, and restricted affect (Beebe & Lachmann, 1992; Perry, Pollard, Blakely, Baker, & Vigilante, 1995; Schore, 1994). The internalization of such interactive patterns may interfere with the developing child's optimal regulation of arousal, and thus compromise his or her capacity to stay attentive and to process socio-emotional information and regulate bodily states, particularly when under heightened emotional stress. This is manifested in adulthood as an impaired ability to maintain interpersonal relationships, cope with stress, and regulate emotions (Beebe, Jaffe, & Lachmann, 1992; Bradley, 2003; Schore, 1994; Spezzano, 1993). These clinical features were pronounced in Peter's case.

The view that the origins of adult psychopathology lie primarily in early environmental failure has received increasing support from the scientific community, particularly in the light of neuroscience evidence detailing the impact of disorganized attachment and cumulative trauma on the child's neurological and emotional development. Indeed, findings indicate that the effects of early trauma on the developing brain are very similar to the dysfunctions found in the brains of adult schizophrenics, as well as in those diagnosed with post-traumatic stress disorder and dissociative disorders. The evidence that children's immediate social environment affects brain development would now appear to be unequivocal (Mancia, 2006; Panksepp, 2001; Siegal, 2001). Such findings challenge biogenetic explanations of mental illness and support psychosocial explanations (Read, Goodman, Morrison, Ross, & Aderhold, 2004).

CONCLUSION

Cumulative trauma, then, sets the child on a developmental trajectory that may culminate in psychological breakdown and criminality in later life. From this perspective, the role of the caregiver as mediator, reflector, interpreter, and moderator of the child's mind cannot be overemphasized. As Fonagy et al. (2004) observe, disturbed, unresponsive, and abusive parents obliterate their children's affective experience. The lack of attuned mirroring and marking of affective states leaves the child with an inner life that is experienced as barren and unknowable. Such feelings of alienation and isolation become fundamental to a fragmented and empty sense of self and to the failure to develop sustaining and nurturing relationships with others. In short, affects that are not held in mind by the caregiver or, more significantly, are misrepresented or distorted, remain diffuse, terrifying, and unrepresentable. This may lead to a range of borderline phenomena and criminal pathology of the self in later years (Fonagy 1999a; Fonagy & Target, 1996; Fonagy et al., 1997, 2004; Holmes, 1999a; Schore, 1994, 2001). Given this, it may be more productive to view symptoms of post-traumatic stress disorder, dissociative disorders, schizophrenia, borderline personality disorder, and so on as related components of a long-term process that begins with adaptive responses to early traumatic experiences, rather than persisting with the current practice of separating the trauma/abuse sequelae into discrete categories of "disorder" (Read et al., 2004). In essence, it is argued that cumulative trauma in infancy, consisting of oscillating states of hyper-arousal and dissociation, impacts the child's resilience and becomes the template for adult post-traumatic stress disorder (Perry et al., 1995; Schore, 1994, 2011).

Chapter 4

Memory, Trauma, and Dissociation

The Reemergence of Trauma-Related Childhood Memories

INTRODUCTION

As I noted in the previous chapter, Janet coined the term *dissociation*, using it to describe a changed state of consciousness in patients who had suffered traumatic experiences. He considered post-traumatic hysteria to be a disorder of the biographical function of memory processing, arguing that traumatic memories are automatically reactivated and reenacted under state-specific trigger conditions. He suggested that the traces of the traumatic memory cannot be expunged until they have been translated into a personal narrative. However, while seeing traumatic memories as being reproductive, Janet argued that they are vulnerable to post-event modifications and should not be considered as exact reflections of the original traumatic events (Brown & van der Hart, 1998).

Following Janet, pathological dissociation may be defined as an altered, detached state of consciousness, which is automatically induced as a mental defense against psychological trauma involving pain, danger, terror, and helplessness. The traumatic experience has the effect of overwhelming and disorganizing the person's normal fight/flight responses with the consequence that part of mental functioning becomes separated from other activities. In such situations, events become disconnected from their ordinary meaning and perception is distorted, with partial loss of memory occurring. Experience takes on a dreamlike, unreal quality and the traumatized person feels as though the event is not happening to him or her (Herman, 1992; van der Kolk, 1989, 1994).

From a relational perspective, Davies and Frawley (1994) and Bromberg (1998) have respectively shown how a relational matrix characterized by trauma and abuse can lead to the development of multiple self-states. Here, traumatic experience is dissociated and encapsulated within the personality as a separate, non-reflective reality cut off from authentic human relatedness. In a review of a number of empirical studies, Boon and Draijer (1993) assert that dissociative identity disorder (DID) can be considered to be a specific and complicated post-traumatic stress disorder which develops in early childhood in response to severe and chronic abuse. Brown and van der Hart (1998) cite a number of studies showing that total amnesia has been reported in cases of sexual abuse in childhood, in combat trauma, in extreme experiences in concentration camps, in torture, and in cases of robbery. However, as Wachtel (2008) observes, the mental defense of dissociation refers to an overlapping set of phenomena, not to a single phenomenon. Thus, in less extreme instances of trauma, dissociation may be expressed in subtle, nuanced ways, and in varying degrees in everyday experience, depending on the person's particular state of mind and relational and cultural context.

A NEUROSCIENCE PERSPECTIVE

As we have seen, the current view from neuroscience holds that memory is composed of parallel, interacting systems. This is seen as providing potentially fertile ground for the operation of dissociative processes (Schacter, 1996). With regard to adults, dissociation in reaction to a traumatic event represents a negative expression of brain plasticity resulting from an uncontrolled cascade of stress-related neurochemicals which may lead to the failure of the explicit memory system. This is reflected in the disruption of learning, memory, and neural network organization (Cozolino, 2002, 2006; de Zulueta, 1993; Herman, 1992; van der Kolk, 1989, 1994; Wilkinson, 2010). However, dissociation does not erase traumatic memories, but severs the links among the different memory systems. As a consequence, aspects of the past or periods of ongoing experience become detached from conscious awareness, and the dissociated traumatic experience is encoded and stored in the systems of implicit/procedural memory as sensory fragments with no linking narrative (van der Kolk, 1994; Schacter, 1996; Schore, 2001; Pally, 2005).

Dissociation and concomitant altered states of consciousness make a traumatic experience difficult to recall consciously. Indeed, the most common post-traumatic symptom is unbidden recollection of the trauma in the form of flashback memories, which occur in the context of emotional disturbances. The amygdala and stress-related hormones play a special role in emotional memories. The amygdala is an almond-shaped structure located deep within the medial temporal lobes of the brain that form part of the limbic system. Evidence suggests that the maturation of the limbic system is experience-dependent and directly influenced by the caregiver–infant relationship (Schore, 1994). Research indicates that the amygdala is particularly involved in the fight/flight fear response and in emotional processing and implicit memory (Ledoux, 1994, 1996). Given these factors, memory for trauma differs in important ways from ordinary memory. Indeed, findings suggest that flashback and somatic memories are heavily influenced by expectations, beliefs, and fears which are not recognized as past memories activated in the present. Rather, they are experienced as happening in the here-and-now. Given this, the contents of a flashback memory may say more about what a person believes or fears about the past than about what actually happened (Pally, 2005; Schacter, 1996). The difficulty in consciously recalling traumatic memories makes it more likely that a person will manifest behaviors and symptoms that reflect implicit memory for dissociated experience (van der Kolk & van der Hart, 1989). As an example of this, Schacter (1996) cites Terr (1981), who found that children who had been traumatized in a violent school bus kidnapping enacted the trauma in their play, fears, and other nonverbal behaviors.

In reviewing the research on sample populations diagnosed as suffering from dissociative disorders, Steinberg (1993) concludes that five primary symptoms are involved: amnesia, depersonalization, derealization, identity confusion, and identity alteration. She recommends that these dissociative symptoms be routinely evaluated when interviewing patients with histories of trauma. Davies and Frawley (1994) take the view that dissociation exists on a continuum with DID representing the most extreme form of this defense. This opinion is shared by Mollon (1996) who, while acknowledging the startling clinical phenomena of DID, contends that the disorder "...inherently involves pretense and simulation..." (p. 114). Further, he points to the overlap between DID and other psychiatric disorders such as borderline personality disorder, antisocial personality disorder, and somatization disorder. In this context, Mollon questions whether DID should be conceptualized as part of a broad grouping of trauma-based psychiatric disorders, or as a unique form of personality organization deriving from dissociative and post-traumatic factors.

THE PSYCHOBIOLOGY OF TRAUMA

As previously noted, a psychobiological perspective, as proposed by van der Kolk (1989, 1994), understands altered states of consciousness as resulting from the release of endogenous opioids within the central nervous system, a reaction that is triggered by the traumatic event itself. Bessel van der Kolk has been involved in trauma research since the 1970s and has explored these processes in depth. His work integrates developmental, biological, psychodynamic, and interpersonal aspects of the impact of trauma and its treatment. Influenced by van der Kolk's research, de Zulueta (1993) thinks it probable that a similar psychobiological reaction is involved in disordered attachment behavior, seeing this as being activated by the trauma of separation and loss.

In reviewing studies pointing to the underlying physiology of attachment, van der Kolk (1989, 1994) suggests that endorphin releasers are laid down in the early months of life in the context of attachment to caregivers with different styles of caregiving. Indeed, neurobiological data indicate that mother–infant interaction activates specific neuro-endocrine systems. For example, the stress response entailed in avoidant behavior appears to be maintained by the release of catecholomines and cortisol, the main stress hormone, whereas attachment and nurturing behavior seem to depend upon the availability of oxytocin and vasopressin, positive neuropeptides associated with loving physical touch (Mancia, 2006; Siegal, 2001; Siegal et al., 1999). Van der Kolk (1989, 1994) concludes that affectively intense experiences accompanied by the release of such neurochemicals come to be associated with states of both security and trauma. Moreover, as Herman (1992) points out, dissociated traumatic states may become frozen in time.

THE REEMERGENCE OF TRAUMA-RELATED CHILDHOOD MEMORIES

As has been well-documented, all of us are subject to childhood amnesia in that we remember nothing prior to the ages of 2 or 3 and little prior to the ages of 5 or 6. As noted above, this is because the neural networks that support explicit memory, the hippocampus and temporal lobes, develop more slowly than those that support implicit memory, the basal ganglia, cerebellum, and amygdala, which are almost fully developed at birth (Pally, 2000; Rose, 2005). As previously noted, the amygdala is at the center of the fear regulation system and is particularly involved in implicit learning of intense, emotionally charged experiences (LeDoux, 1994, 1996).

There may be an evolutionary reason for this, in that for survival purposes infants need to possess the capacity to experience fear and anxiety in order to signal danger, distress, and their urgent need of protection. However, as a consequence of the amygdala being centrally involved in implicit learning *and* emotion regulation, the infant is born not only with the capacity to learn and remember enacted experience, but also with an exquisite vulnerability to being overwhelmed by frightening experiences. Such experiences are encoded in the systems of implicit memory and may reemerge in emotional contexts that cue the retrieval of traumatic memories (Mancia, 2006; Perry et al., 1995; Schacter, 1996; Schore, 1994, 2001; Turnbull & Solms, 2003; van der Kolk, 1989, 1994; van der Kolk & Fisler, 1995). Farhi (2010) and Milner (1969) go so far as to argue that trauma may be experienced in the womb and be carried into adult life. Neuroscience research supports the idea that preverbal, presymbolic experiences in infancy become represented in adult brain systems and affect the person's functioning throughout life (Damasio, 1999, 2003; LeDoux, 1994, 1996; Mancia, 2006; Pally, 2000, 2005; Siegal, 2001; Turnbull & Solms, 2003). Indeed, findings indicate that vulnerability to, and resilience against, adult post-traumatic stress is vitally affected by early traumatic experiences that have been indelibly imprinted in the infant's implicit memory (LeDoux, 1989; Perry et al., 1995; Schore, 1994, 2001; van der Kolk & Fisler, 1995; Wilkinson, 2010). Moreover, as previously noted, implicit effects of past experiences may shape our emotional reactions, preferences, and dispositions—key elements of personality (Grigsby & Hartlaub, 1994; Schacter, 1996).

Findings, then, show that the amygdala plays a specific role in both fear conditioning and implicit learning and that the later developing hippocampus plays a specialized role in the neural networks that support explicit memory (LeDoux, 1994; Mancia, 2006; Pally, 2005; Rose, 2003; Schacter, 1996). Given this, fear and anxiety experienced in early childhood are subject to a form of amnesia and thus may lay dormant for years (LeDoux, 1994). However, the procedural and emotive aspects of such experiences are still working within us and may suddenly be reactivated when we are exposed to a new traumatic stress. Typically, we have no meaning for how we initially acquired the fear. Again, this reflects the operation of implicit memory and the normal amnesia characteristic of the first years of life (LeDoux et al., 1989; Pally, 2005; Schacter, 1996; Turnbull & Solms, 2003).

Informed by research, Schacter (1996) speculates on the neurochemical reasons for the sudden reemergence of childhood trauma in later life. Accepting that early trauma is encoded in implicit memory in brain circuits outside or dissociable from the hippocampal system, as the latter system develops, the childhood fears may recede into the background. When, however, we experience a new psychological trauma, our brains release an uncontrolled cascade of glucocorticoids, excessive exposure to which can damage the hippocampus, which has a high number of glucocorticoid receptors, thereby contributing to memory-related abnormalities. The bombardment of stress-induced glucocorticoids temporarily suppresses the hippocampus and enhances amygdala activity. As a result, non-hippocampal systems may become more active, allowing hidden implicit memories such as long latent childhood fears to suddenly resurface (LeDoux, 1994; LeDoux et al., 1989; Mancia, 2006; Schacter, 1996).

Indeed, research shows that the dysregulation of fear-states in early life results in a permanent sensitivity to even mild stress in adulthood with the individual being unable to terminate a stress response in time to prevent an excessive reaction (Perry et al., 1995; Schore, 2001). Moreover, it is now thought that traumatic early life events predispose certain individuals to later psychiatric disturbance when they are re-challenged with a matching event, or experience a recurrence of the original stressor (Perry et al., 1995). These findings reflect a trauma-induced deficit in the brain's right orbitofrontal systems and concomitant difficulty in inhibiting responses related to orbitofrontal dysfunction. As a result of such dysfunction, affective information implicitly processed in the right brain is inefficiently transmitted to the left hemisphere for semantic processing. Thus, the individual is more likely to behave impulsively and aggressively in situations of stress and arousal (Bradley, 2003; Schore, 1994, 2001). The way in which the individual subjectively interprets traumatic and abusive experiences is, needless to say, central to the modulation of affective arousal and to the development of symptoms and disorders (Herman & van der Kolk, 1987; van der Kolk & Fisler, 1995).

CLINICAL ILLUSTRATION

"Michael" killed his estranged wife "Anna," hitting her head repeatedly with a claw hammer in an explosive rage after confronting her about "the accusations she was making about me to the children." He was 49 at the time and had been married to Anna for 20 years. The couple had four children aged between 10 and 18 years.

Michael's parents separated when he was age 4. He soon lost contact with his father and paternal grandparents after his mother remarried. He became estranged from his mother when she and his stepfather became preoccupied with running a small business, and he developed a substitute attachment with his maternal grandmother, since she was now chiefly responsible for his upbringing. Michael had nothing in common with his stepfather and their relationship was distant and strained. His relationships with his parents deteriorated further when his half-sister was born because he felt they favored her over him. This situation seemed to reinforce Michael's sense of rejection and foster a nascent misogynistic attitude. At about that time, a friend of his grandfather's sexually abused him. He frequently ran away from home and suffered from persistent enuresis. He had 6 months therapy with a child psychiatrist at that time.

In early adulthood Michael became engaged to Clare, who precipitately broke off the engagement. On subsequently meeting Clare by chance in the street, they argued, and Michael stabbed her in the chest with a hacksaw blade. He was convicted of grievous bodily harm (GBH) and imprisoned. On his release a spate of offending behavior occurred, culminating in a 4-year sentence of imprisonment for offences of robbery, possession of a firearm, and GBH with intent.

Michael's criminal activity ceased following his marriage to Anna. In the 4 years prior to his killing her, tension mounted in the marriage. He was working long, unsocial hours, and Anna suspected him of having an extramarital affair. They led increasingly separate lives, rarely having sex and frequently arguing. Their problems were exacerbated by Anna's excessive drinking and his controlling behavior. Michael's grandmother and mother both died during this time causing him intense distress. He was reluctant to share the money he inherited with Anna because he suspected that she would use it to "leave me."

The couple tried but failed to reconcile their differences. Michael was hospitalized with depression after a suicide attempt. Within 2 weeks of being discharged, Anna accused him of raping her, and he was arrested and remanded in custody for 3 months. During his time on remand, Anna filed for divorce. Four days after his release, he went to see Anna and killed her when she refused to talk to him, attempted to phone the police, and flee from the house. Afterward, Michael explained that "all my anger and frustration suddenly burst out." The police were called and found Michael sitting in his car outside the family home. He was convicted of manslaughter and sentenced to 7 years' imprisonment.

Michael spoke of loving Anna and of not wanting them to separate and divorce. However, he felt that she had provoked him by alleging rape, by tarnishing his name with their children, by withdrawing sexually from him, and by planning to divorce him, leaving him feeling shamed and humiliated in her's and the children's eyes. Michael seemed emotionally detached and unable to empathize with Anna, but he was deeply distressed by "the grief I've caused my children," when he had wanted to give them the "perfect childhood I didn't have."

Michael's formative experiences would seem to have consisted of both cumulative developmental trauma deriving from interaction with unresponsive caregivers and dramatic trauma in the form of loss, abandonment, broken attachments, and sexual abuse. These experiences are likely to have impacted negatively on his neurological development. In the absence of appropriate help to process these experiences, it would seem that he developed a disorganized pattern of attachment and concomitant difficulty in regulating emotional states associated with rejection and abandonment. In childhood, he expressed his anger and distress by running away from home and bedwetting, whereas in adulthood it was enacted in violent crime.

Michael's secure-enough attachment to Anna enabled him to contain his fear and anxiety, and his offending behavior ceased. However, it appears that he was defending against unresolved childhood trauma by controlling Anna and idealizing the relationships with his children. While Anna was emotionally available to him such defenses and coping strategies kept his fear and anxiety within manageable proportions. However, perceiving that Anna was intent on leaving him activated Michael's multiple, incoherent representational model, together with an uncontrolled release of stress-related neurochemicals and the reemergence of dissociated traumatic childhood experiences. Lacking a coherent strategy to deal with separation and loss, Michael's behavior became increasingly disorganized. His coping strategies, mental defenses, and capacity to mentalize and regulate emotional and bodily states were overwhelmed, resulting in an explosive murderous rage. His attack on Clare when she had rejected and abandoned him may also be seen as indicating that loss activated an incoherent representational model deriving from dissociated childhood trauma and disorganized attachment to his early caregivers.

Thinking about Michael's early experiences in the context of neuroscience research, van der Kolk & Fisler (1995) found that childhood trauma results in more pervasive biological dysregulation than adult trauma. Significantly, their research shows that people who have a history of childhood trauma experience greater difficulty in regulating internal states than those first traumatized in adulthood. Genetic variables notwithstanding, infant and trauma research may help to elucidate the question as to why individuals respond differently to the same or qualitatively similar traumatic incident. As noted above, researchers have demonstrated that securely attached children develop the capacity to stay attentive and responsive to the environment and use error-correcting information to reflect on their experience and construct a coherent narrative (Main, 1991; Main et al., 1985; Solomon, George & De Jong, 1995). Thus, the stressful experience remains available for processing via the systems of explicit memory. Secure/autonomous individuals may, therefore, possess the resilience and mental resources to process information more readily in the aftermath of a traumatic event without developing full-blown post-traumatic stress disorder than unresolved/disorganized subjects whose ability to regulate states of arousal was compromised during early development.

As previously noted, children subjected to misattuned, insensitive, and over-arousing caregiving may typically inhibit responsivity and enter prolonged and severe states of withdrawal (Beebe et al., 1992) as an "emotional regulation strategy" (Schore, 1994). It would seem reasonable to hypothesize, therefore, that an individual with an unresolved state of mind with respect to childhood trauma, and concomitant incapacity to regulate psychobiological states in moments of stress, may be more vulnerable to subsequent trauma and its sequelae than an individual with a secure/autonomous state of mind.

From a neurobiological perspective, then, trauma-related childhood memories such as Michael's are encoded and stored in the systems of implicit/procedural memory and may reemerge in stress-inducing social contexts in adulthood such as separation and loss that cue the retrieval of these indelibly imprinted emotional memories (LeDoux, 1994, 1996; LeDoux et al., 1989; Pally, 2000, 2005; Schacter, 1996; Schore, 1994; van der Kolk & Fisler, 1995).

Chapter 5

Psychoanalysis and the Internal World

How Different Theories Understand the Concept of Mind[*]

INTRODUCTION

From the 1930s onward, psychoanalysis has seen a paradigmatic shift away from Freudian drive theory towards a relational perspective. The work of Fairbairn, Melanie Klein, Winnicott, and Balint provided momentum to this shift, which gave rise to the development of British object relations theory. The British Psycho-Analytical Society was in a state of flux at this time, reflecting fierce disagreement between the Kleinian and Freudian camps about theoretical issues. These disputes were fuelled by the arrival in Britain in the 1940s of a group of psychoanalysts from Vienna which included Sigmund Freud and Anna Freud (Holmes, 1993).

A compromise was agreed in 1944 following what became known as the Controversial Discussions. This resulted in the Society being divided into three groups—the Kleinians, the Freudians, and the Independents. The Discussions reflected longstanding tensions and disagreements between the way in which British psychoanalysis had developed, as influenced by Klein, and the more traditional approach favored by the supporters of Sigmund Freud and his daughter, Anna. A major aspect of the dispute between Anna Freud and Melanie Klein focused on the principles of child analysis (Grosskurth, 1986; King & Steiner, 1991).

Bowlby became increasingly disenchanted by the lack of scientific rigor characterizing psychoanalytic thinking. He thought that neither Melanie Klein nor Anna Freud understood the nature of the scientific method and the importance of empirical evidence (Knox, 2003; Schwartz, 1999). He took particular issue with the Kleinian theory because of its emphasis on the role of unconscious fantasy in the etiology of neurotic and psychotic symptoms at the expense of environmental factors, especially in relation to clinical issues of separation and loss. In an attempt to provide psychoanalysis with scientific legitimacy, Bowlby turned to the newly emerging

---

[*] Portions of this chapter appeared in an earlier form in *Attachment*, 1(1), 2007, pp. 71–77. Reprinted with kind permission of Karnac Books.

science of ethology. By linking the latter to neo-Darwinian evolutionary biology, he developed the idea that social as well as intrapsychic behavior could be instinctive, that the child becomes attached to the person with whom he or she has the most interactions, and not necessarily to the person who feeds him or her. Bowlby therefore suggested that human relationships could be the subject of empirical observation. His basic hypothesis, and that underpinning the development of attachment theory, is that the baby has an innate psychobiological system that motivates him or her to form an emotional bond with the primary attachment figure who in Western societies is, more often than not, the mother (Bowlby, 1958, 1973). Moreover, his clinical experience led him to propose that when deprived of this relationship through separation and loss, the resultant fear, anxiety, and distress has a deleterious and long-lasting effect on the infant's overall physical and psychological development. For Bowlby, then, attachment is a goal-corrected instinctual system and separation anxiety a purely instinctive reaction to an external danger which activates a distinct behavioral system.

Quinodoz (1993) acknowledges that Bowlby's approach poses a challenge to psychoanalytic theory, but considers that his reevaluation of this theory with its introduction of control systems and instinctive behavior departs from the specific field of psychoanalysis and comes closer to experimental psychology. Quinodoz's views encapsulate many aspects of the critiques that were leveled against Bowlby by major figures in the world of psychoanalysis following the launch of attachment theory in the late 1950s (Bowlby, 1958). It may, however, be said that Bowlby contributed in no small measure to his being ostracized by failing to acknowledge and engage with colleagues whose views had much in common with his own thinking. For example, Anna Freud and Dorothy Burlingham (1944) had already established that the child has an instinctual need to be attached to the mother (Fonagy, 1999d). Moreover, Freud's (1905a) observations of children led him to conclude that their anxiety was an expression of the loss of the person they loved. The main difference between Bowlby and Freud centered on the theory underpinning drive theory. Whereas Freud saw love relations as dependent upon the primary need for drive satisfaction, Bowlby, influenced by Fairbairn (1946), argues that the child's primary motivation consists of the need to form an emotional attachment to the mother (Hurry, 1998).

Although Bowlby (1984, 1988) theorized the etiology of aggression, attachment theory may legitimately be criticized for omitting the importance of sexuality as a motivating factor in human behavior. Attempts to rectify this omission have been made in recent years, most notably by Lichtenberg (2007, 2008). This notwithstanding, the essence of the dispute between attachment theory and psychoanalysis that arose some 60 years ago focused on what Bowlby (1988) saw as the reluctance in analytic circles to examine the impact of real-life traumatic events in the genesis of pathology. Instead, classical thinking emphasized drive theory, unconscious fantasy, and the death instinct.

From the very beginning, then, attachment theory was informed by a range of disciplines: object relations theory, ethology, evolution theory, and developmental psychology. Contemporary attachment theory has continued in this vein, broadening its theoretical base to encompass cognitive science, cybernetics, social learning theory, linguistics, narrative theory, personality theory, philosophy, and sociology. Holmes (1996) suggests that attachment theory has the potential to synthesize the most productive ideas from these various disciplines into a coherent new paradigm. Mitchell (2000), too, emphasizes convergence and integration, stating: "At this point in the evolution of psychological ideas, attachment theory and psychoanalytic theory, rather than offering alternative pathways, offer the exciting possibility of a convergence that is mutually enriching" (p. 102).

PSYCHOANALYTIC THEORIES
OF THE INTERNAL WORLD

In broad terms, the internal world refers to the organization, structures, and functioning of the mind and has been conceptualized in a variety of ways by different theorists. Psychological theories of the mind are inevitably linked to what philosophically is termed the mind–body problem. Here, the dichotomy is whether to approach the mind from an objective point of view, that is, the workings of the brain, or from a subjective point of view—as a psychology of personal experience (Hinshelwood, 1991). The following section briefly outlines the thinking of some of the major theorists in psychoanalysis. For a comprehensive exposition of the development of object relations theory, I would warmly recommend Greenberg and Mitchell's *Object Relations in Psychoanalytic Theory* (1988); for a history of psychoanalysis in Europe and America, Schwartz's *Cassandra's Daughter* (1999).

Sigmund Freud

Freud (1911), on discussing the topic of mental functioning in terms of drive theory, drew a distinction between primary and secondary processes. Primary process relates to the unconscious system and method of functioning. Here, infantile instinctual wishes and desires of a sexual and aggressive nature are the source of unconscious fantasy and determine the content of internal objects. Instinctual impulses are repressed and become subject to mental defenses of displacement, condensation, and symbolism. However, repressed material returns in altered form and is expressed through, for example, dreams, parapraxes, and psychosomatic symptoms. As the child matures and undergoes a process of socialization, sexual and aggressive impulses are brought under the sway of the reality principle. This principle characterizes the secondary process and incorporates the mature mental defense of sublimation whereby prohibited wishes and desires are channeled into culturally acceptable activities. For Freud, psychopathology is an external manifestation of unconscious neurotic conflict between an instinctual wish that is seeking discharge and a moral imperative, or between two contradictory emotions, such as ambivalent feelings of love and hate. Conflict is also given a central place in Freud's later structural theory of mind, operating among the psychical agencies of id, ego, and superego (Laplanche & Pontalis, 1988).

It may be seen, then, that Freud's concept of mental life is both physiological, in terms of biological instincts and impulses, and psychological, in terms of the personal meanings that the developing infant comes to attribute to his or her instinctual life, and the way in which these meanings are assumed to motivate subsequent behavior and activities. Hinshelwood (1991) argues that Freud's view on the mind-body problem reflects the philosophical position known as psychophysical parallelism. This position holds that there is both a mind and a brain, and that each work in their own particular ways. Hinshelwood suggests that Freud's approach to this problem, as found in his writings, indicates a conflict between Freud the scientific neurologist and Freud the humanist psychologist, and that Freud never quite managed to extricate himself from the physiological psychology that was his starting point.

Anna Freud

Anna Freud remained faithful to her father's psychoanalytic theory, but placed greater emphasis on the ego and its functions than Freud. She argues that it is from the ego that we observe the work of the id and the superego and, indeed, of the unconscious generally. Her focus on the ego led to the development of ego psychology, and she brought together a group of child psychoanalysts that included Margaret Mahler and Erik Erikson (Edcumbe, 2000).

Anna Freud devised the concept of "developmental lines" to chart the progress of normal growth from dependency to emotional self-reliance. Her thinking combined drive theory with the more recent emergence of object relations theories, and she emphasized the importance of parents in child developmental processes. This emphasis was informed by her work at the Hampstead Child Therapy Clinic in London, which she helped to found in the 1940s (Freud & Burlingham, 1944). Her observations of children separated from their parents during the Second World War helped her to understand their need to attach to substitute parents and also the development both of defense mechanisms and of the ego and superego (1968).

Melanie Klein

As noted above, Anna Freud and Melanie Klein profoundly disagreed on theoretical issues. Klein's model of the mind elaborates on Freud's assumptions. Her theory posits that we live in two worlds consisting of inner psychic reality and external reality. The internal world is built up through the introjection of objects and comes to be experienced in as real and concrete a fashion as the outside world (Klein, 1935, in Spillius, 1988a). Klein views the mind as also consisting of mental representations which include memories, ideas and, most significant of all, unconscious fantasies. Body-based sensations are linked to unconscious fantasies in relation to internal objects as well as to paranoid fears of actual external objects. Indeed, for Klein internal objects are the very stuff of unconscious fantasy, a level of psychology that is closely linked to biological functions and bodily contents. Furthermore, in Klein's formulation, identity itself is deeply bound up with the internalization, introjection, or incorporation of objects, with the degree of hostility towards these objects in the internalizing fantasies, and in the resulting alienation from, or assimilation to, the internalized objects. These representations together with relations with introjected objects, constitute the psychic structure of the Kleinian inner world.

As Hinshelwood (1997) points out, Klein was the first theorist to describe the forms that childhood anxieties took, conceptualizing these as objects and part-objects in the child's inner world. She also insisted on the significance of the parent–infant relationship from the very start of life for the development of the human psyche. Klein developed play technique with young children from the 1920s onward, using drawings and a small array of simple toys. She found that the invitation to play quickly produced in the child the expression of acute anxieties. The use of male and female toy figures pointed towards relations with and between internal objects. For Klein, these configurations showed unconscious fantasies active in the child's mind. She linked the fate of the toy figures to the child's worries about what would happen in reality between the child and the important people in his or her life (Segal, 1988; Steiner, 1989).

Klein would speak to the child about his or her worries in a direct manner. She found that children were remarkably responsive to being taken seriously. Correct interpretations brought the alleviation of anxiety. Klein sought to understand the child's own logic and found a consistent unconscious content in anxious play, which she related to deeper unconscious meanings in the child's mind. The process starts with the child's play, proceeds to a direct and explicit interpretation, and results in a response of some kind in the further play of the child. The sequence is anxiety–interpretation–response. The alleviation of anxiety and the immediate change in the character and content of the child's play were important markers for

Klein in assessing the validity of her interpretations and of the technique itself (Hinshelwood, 1994; Spillius, 1988b; Steiner, 1989).

In Klein's formulation, splitting allows the ego to emerge out of the chaos of the paranoid-schizoid position and to order its emotional experiences and sensory impressions. This is a precondition of later integration and the basis of the faculty of discrimination—the capacity to differentiate between good and bad. The leading anxiety in the paranoid-schizoid position is that of persecutory objects getting inside the ego and overwhelming and annihilating both the ideal object and the self. This position is termed *paranoid-schizoid* because the leading anxiety is paranoid, and the state of the ego and its objects is characterized by splitting, which is schizoid (Klein, 1945). In addition to splitting, manic defenses against overwhelming persecutory anxiety include denial, idealization, and projective identification. With regard to the latter, parts of the self and parts of internal objects are split off and projected into an external object which, in unconscious fantasy, then become possessed by, controlled by, and identified with the projected parts. The aims of projective identification are manifold and include the avoidance of separation from the ideal object and an attempt to gain control of the bad, persecutory object. The effects on the self, however, are feelings of depletion and desolation. In the depressive position, the manic defenses are primarily directed against psychic reality, specifically the experience of depressive guilt and the anxiety consequent on valuing and being dependent on the object whose loss is feared (Hinshelwood, 1994; Spillius, 1988a).

In terms of the child's inner world, fears of persecutors and of the bad mother and the bad father lead him or her to feel unable to protect loved internal objects from the danger of destruction and death. Moreover, the death of good internal objects would inevitably mean the end of the child's own life. Klein sees this situation as constituting the fundamental anxiety of the depressive position because the good internal object forms the core of the ego and the child's internal world. The depressive conflict consists of a constant struggle between the child's aggression and destructiveness (the death instinct) and his love and reparative impulses (the life instinct) (Klein, 1945). In Klein's formulation, the depressive position is never fully worked through. She argues that the anxieties pertaining to ambivalence and guilt, as well as to situations of loss which reawaken depressive experiences, are always with us (Hinshelwood, 1994; Spillius, 1988a).

In a contribution to the Controversial Discussions in 1943, Susan Isaacs argued that unconscious fantasy underlies every mental process and accompanies every mental activity. Hinshelwood (1991) suggests that this conceptual framework is informed by the philosophical position of psychophysical interactionism. From this position, the mind is viewed as emerging from the activity of the brain which, in turn, may be manipulated by the mind. This interactive process may be seen in Kleinian theory, which, as we have seen, postulates that biological processes are mirrored in activities of the mind called unconscious fantasies. Equally, this theory holds that unconscious fantasies mold both the personality of the developing infant and his or her social world.

From this perspective, it is suggested that the infant exists in a world of so-called primitive emotions and, therefore, introjected objects are initially experienced in an emotional rather than a physical way. The distinction between mind and body comes about in the course of development and is generated psychologically by a process of splitting. This process creates a psychical space within which the infant may experience the physical and the psychological. Hinshelwood (1991) therefore concludes that Kleinian theory assumes an interaction between physical events and psychological events and that each will influence the other.

Writing from a relational perspective, Greenberg and Mitchell (1988) question the degree to which Klein focuses on aggression at the expense of other motives. In line with the views of Fairbairn, Winnicott and Bowlby, the authors contend that Klein's theoretical formulation is over-generalized and privileges unconscious fantasy over real people and events. Moreover, because Klein views psychopathology as arising predominantly from internal, constitutional sources she tends to derive good objects from outside and bad objects internally. Greenberg and Mitchell argue that this tendency minimizes the importance of parental anxiety, ambivalence, and character pathology in the etiology of the child's psychopathology. In contrast, the parents in Klein's formulation are seen as important primarily because they represent universal human attributes. This theoretical position is reflected in Klein's presentation of relationships as constitutional and universal—as being a direct and predetermined result of the nature of the drives, particularly of constitutional aggression in the form of the death instinct. The idea that problematic features of the parents' own personalities and difficulties in living may contribute in a more direct and immediate way to the original establishment of bad objects, and thus to the beginnings of psychopathology in the child, is missing from Klein's formulation of the internal world. Greenberg and Mitchell argue that in deriving all salient emotional factors from inside the child's own mind, Klein fails to give due weight to the extent to which depressive anxiety and guilt often stem from actual parental suffering and difficulties.

Ronald Fairbairn

Fairbairn lived and worked in Edinburgh and thus was far away from the political maelstrom going on in London in the 1940s. However, he had a profound influence on the development of object relations, developing his theories independently from the Kleinian mainstream as a member of the Middle Group. Indeed, Klein accused him of not following Freud, and of giving insufficient weight to hate and aggression in his theories (Schwartz,

1999). For Fairbairn, however, the problem of human development was not hate, but love. His clinical experience led him to argue that failures in the external world could produce the intrapsychic structures described by Klein. He made a significant move away from drive theory in the mid-1940s, contending that human beings are object-seeking rather than pleasure-seeking (Fairbairn, 1946).

More generally, Fairbairn postulates that feelings of security vitally influence the manner by which the infant affectively relates to internalized, split off idealized objects, and rejecting objects. In a marked shift away from the Kleinian emphasis on unconscious fantasy, he acknowledged the subject's real experience, averring that insecurity stems primarily from separation anxiety and the conflicts attendant on a persisting state of "infantile dependence." He suggests that this type of anxiety is a causative factor in the development of "schizoid" aspects of personality which engender a sense of futility and hopelessness in the subject's inner world of object relations. Such a person, he contends, lacks the capacity to differentiate self from other and thus is unable to attain a state of "mature dependence" (Fairbairn, 1996). As Mitchell (2000) observes, Fairbairn's "important contributions of the 1940s and early 1950s remained almost completely unrecognized until Harry Guntrip began to make them more accessible in the very different climate of the 1970s" (p. 79).

Margaret Mahler, Fred Pine, and Anni Bergman

The development of relations with objects is also central to Mahler and her colleagues' (Mahler, Pine, & Bergman, 1985) theory of the way in which the infant's inner world is structured and organized. The authors' observations of mothers and their infants are informed by ego psychology and object relations. As we have seen, this perspective is derived from an integration of classical drive theory and object relations theory stemming from the work of Anna Freud. Ego psychology grants the ego more autonomy and flexibility than drive theory in understanding human behavior. However, the adaptive aspect of this perspective was criticized for emphasizing social conformity to the status quo (Schwartz, 1999).

Mahler et al. (1985) hypothesize that the infant's initial experience is one of symbiotic attachment to the mother. This is followed by a gradual build up of a differentiated inner mental representation of the mother and the self through progressive steps in the development of relations with objects. Mahler et al. conceptualize this developmental progression in terms of a process of separation–individuation that has two distinct but intertwining aspects. Separation refers to the process whereby the infant gradually forms an intrapsychic self-representation distinct and separate from the mental representation of the mother; individuation refers to the infant's attempts to form a unique individual identity.

Mahler et al. (1985) argue that the process of separation–individuation leads to a normative "rapprochement crisis" in the second year of life. This is characterized by behavior that alternates between avoidance and pursuit of closeness with the mother. The authors' observations show that the process of separation–individuation is forestalled when the mother keeps the infant in a dependent position so as to meet her own symbiotic needs or, alternatively, pushes the infant precipitately into autonomy. By contrast, they found that the infant's autonomous strivings are facilitated by the mother's continuing emotional availability.

From an attachment theory perspective, the child's ambivalent or avoidant behavior noted by Mahler et al. (1985) would not be seen as "normative," but rather as indicating the development of insecure attachment. Indeed, Lyons-Ruth (1991) suggests that the first 2 years of life should be reframed as an attachment–individuation process rather than as an attachment–separation process. Bowlby (1973), in comparing attachment theory to the process of separation–individuation, points out that his usage of the word *separation* differs from that employed by Mahler (1969). Whereas she uses the term to refer to a process of differentiation on a psychological level, Bowlby's use of the term implies that the infant's primary attachment figure is inaccessible in a physical sense. Nevertheless, he agrees with Mahler's (1969) theoretical proposition that self-confidence, self-esteem, and pleasure in independence develop out of trust and confidence in others, specifically through the infant's experience of an emotionally available mothering person.

Phyliss and Robert Tyson

Tyson and Tyson (1990) also embrace an ego psychology perspective. However, they adopt an integrative approach to describe the child's early development. This is informed by Freud's early affect-trauma model, infant research, ego psychology, self psychology, and object relations theories. The authors stress the significance of affects in structuring the infant's internal world. Affects are defined as mental structures that have motivational, somatic, emotional, expressive, and communicative components, as well as having an associated idea or cognitive component. The good enough, attuned caregiver is responsive to the infant's differentiated affective behavioral patterns and discrete emotional expressions. During the course of such continuous interactions between mother and infant, ideas and memories take on mental representation for the infant, who also constructs wishes and fantasies. The Tysons (1990) argue that affective behavioral responses and their physiological counterparts come to be associated with these ideas and fantasies. Through this process, the infant's behavior and the response of the caregiver begin to take on meaning for the infant. Thus, the connection between affective behavioral response patterns on the one hand, and memories and ideas, both conscious and unconscious, on the other, develops into an inner psychological experience endowed with individual meaning.

Tyson and Tyson (1990) make the point that once a feeling has come to be linked with an idea it has the potential to be verbalized. Feelings or affective states are then more easily recognized, defended against, and controlled by the ego. Extending Spitz's (1959) model of ego formation, the Tysons argue that, given optimal development, affects come to serve a signal function enabling the child to master and regulate his or her own affects, instead of being overwhelmed by their disorganizing effects. According to the Tysons' integrated conceptual framework, the use of signal function comes about through the child's successful internalization of, and identification with, the mother's organizing and regulating functions. The authors therefore contend that the achievement of signal function indicates the accomplishment of an important developmental step. However, following Kohut (1971), the Tysons argue that where there is a failure of parental empathy or traumatic interference of one form or another, this process is disrupted and the development of a coherent sense of self is compromised leading to a fragmentation of experience and, therefore, of personality. From this perspective, psychopathology is viewed in interpersonal terms and traumatic affect as playing a part in organizing mental functioning, in that painful affect may become a significant motivating force in the manifestation of psychopathology.

Donald Winnicott

By the end of the 1950s, the British object relations school was in competition with Freud's and Klein's instinctual paradigm. Following the Controversial Discussions, Winnicott positioned himself in the Middle or Independent Group, that is, between the Kleinians and the Anna Freudians. Winnicott was a pediatrician prior to training as a psychoanalyst. His work with children and their mothers influenced many of his concepts, as discussed below, such as the holding environment, transitional objects, the good enough mother, and the importance of play, which he considered as taking place in the potential space between the infant and the mother. Indeed, in clinical work with adults he viewed the initial task of the therapist as that of enabling the patient to become able to play and be creative. Moreover, for Winnicott (1988) cultural experience was a third area deriving from this very capacity to play. The ability for creative play is linked to the development of the "true self," which Winnicott (1960) saw as the instinctive core of the personality and as flourishing in response to the repeated success of the mother's responsiveness to the infant's spontaneous gestures. By contrast, the "false self" is overly compliant to external demands and to the gestures of the mother who is not good enough. The primary function of the false self is to protect the true self from threat and destruction.

Winnicott disagreed with Klein's insistence that ambivalence and aggression are biologically inherited, and he saw her as being temperamentally incapable of relating her observations to real-life experience (Schwartz, 1999). For her part, Klein thought that Winnicott did not understand her theories. On one occasion, she is said to have referred to him as "that dreadful man." While Klein's theories about child development jarred with Winnicott's long experience in pediatrics, he acknowledged that they made the child's inner psychic reality very real (Kahr, 1996). Notwithstanding these disagreements, Winnicott (1988), in a somewhat similar way to Klein, sees Freud's primary and secondary processes as complementary, rather than in opposition. Moreover, he envisages a similar outcome to that proposed by Mahler et al. (1985), though the process of psychological separation expounded by him is characteristically idiosyncratic. He assumes the existence of a transitional space, viewing this as an intermediate area of experience between mother and child in which imagination and reality coincide. Under optimal conditions of good enough mothering within a holding environment, the infant is gradually disillusioned of subjective omnipotent fantasies, leading to an integration of personality and a sense of continuity within an objective reality. In Winnicott's theory of mind, transitional objects, in the form of a favorite teddy bear or blanket, are used by the infant to bridge the space between inner and outer reality. Such phenomena provide a non-compliant solution to the loss of omnipotence and assist the child to separate from the merged state with the mother. A key aspect of the mother's role is to mirror or reflect back the child's own being, thereby facilitating the development of an authentic sense of self. In a critique of this aspect of Winnicott's theoretical position, Bowlby (1969) construes transitional objects as substitute attachment figures, arguing that the child redirects or displaces his or her attachment behavior onto such objects because the "natural" object, that is the primary caregiver, is not emotionally or physically available.

Fonagy (1998) considers Winnicott's description of the "capacity to be alone" as constituting a central aspect of the process of change. Winnicott (1958) argues that being alone in the presence of someone is based on the assumption that the other "is available and continues to be available when remembered after being forgotten" (p. 55). As we have seen, for Winnicott, this capacity is gradually built up within an environment that is good enough. It becomes part of the child's personality through a process of introjection and, thereby, is equated unconsciously with the internalized comforting presence of the mother. An important aspect of this developmental process is a shift from a state of "ruthlessness" to a state of "ruth," reflecting the infant's capacity to recognize the other as a separate person.

Winnicott (1969) links this process to a theory of "object usage" during which the infant destroys the object, only to find that it survives.

Much of Winnicott's thought would seem to resonate with the philosophical writings of Sartre from an existentialist perspective, and Husserl, Heidegger, and Merleau-Ponty from a phenomenological perspective. Phenomenology is concerned with the description of pure subjective experience—the phenomena of consciousness. Consciousness is viewed as being the bearer of experience. These writers stress the significance of direct awareness of subjective experience and draw a distinction between authentic and inauthentic modes of being or existence. For example, Heidegger (1962) argues that a sense of self is accomplished through a process of "being-in-the-world." This process is underpinned by a doctrine of intentionality and characterized by the subject's active participation and involvement in the world. Similarly, Merleau-Ponty (1945, in Copleston, 1979) suggests that the body-subject exists in a milieu in which its perceptual behavior is in dialogue; that a dialectical relationship exists between the subject and his or her environment. For Merleau-Ponty, perceptual experience consists of the exceptional relation between the subject and its body and its world. The influence of Heidegger's thinking about the "dreadful that has already happened" may also be seen in Winnicott's final paper, "Fear of Breakdown" (1974). Moreover, the pathology of Winnicott's (1960) false self concept may be equated with Heidegger's inauthentic existence, and the concept of the true self with Heidegger's description of authentic "being-in-the-world."

Christopher Bollas

Christopher Bollas is an American psychoanalyst who divides his time between London and North Dakota. He is a member of the British Psycho-Analytical Society and a theoretical contributor to the Independent Group. However, he is a great admirer of Bion as well as of Winnicott. Indeed, he incorporates aspects from diverse analytic approaches into his thinking.

Bollas (1987) contends that the infant's internal world is structured, in part, by both Freud's notion of primary process and Kleinian concepts of unconscious fantasy. He suggests that during the early stage of development the infant experiences the mother as a transformational object associated with an intersubjective process. He subscribes to the view that no clear distinction exists between internal and external perception at this time. In using the concept of intersubjectivity, Bollas, too, is emphasizing the phenomenological element of experience—the process by which the infant–mother dyad participate in and identify with their respective inner subjectivities, thereby creating a shared psychological experience. For Bollas, the process of intersubjectivity "instructs" the infant into the logic of being and relating. This is achieved by means of the mother's countless exchanges with her child. However, the earliest levels of psychic experience are not readily available for mental representation or symbolic processing leading Bollas to call this form of "knowledge" the "unthought known." As noted in Chapter 2, this term stands for everything that on some deep level is known, such as moods, somatic experiences, and personal idiom, but which has not yet been thought, in that the phenomena have remained unavailable for mental processing.

On discussing the unthought known, Bollas links Winnicott's concept of the true self and Freud's concept of the ego to the notion of primal repression. He argues that the primal repressed must be the inherited disposition that constitutes the core of the personality. He suggests that: "At the very core of the concept of the unthought known, therefore, is Winnicott's theory of the true self and Freud's idea of the primary repressed unconscious" (p. 278). Bollas argues that the unthought known becomes thought through object relations: "It is only through the subject's use and experience of the other that mental representations of that experience can carry and therefore represent the idiom of a person's unthought known" (p. 280).

This aspect of Bollas' theory has resonances with D. B. Stern's (1997) concept of "unformulated experience." Unformulated experience is composed of vague tendencies and refers to "content without definite shape" (p. 39). Stern suggests that: "The way in which each of us shapes moment-to-moment experience is the outcome of our characteristic patterns of formulation interacting with the exigencies of the moment" (p. 38). Given this "the resolution of the ambiguity of unformulated experience is an interpersonal event" (p. 38).

Wilfred Bion

Bollas' concept of the unthought known would also seem to be influenced by Bion (1984), who argues that we all have sense impressions and emotional experiences. Bion suggests that there is a specific function of the personality which transforms sense impressions and emotional realities into psychic elements. These then become available for mental work by such means as thinking, dreaming, imagining, and remembering. Bion terms the latter "alpha elements," and the process by which they are transformed, "alpha function." This process requires the mother to enter a state of calm receptiveness—a state of mind Bion (1984) terms "reverie." The mother is thereby amenable to containing the infant's inchoate state of mind and thus able to give meaning to the anxiety and terror inserted into her in unconscious fantasy by means of projective identification. "Beta elements," on the other hand, consist of untransformed sense impressions and emotional experiences. These elements are experienced as split off, unintegrated "things-in-themselves" and are therefore evacuated by means of projective identification, leaving the self feeling depleted, fearful of persecution, and in a state of "nameless dread." Bion (1990) developed Klein's concept of projective identification, arguing that it may function as a form of normal communication between subject and object, as well as being a sadistic pathological act of expulsion of split off, disowned parts of the self experienced as intolerable.

Thomas Ogden

Ogden (1994), also writing from a Kleinian perspective, and, like Bion, seemingly influenced by phenomenology, posits that the paranoid-schizoid and depressive positions are, in essence, states of being which coexist dialectically. These defensive organizations consist of constellations of fantasies, relations with objects, and characteristic anxieties and defenses (Joseph, 1994). Ogden, in line with Bion (1990), argues that there is a continuous interplay between these two defensive organizations, rather than one largely transcending the other, as postulated by Klein. Furthermore, Ogden suggests that this interpenetrative process is also in operation between conscious and unconscious states of mind, and between the past and the present. He concludes that our experience of inner and external reality is vitally affected by this dialectical interplay, as this process indicates a coexistence of multiple states of consciousness.

Jessica Benjamin

Along a similar theoretical line of thought to Bollas (1994), Benjamin (1992) equates the development of mind or inner reality with the experience of the self as a subject in relation to the subjectivities of others. This form of intersubjectivity assumes that a "shared reality" comes to be established by means of a subtle intertwining of both intrapsychic and interpersonal processes. Both Benjamin (2004) and Ogden (1994) suggest that something unique emerges from the meeting of two subjectivities. The emergent property of the therapeutic dyad is termed the "analytic third," a property that can take many and various forms (Aron, 2008). For Ogden (2004), the analytic third is generated intersubjectively and consists of the jointly created unconscious life of the analytic pair. Benjamin (2004) argues that a cocreated shared intersubjective "thirdness" helps to break down sterile, complementary aspects of the therapeutic relationship that characterize impasses and enactments. The restoration of thirdness facilitates mutual recognition.

Stephen Mitchell

For Mitchell (1993), interactional processes of the type described by Benjamin (1992), Ogden (1994), and Bollas (1987) give rise to a manifold organization of self or mind patterned around different self and object images and mental representations, as derived from different relational contexts. Psychological meaning is negotiated through interaction in the relational field, rather than regarded as universal and biologically inherent, as in drive theory (Mitchell, 1988). Indeed, Mitchell (1993) suggests that relational theories would seem to have been confirmed and validated by recent infant research on the communication of affect between mother and infant, as I describe in Chapter 6. These findings indicate that the mother's emotions in some way become part of the infant's emotional experience, thereby supplying the tone and contours that make up the world in which the baby lives (Beebe & Lachmann, 1992).

Mitchell (1993) points out that the model of mind or self found in relational theories emphasizes its multiplicity and discontinuity, with experience portrayed as being embedded in particular relational contexts. He therefore argues that psychic organization and structures are built up through, and shaped by, the interactions we have with different others, and through different interactions with the same other. From this position, Mitchell suggests that our experience of self is discontinuous and composed of different selves with different others, rather than consisting of a singular entity. Moreover, at times we may identify with an aspect of our self or with an aspect of the other, and this will affect the way in which we organize experience and construct our sense of meaning.

Somewhat paradoxically, Mitchell argues that despite the discontinuous aspect to our experience, we nevertheless retain a sense of self as enduring and continuous. He depicts this in Winnicottian terms as consisting of an unbroken line of subjective experience which forms the core of the personality. However, if it is accepted that the self is both multiple and discontinuous and integral and continuous, a creative tension arises requiring a balance to be struck. As Mitchell puts it, "where there is too much discontinuity there is a dread of fragmenting, splitting and dislocation. On the other hand, where there is too much continuity there is a dread of paralysis and stagnation" (p. 116). In formulating this paradox, Mitchell acknowledges Winnicott's (1988) concept of the true and false self. As I note in Chapter 3, Mitchell also refers to McDougall's clinical description of "normopathic" characterological traits (McDougall, 1990) and to Bollas' (1994) concept of the "normotic" personality, suggesting that pseudonormality is the clinical problem of our time. The clinical picture depicted here would seem to mirror the bleak and desolate aspect of our own existentialist experience and constitute what Sartre (1966) refers to as "bad faith," that is, the turning away from an authentic form of existence and choosing, instead, to become a passive subject of external influences.

INTERSUBJECTIVITY AND THE INTERNAL WORLD

As we have seen, relational and interpersonal theorists view the internal world as developing through a process of intersubjectivity. For Mitchell (1988), all meaning is generated in "the symbolic textures of the relational matrix" (p. 62). He conceptualizes the relational matrix in broad, paradigmatic terms, seeing it as integrating the theories of Bowlby, Fairbairn, Klein, Winnicott, and Kohut. Mitchell (1993) argues that the dynamics and life history of the person in analysis are actually cocreated by the analyst's participation during the course of the therapeutic process. This assumption constitutes a shift in theory, with truth now being viewed in terms of narrative intelligibility and discourse coherence, rather than historical veracity. Thus, there is no singular correct version of reality, and experience may be understood in various ways. Moreover, the distinction between fantasy and reality that became a problem for Bowlby because of its link with drive theory is not drawn so sharply in current psychoanalytic theorizing. Indeed, it is generally accepted that "reality is encountered, inevitably, *through* imagination and fantasy. Fantasy and actuality are not alternatives; they interpenetrate and potentially enrich one another" (Mitchell, 2000, p. 84, emphasis in original).

From a postmodern perspective, as articulated by Mitchell (1993), the past is not reconstructed, but coconstructed and given meaning in the here and now, with reality being mediated by personal narrative. It follows, therefore, that in the analytic situation the patient's inner world of experiences, associations, and memories can be integrated or organized in many different ways. Mitchell argues that the scheme arrived at is a dual creation, shaped partly by the patient's material, but also inevitably molded by the analyst's patterns of thought, theory, and systems of ideas. He goes on to stress the enormous importance that the analyst's theory has on the analytic process, arguing that the theory itself influences what is seen in the clinical material and also shapes and organizes it.

From this standpoint, the therapeutic process is redolent of the subtle intersubjective process that takes place between the mother and the child, which is assumed to structure, shape, and organize the child's internal world. It is, therefore, perhaps not surprising that Mitchell, in a similar way to Winnicott (1988), views the mother–infant relationship as the prototypical therapeutic model.

HERMENEUTICS VERSUS EMPIRICISM?

Mitchell's thinking in regard to the therapeutic process is influenced by hermeneutic interpretive theory, a discipline closely associated with phenomenology. Recent exponents of this theory are Heidegger (1962), Habermas

(1972), and Gadamer (2007). In broad terms, a hermeneutic may be defined as a set of practices or techniques used for the purpose of revealing intelligible meaning (Shotter, 1986, cited in Harré & Lamb, 1986). The task in the hermeneutic tradition is to understand the subjective inner reality of the mind by reference to the person's historical and cultural context. This approach requires a splitting of reality into two: an outer reality to be explained causally and an inner reality which needs to be understood, that is given meaning. Hermeneutics, then, may be seen as acting to reveal the hidden subjectivity, intentions, and purposes of the inner world. The approach involves drawing a distinction between historical truth and narrative truth, between real events and events that may or may not have occurred, but which may be regarded as "true" by the individual in a psychological, subjective sense. Shotter (1986) suggests that the recent renewal of interest in hermeneutics reflects the view that empiricism is an inadequate approach to use in the understanding of mental phenomena.

The inner world as portrayed by attachment theory would seem to have little space for the stuff of primary process such as dreams, fantasies, wishes, and desires. Indeed, Bowlby's view of hermeneutics in relation to psychoanalysis was trenchant and dismissive, as summed up by his terse comment that "There are people who think psychoanalysis is really a hermeneutic discipline. I think that's all rubbish quite frankly" (Bowlby et al., 1986, quoted in Holmes, 1993, p. 145). It is of interest to note, therefore, that attachment theory's position would seem to have shifted in this respect in that hermeneutic interpretive theory may now be seen to be embraced in the form of narrative theory, metacognitive knowledge, and self-reflexivity (George et al., 1984; Main & Goldwyn, 1995). (I examine Main and her colleagues' work in respect of the Adult Attachment Interview (AAI) in the following chapter, and expand on the clinical usefulness of adult attachment research in Chapters 8 and 10.) Being conversant with such research may enable the clinician to tap into implicit/procedural memory, in the form of non-optimal representational models, and thus creatively coconstruct with the patient the way in which his or her early intersubjective and phenomenological experience is being repeatedly enacted in the here and now. Indeed, as Mitchell (2000) notes in relation to research utilizing the AAI, the "emphasis in recent conceptualizations of attachment bears close resemblance to the importance in recent psychoanalytic theorizing of the themes of hermeneutics, constructivism, and narrativity" (p. 85).

More generally, the integration of narrative theory into attachment theory would seem to be a yet further example of the interplay between theory informed by prospective empirical infancy research, on the one hand (Ainsworth et al., 1978), and theory developed retrospectively from clinical phenomena with adults, on the other hand. Therefore, hermeneutics, applied empirically in order to interpret or code a semi-structured AAI, may be viewed as bridging the divide between empiricism and phenomenology. This paradigmatic shift would appear to lend weight to the respective claims of Mitchell (1993) and Holmes (1996) that integration is taking place between the different relational approaches. Indeed, adult attachment research data are increasingly being used to inform clinical work with individuals and couples, as are empirical findings from developmental studies and neuroscience.*

The argument between those who staunchly advocate either empiricism or hermeneutics would seem to be missing the point, in that it is not a matter of choosing one over the other. Indeed, as Aron (2009) points out, Freud's greatness lay in his ability to bring together the sciences and humanities of his time to form a creative new discipline that transcended such polarities. In emphasizing the need for a dialogue between different systems of epistemologies, Aron (2009) states: "I do think that psychoanalysis needs to be in contact with other disciplines. We cannot function in isolation. Whether you favor hermeneutics or empirical science, we have to be in discussion with other fields. . . ."

A certain convergence between postmodern theory, attachment theory, infant research, neuroscience, and psychoanalysis is noted by Teicholz (2009). Ogden (1994), however, is somewhat more cautious in this regard, viewing psychoanalytic theory as characterized by "an uneasy coexistence of a multiplicity of epistemologies" (p. 193). Indeed, he suggests that the task of theoretical integration needs to be accomplished at the level of the individual practitioner. He argues that clinicians need to develop their thinking within the context of different systems of ideas which together "in a poorly integrated way constitutes psychoanalysis" (p. 193).

THE PROBLEM OF INTEGRATING NEUROSCIENCE AND PSYCHOANALYSIS

As we saw at the beginning of this chapter, Freud's concept of mental life is both biological and psychological, reflecting the fact that he was both a scientific neurologist and humanist psychologist. To briefly recap, Hinshelwood (1991) critiques Freud's theory for failing to overcome the mind–body problem, which holds that there is both a mind and a brain, with each working in their own particular ways. This, in turn, reflects the philosophical position of psychophysical parallelism. Hinshelwood sees this problem as being resolved in Kleinian theory, which views the mind as

---

* See Beebe & Lachmann (2002); Beebe et al. (2005); Bowlby (1988); Bruschweiler-Stern et al. (2002, 2007); Cozolino (2002, 2006); Diamond & Kernberg (2008); Johnson (2004); Lichtenberg (2007, 2008); Lyons-Ruth et al. (1999); Mancia (2007); Pally (2000, 2005); Renn (2003, 2006); Shimmerlik (2008); Slade (1999); Stern et al. (1998a, 1998b); Target (2008); Teicholz (2009); Turnbull & Solms (2003); van der Kolk (1989, 1994); van der Kolk & Fisler (1995); Wallin (2007); and Wilkinson (2010).

emerging from the activity of the brain which, in turn, may be influenced by the mind. Thus, Kleinian theory assumes an interaction between biological events and psychological events, and that each will influence the other. This conceptual framework is informed by the philosophical position of psychophysical interactionism. I have argued that this philosophical position underpins all relational perspectives.

We see, then, that the link between our psychic life and biology is nothing new, and that this was of great interest to Freud. While acknowledging the essential differences between psychoanalysis and the empirical sciences, and that mental life and biology cannot be conflated, it may be accepted that what emerges from one field may influence the other; that biology and psychology interpenetrate and may be used to inform one another. This was certainly Freud's position and, indeed, Bowlby's in developing attachment theory. Being open to exploring the potential links between different epistemologies or systems of ideas reflects the view that no single paradigm or methodology can explain the complexity of the human mind (Green, 2003). For example, the finding that the brain is shaped and sculpted by experience in the environment and retains plasticity across the life span (Edelman, 1987, 1989; LeDoux, 1994; Rose, 2003, 2005; Schacter, 1996) has important implications for psychoanalysis, not least that new relational experiences can effect therapeutic change (Cozolino, 2002, 2006; Green, 2003; Main, 1991). As we know from the history of psychoanalysis, all disciplines have their disagreements and disputes. Research findings supporting brain plasticity and the dynamic nature of memory challenge reductionist views from neuroscience that compares the human brain to a digital computer or mechanical filing system.

More generally, it may be argued that whatever psychodynamic model of mind we hold, it needs to be congruent with our present state of knowledge. If a psychoanalytic model draws on too narrow a range of organizing principles it, too, may be seen as being reductionist and as failing to do justice to the complexity of the human mind (Green, 2003). In this context, Turnbull and Solms (2003) argue that no topic is of more importance for psychoanalysis than a neuroscientific understanding of the dynamic nature of human memory. Indeed, Solms (cited in Pally, 2000) argues that the neuroscience literature on memory, emotion regulation, and perceptual processing may provide insights into clinical phenomena such as transference, projection, and projective identification. The Boston Change Process Study Group (BCPSG) argue that their own exposure to, and engagement with, ideas from empirical disciplines, such as cognitive science, have illustrated aspects of therapeutic action in the implicit/enactive domain that might otherwise have remained invisible (BCPSG, 2008). Green (2003) and Teicholz (2009) respectively contend that a convergence is occurring between psychoanalysis and neuroscience and that integration is on the agenda.

This notwithstanding, legitimate concerns exist about such a process of integration. For example, Modell (2008) sees a risk in employing the terminology of cognitive science, such as implicit memory, because this may lead to a confusion of memory categories and the loss of the unique knowledge obtained from psychoanalytic practice. For similar reasons, Westen and Gabbard (2002) suggest that simply importing concepts from cognitive neuroscience into psychoanalytic discourse, such as implicit/procedural memory, may do psychoanalysis a disservice. The authors argue that integration implies a two-way process. Another important concern is that the focus on individual subjectivity may be lost by the integration of psychoanalysis and the empirical sciences. However, Mancia (2006) and Panksepp (1999) respectively suggest that the time is ripe for a productive dialogue between the two disciplines characterized by cooperation, mutual influence, and reciprocal contributions to understanding the mind's functions.

In my view and despite the development of neuro-psychoanalysis, we are a long way from developing a meta-theory that integrates psychoanalysis and neuroscience. Moreover, I am not sure that such a development would be entirely desirable. Rather, I would endorse Ogden's (1994) sentiments, as noted above, that theoretical integration is best accomplished by the individual practitioner. Admittedly, this is an arduous and time-consuming task. Indeed, I have spent many a long hour sifting through theories and empirical findings, discarding many, but embracing those with which I felt an affinity and which, therefore, are in some way personally meaningful and of potential clinical use to my patients. The key consideration here is that what we take on board, from whatever discipline, becomes an authentic expression of our unique personality and may be used to deepen our understanding of our patients' phenomenological experience.

The following may be seen as an example both of my own process of individual integration (Ogden, 1994) and of how the theories that I embrace influence what I see in clinical material (Mitchell, 1993). The example consists of the thoughts and associations I had after reading a clinical vignette by Wallin (2007) of his work with "Ellen." Wallin writes:

> I'm feeling calm, quietly taking in her presence without experiencing the familiar internal pressure to quickly respond. Staying with her, I'm also turning my attention to my breathing and my body. I have the not unfamiliar sense that I'm "knowing" her through my belly: My "gut sense" is that, as I'm relinquishing the lead, she's taking it. (p. 321)

Wallin is working from an attachment perspective and also bringing a "mindfulness" approach to bear on his experience of being with Ellen. For me, his sense of "knowing" Ellen through his belly and of allowing his "gut sense" to inform the interaction (allowing Ellen to take the lead) may be seen as an example of body countertransference. From my reading of the neuroscience literature, my particular understanding of body countertransference is informed by the knowledge that there is an entire nervous system in the gut—the enteric nervous system—with nigh on as many neurons as the brain (Rose, 2005). As well as emphasizing the interconnectivity of brains and bodies, Rose (2005) suggests that we do, indeed, often feel with our bowels!

To my mind, the existence of the enteric nervous system adds credence to Damasio's (1999) assertion that the source of feelings lie in the internal milieu and viscera of the body—that the body is the main stage for the emotions and for what Damasio calls "background feelings." Moreover, I would suggest that the experience of "embodied simulation" that occurs when the mirror neuron system is activated has a part to play in understanding body countertransference (Gallese, 2009). As Wallin's example suggests, bringing focal attention to bear on our bodies in a mindfulness way may help us to become consciously aware of such background moods and feelings in ourselves and inform what is occurring between therapist and patient in the implicit/enactive mode of experiencing (Bruschweiler et al., 2002, 2007; Lyons-Ruth et al., 1998; Stern et al., 1998a, 1998b).

Similarly, I often find that when the dialogue in a session has touched upon an issue that is too painful, threatening, or overwhelming for the patient to think about and symbolize, there may instead be a motoric discharge of the dissociated affect. A common example of the bodily discharge of a state of mind that cannot be mentalized is the vigorous shaking of a leg. Other examples are facial contortions, the rapid crossing/uncrossing of legs, the wringing of hands, becoming suddenly fidgety, blushing and/or the appearance of red blotches on the throat, and attempts at self-soothing such as stroking the face or hair. Following Freud (1914), neuroscience findings indicate that the somatization and behavioral manifestation of traumatic experience is itself a form of memory expressed by the body (van der Kolk, 1989, 1994).

In my own clinical practice, if the timing feels right and I sense that the patient will not feel shamed, persecuted, or impinged upon, I might draw attention to his or her bodily behavior, linking this to what we were discussing at the specific point in the session that such behavior became manifest. I might also share my own bodily experience in the context of our interaction and of what I had observed in the patient's expressive bodily display. I have found that developing mutual awareness of this kind, and sharing bodily as well as emotional experiences can facilitate the process of transforming right-brain, body-based experience into left-brain, subjective states of consciousness. Via this process, visceral-somatic experiences may become available for verbal reflection and elaboration (Schore, 1994). This aspect of therapeutic action is also informed by my familiarity with van der Kolk's (1989, 1994) research into the psychobiology of trauma, and the finding that traumatic experience gets locked into the body.

More generally, in a given context I might ask the patient to describe what he or she is experiencing bodily—tightness in the chest, constriction of the throat, tension in the neck or shoulders, restriction in breathing, butterflies in the stomach. We would then wonder together what such bodily states might represent in emotional terms—anxiety, fear, shame, hate, anger, disgust, sadness, despair. Not infrequently, a patient whose childhood productions were routinely squashed as inadequate or shameful may, paradoxically, become dysregulated by positive experiences associated with pride, joy, and interest-excitement. Patients who, for reasons of cumulative developmental trauma or dramatic abuse, have developed alexithymia or dissociation may, when asked what they are feeling, routinely respond with a thought—for such patients thoughts are habitually equated with feelings. These patients often have difficulty linking emotions to a given interpersonal context, particularly when in a stressed psychobiological state. This may, in turn, leave them feeling confused about what other people's behaviors really mean—the capacity to mentalize is compromised by the dysregulation of bodily and emotional states. Introducing the language of emotions into the therapy, and helping the patient to appraise what he or she is feeling, can be powerfully transformative, enhancing the capacity to regulate bodily and affective states and thus mentalize one's own and the other's emotional and intentional states of mind under increased levels of stress. The therapeutic benefit of integrating a sensorimotor perspective with the emotional and cognitive aspects of clinical work with traumatized individuals has been elaborated by Ogden and her colleagues (Ogden, Minton, & Pain, 2006).

Chapter 6

Attachment and Intersubjectivity

Developmental Perspectives
on the Internal World[*]

AN ATTACHMENT THEORY PERSPECTIVE

John Bowlby studied psychology at Trinity College, Cambridge, following which he trained in adult psychiatry at the Maudsley Hospital. He qualified as a psychoanalyst in 1937 at the age of 30. As noted in Chapter 5, Bowlby launched attachment theory in the late 1950s in response to what he saw as questionable ideas about childhood development and a lack of scientific rigor in psychoanalytic thinking in the 1930s and 1940s (Holmes, 1996). Despite the ethological and biological dimensions of attachment theory, the genesis of Bowlby's work was psychoanalysis, and he acknowledged his debt to Freud, Klein, Fairbairn, and the British object relations school (Bowlby, 1969). Bowlby was particularly influenced by Fairbairn's account of separation anxiety and the way in which the infant's actual experiences with others structures his or her representational world of object relations.

Bowlby was born in 1907 into an upper-middle-class Edwardian family. His father was a surgeon general in the British army and was appointed Royal Surgeon to King Edward VII and King George V. Bowlby saw little of his mother, who left his care largely to the family's nanny and other servants. As a young child, Bowlby was devastated by the loss of his beloved nanny when she left the family's service, as she seems to have become his primary attachment figure. At the outbreak of the First World War in 1914 when Bowlby was 7 years old, he was sent to boarding school (Holmes, 1993). Given these autobiographical facts, it is perhaps not surprising that Bowlby went on to develop his theory about attachment, separation, and loss.

It is often overlooked that the genesis of attachment theory is rooted in Bowlby's interest in understanding the origins of delinquent behavior in young children (Bowlby, 1944). The research for his study into the character and home life of 44 juvenile thieves was carried out in the late 1930s at a London Child Guidance Clinic where he worked as a psychiatrist. During

---

[*] Portions of this chapter appeared in an earlier form in *Attachment*, 4(2), 2010, pp. 146–168. Reprinted with kind permission of Karnac Books.

this time he was training as a child psychoanalyst and his supervisor was Melanie Klein, whose influence on Bowlby I detail below.

Although the 44 thieves' paper predates the launch of attachment theory by a good number of years, many of the themes that were to become central to Bowlby's life's work were already present (Holmes, 1993). In particular, Bowlby drew attention to the "emotional traumas" that had occurred during the first decade of the child's life, seeing his or her emotional disturbance and delinquent behavior as reactive to an adverse home environment and the disruption in family relationships. In exploring the child's phenomenological experience, Bowlby took a full and detailed history, paying special attention to the emotional atmosphere in the home. Instead of privileging unconscious fantasy, he stressed the significance of the child's real-life experiences and emotional relationships, arguing that these factors vitally influence the development of the child's character, internal object relations, and capacity for object-love. In this context, Bowlby implicated the parents' conscious and unconscious attitude towards their child, noting that this was often marked by ambivalence, rejection, and unacknowledged hatred and hostility (Bowlby, 1944; Renn, 2007). But the factor to which he gave most weight was the young child's prolonged separation from the mother or foster mother, viewing this as the cause of "appalling damage" because it shattered the "emotional bonds which usually unite mother and child" (p. 112). As Bowlby noted, when eventually reunited, the child felt like a "lost soul" and the mother as though she had "lost her child" (p. 112).

Bowlby points out how lightly early separations were treated by most workers in the field of juvenile delinquency. He advocates adopting a position of active inquiry into emotional traumas, stating: "My experience has shown me again and again that if these factors are not looked for they are not found...." (p. 20). Commenting in passing on adult offenders, he criticized the prevailing attitude among lawyers, judges, the press, and psychiatrists for failing to take into account the early environment and current circumstances of the person in understanding his or her criminal behavior (Bowlby, 1944; Renn, 2007).

Of the 44 children interviewed by Bowlby, 14 were diagnosed as "affectionless characters." To my mind, the section detailing the experiences of affectionless children constitutes the heart of the paper (Renn, 2007). In addition to stealing and truanting, many of these children were aggressive and bullying. With respect to some, Bowlby formed the impression that "they might easily develop into desperate and dangerous criminals" (p. 38). While Bowlby considers that mothers have greater influence than fathers in their children's early years, in some of the cases studied he concluded that the father's malign influence was of outstanding importance in contributing to the child's unfavorable character development. In the majority of cases, however, he found a high degree of association between the affectionless children and prolonged mother–child separation. In consequence of lacking affectionate relationships with loved objects in early life, the children were distinguished from their peers by being isolated and emotionally indifferent and unresponsive in their personal relationships. Regardless of the real qualities of the mother, the child who has experienced a prolonged separation tends to distort his perceptions, seeing her as a faithless, malicious, and hateful person and himself as a bad, unlovable object (Bowlby, 1944; Renn, 2007).

As Bowlby discovered, the characteristic avoidance and indifference of affectionless children was a form of self-protection against the risk of their ever again experiencing feelings of disappointment, rage, and longings for the lost or unavailable person. However, he noted that "behind the mask of indifference is bottomless misery and behind the apparent callousness despair" (p. 39). Stealing, however unconsciously motivated, was a way of fulfilling hopes for "libidinal satisfaction," in that the objects stolen were felt to be the symbolic equivalent of the mother's love. But, as Bowlby notes, the act of stealing was also aggressive, being motivated by the deprived child's intention to inflict suffering on the other in equal measure to the suffering that had been inflicted upon him (Bowlby, 1944; Renn, 2007).

Bowlby's contribution to the field of juvenile delinquency gradually waned in the years following the Second World War, but his interest in the effects on children of real-life events continued apace with a research focus on separation and loss. As noted above, this culminated in the launch of attachment theory in the late 1950s (Bowlby, 1958). Since that time, attachment theory has been in a continuous process of development and refinement, a process informed by a wealth of empirical studies.

Bowlby (1969) sets out his position on the inner world by quoting approvingly the philosophical view of mind expounded by Hampshire (1962). The latter asserts that "patterns of behavior in infancy ... must be the original endowment from which the purely mental states develop" (cited in Bowlby, 1969, p. 6). On articulating his thinking about psychopathology in general, and aggression in particular, Bowlby (1969, 1979) points out that Freud's major theoretical formulations consistently center on trauma and on an understanding of how intrapsychic conflict between sexual and ego instincts and life and death instincts, expressed as the ambivalent conflict between love and hate, comes to be satisfactorily regulated (Freud, 1915, 1923). Following Klein (1940), Bowlby (1960, 1969, 1973) drew a connection between pathological childhood mourning and psychiatric illness in adulthood. Klein's view that certain mental defenses in early childhood are directed against "pining" for the lost object was particularly influential in his thinking. However, Bowlby (1958, 1960, 1969, 1973) eventually discarded the dual-drive theory of sexuality and aggression. Influenced by Fairbairn (1946), he argued that a biologically based "drive" for attachment was more compelling. In a direct and bold challenge to classical theory, he proposed that it is the particular quality of love and security provided by the mother that helps the child to regulate the basic conflict between love and hate.

As Bowlby developed his theory, he hypothesized that human beings are born with a primary psychobiological system that motivates them to seek proximity, comfort, and support from protective others (Bowlby, 1969, 1973). Thus, whereas Klein (1940) regarded aggression as an expression of the death instinct and anxiety as resulting from its projection, Bowlby (1969, 1979) found this formulation unconvincing, arguing that accounts of aggression that step outside of biology are remote from clinical observation and experience. Instead, he contended that aggression and destructiveness are secondary, viewing such behavior as the result of a traumatic disturbance in the infant–mother relationship, and as being activated by the actual or threatened loss of the attachment bond to the mother.

While initially empirical observation focused on the infant's acute distress when separated from the mother as expressed by protest, despair, and emotional detachment (Bowlby, 1980; Robertson & Robertson, 1989), extensive evaluation of Bowlby's hypothesis of maternal deprivation by Rutter (1981, 1997) in the 1970s and 1980s suggested that a far more complex set of social and psychological factors were in operation. As Holmes (1993) points out, Rutter's work prompted a move away from a simplistic event-pathology model to an appreciation of the subtle nature and quality of the child's attachment to the mother or primary caregiver.

The Basics of Adult and Infant Attachment Research

The work of Bowlby and his collaborators inspired wide interest in infant research, a field of study that continues apace. Main, Kaplan, and Cassidy (1985) emphasize that Bowlby's theory includes the consideration of representational states, as well as focusing on the role of early trauma and early parent-child interaction patterns in the development of anxiety and defensive processes. Indeed, when conceptualizing the inner world from an attachment theory perspective, Bowlby (1973, 1980) looked to cognitive psychology, drawing specifically on the concepts of episodic and semantic memory (Tulving, 1983), and internal working models (Craik, 1943), which he came to view as integral components of the attachment behavioral system. This holds that cumulative experiences are internalized to form internal working models (IWMs) which guide expectations and perceptions, thereby serving as templates for future relationships. Although resistant to change, IWMs are open systems and may be updated and revised in the light of new experience, both influencing and being influenced by later social relationships (Bowlby, 1973, 1980; Fonagy, 1999b; Peterfreund, 1983). In attachment theory, the concept of the IWM or representational model replaces that of the internal object (Knox, 2003). The key role of representations of real experiences in the formation of implicitly encoded mental models has support from empirical science (Bucci, 1997; Edelman, 1987; Schacter, 1996). Knox (2003) argues that Bucci's (1997, 2011) concept of "emotion schemas" is all but identical to Bowlby's (1977, 1988) IWMs, and that Edelman's (1987) theories of "neural Darwinism" and "neural maps" provide the neurobiological basis for both of these psychological constructs.

Research findings, then, from cognitive psychology and cognitive neuroscience would seem to confirm both the validity of Bowlby's theory of attachment and the connection between the child's interpersonal relations and his or her internal world; namely that a secure attachment tie to the mother or primary caregiver functions to integrate the child's personality (Bowlby, 1958). For example, extended mother–child separations of a month or more before the age of 5 have been linked to increased symptoms of borderline personality disorder (BPD) in adolescence and adulthood (Crawford et al., 2009).

The two main methods used in attachment research are the Strange Situation procedure (Ainsworth et al., 1978) and the Adult Attachment Interview (George, Kaplan, & Main, 1985; Main & Goldwyn, 1995; Main, Kaplan, & Cassidy, 1985). Research utilizing the Strange Situation found that infants display one of four discrete patterns of attachment behavior when separated from and reunited with their mothers in the presence of a stranger. These patterns have been classified as secure, avoidant, ambivalent-resistant, and, more recently, disorganized/disoriented. Studies have shown that these discrete attachment patterns, and concomitant behavioral strategies, can be predicted to a high level of accuracy from the quality of interaction observed between the primary caregiver and the infant during the first year of life (Main, Kaplan, & Cassidy, 1985). These findings demonstrated that a parent's AAI classification predicted the quality of attachment shown by a child to that particular parent. This, in turn, indicates that patterns of secure and insecure attachment organization are transmitted intergenerationally between caregiver and infant and internalized and represented in the form self–other IWMs or representational models. These mental models are thought to mediate the infant's experience of actual relationships, and to guide and direct feelings, behavior, attention, memory, and cognition out of conscious awareness. In attachment theory the main purpose of defense is "affect regulation" and the primary mechanism for achieving this is "distance regulation" (Sroufe & Waters, 1977). This defense is apparent in the different behavioral strategies that insecure infants display in the Strange Situation. Holmes (1993) suggests that both the avoidant and ambivalent strategies employed by infants can be formulated as attachment dilemmas deriving from the need to get close to the attachment figure and the expected dangers of doing so, in terms of rejection, abandonment, or intrusion.

The Adult Attachment Interview (AAI) is a semi-structured interview developed by George, Kaplan, and Main (1985) and based on Paul Grice's "cooperative principle." Grice (1975, 1989), a linguistic philosopher, argues that coherent discourse has four maxims: quality, quantity, relevance, and manner. The AAI provides researchers with a standardized method to assess current adult mental representations of childhood attachment experiences, the influence of these experiences as perceived by the interviewee, and the relationship the interviewee has with his or her parents in the here and now. The participant is also asked about loss of loved ones and about other traumatic experiences. During the interview, the interviewee is faced with the dual task of producing and reflecting upon memories related to attachment, while simultaneously maintaining coherent discourse with the interviewer. High levels of coherence indicate that the interviewee has a "singular" rather than a "multiple" representational model of attachment. A single, internally consistent IWM facilitates the integration of attachment-related information and enables the secure individual to explore a wide range of positive and negative thoughts and feelings (Hesse, 1999; Main, 1991). Attachment status on the AAI has been found to be unrelated to the interviewee's verbal fluency or intelligence in general terms (Crowell et al., 1996).

Following Tulving (1983), Bowlby drew attention to the ways in which information is encoded and stored in distinct systems of memory. As seen in Chapter 2, the episodic component of explicit memory consists of information that is stored in the form of temporally dated autobiographical details. Each remembered event or episode has its own distinctive place in the person's life history. By contrast, semantic memory consists of generalized information about the world and the person's sense of self in relation to significant others. Bowlby postulated that such generalized information is encoded in IWMs and mediates the person's attachment-related thoughts, feelings, and behavior in a largely nonconscious, procedural way. Semantic information may be at great variance with information stored in explicit memory. This gives rise to cognitive and emotional conflict and to gross inconsistencies between the generalizations a person makes about his or her parents and what is explicitly implied or actually recalled in terms of specific episodes. Such conflict and inconsistencies indicate the operation of parallel memory systems and the dissociation of painful affect. The AAI is designed to "surprise the unconscious" and to detect conflict and inconsistencies in the discourse style of the interviewee. Bowlby's theorizing about these different memory systems occurred before the discovery of the implicit memory system. His description of the operation of semantic memory may now be seen as having certain features in common with the operation of implicit/procedural memory.

This notwithstanding, the AAI is designed to operationalize Bowlby's construct of the IWM as a "state of mind with respect to attachment," as expressed in discourse about early relationships. The researcher shifts attention from the *content* of autobiographical memory to the *form of discourse* in which those memories are presented. For example, the mother's state of mind in respect of her attachment history may be classified as secure-autonomous and her child as securely attached, despite her having experienced early trauma in the form of separation, loss, and/or abuse. Such findings indicate the resolution of trauma and the attainment of "earned security" via subsequent secure attachment experiences which, of course, may include a therapeutic relationship (Hesse, 1999; Main, 1991). AAI classifications, then, reveal differences in discourse style, in access to attachment memories, and in ability to coherently discuss past attachment experience. The "secondary strategies" employed by adults at the representational level in terms of their discourse style, as detailed below, can be seen to parallel the behavioral strategies observed by infants in the Strange Situation. Thus, in the defensive framework of affect regulation and distance regulation theorized by Sroufe and Waters (1977), these intrapsychic mechanisms function to keep emotionally distressing memories and ideas at a safe distance from conscious awareness (Dozier, Lomax, Tyrell, & Lee, 2001).

The four patterns of adult discourse observed and codified from AAI transcripts are:

Secure-Autonomous: Adults termed *secure-autonomous* provide discourse that is open, free, coherent, and collaborative, presenting even difficult early attachment experiences in clear and vivid ways. Discourse includes no contradictions between semantic and episodic memories of childhood attachments, a focus on the goal of the discourse task, and rich use of language and expression. The interviewee demonstrates an ability to discuss and reflect upon personal attachment experiences in collaboration with the interviewer without disorganization, lack of memory, or passivity of thought. These interviews are characterized by recognition, acceptance, and forgiveness of imperfections and injustices in parents and in self, reflecting an integration of positive and negative feelings. As noted above, even adults with extreme and abusive attachment histories who have come to understand coherently their early difficulties may provide a coherent and autonomous narrative.

Dismissing: Transcripts coded as *dismissing* tend to be excessively brief and are characterized by notable contradictions in the interviewee's discourse about early attachments with generalized representations of history being unsupported or actively contradicted by episodes. Strong idealization of caretakers is common, along with contradictory and impoverished memories of actual events. The interviews are notable for restriction in coherence and content, indicating a deactivating strategy with respect to potentially painful memories. Some adults in this group minimize the importance of close relationships and derogate or dismiss the influence of attachment experiences, emphasizing, instead, extraordinary self-reliance.

Preoccupied: The transcripts of adults termed *preoccupied* may be excessively long and embellished, including information that is irrelevant to the discourse task. Interviewees are not able to describe their attachment biography coherently and show an inability to move beyond an excessive preoccupation with attachment relationships. There are frequent examples of passive speech, sentences begun and left unfinished, and specific ideas that disappear in vague expressions. The boundaries between present and past and self and other are often confused. There is a diffuse self-concept and a notable inability to reflect upon experience. In some transcripts coded as preoccupied, there is notable anger, passivity, or fear, which is displaced from past childhood events to the present discourse task indicating a continuing intense involvement and preoccupation with attachment experiences. The reliving of the affective experience of historical events interferes with the interviewee's consciousness of the current discourse task.

Unresolved: Transcripts of adults are termed *unresolved/disorganized* when there is evidence of substantial lapses in the monitoring of reasoning and discourse, specifically surrounding the discussion of traumatic events involving loss and physical or sexual abuse. The interviewee may briefly indicate a belief that a dead person is still alive in the physical sense or that this person was killed by a childhood thought. The individual may lapse into prolonged silence, engage in eulogistic speech, or enter a trancelike, dissociated state. Main (1991) suggests that such lapses indicate the existence of parallel, incompatible belief and memory systems regarding an unresolved traumatic event that may have become dissociated. Lapses in the monitoring of reasoning and discourse also suggest the possibility of "state shifts." Here, the individual may enter a peculiar, compartmentalized state of mind involving a particular traumatic experience. Shifts of state of this kind may result in frightened and/or frightening behavior on the part of the parent (Main & Hesse, 1990). Research suggests that parental behavior of this kind results in disorganized attachment in the child.

It should be noted that the unresolved classification is made solely on the discussion of trauma, abuse, or loss experiences and is superimposed on one or other of the three main attachment classifications. Findings from research utilizing the AAI show that psychopathology is associated with non-autonomous patterns of attachment and that people classified as preoccupied and unresolved/disorganized are strongly over-represented in clinical samples.

A long-term study carried out by Main and her colleagues (1985) combined the AAI and Strange Situation methodologies. A follow up study by Main in 1991 demonstrated that the child's discrete pattern of attachment organization has, as its precursor, a characteristic pattern of caregiver–infant interaction and its own behavioral sequelae. Thus, as predicted 5 years previously, there was a significant match between the mother's and her child's attachment classifications. In the main, secure/autonomous mothers had infants who were securely attached; those with a dismissing state of mind had avoidant infants; while preoccupied mothers had ambivalent-resistant infants. There was a strong correlation between mothers whose discourse transcript was classified as unresolved in respect of trauma and disorganized/disoriented infants.

Findings from attachment research indicate that once patterns of attachment behavior are established they tend to become actively self-perpetuating. As a consequence, malignant events relevant to attachment may cause difficulty in integrating information. The authors emphasize that a parent's sensitive responsiveness has consistently been found to be the best predictor of security of attachment at 1 year of age. By contrast, parental rejection is predictive of infant avoidance and a parent's inconsistent response predicts ambivalent-resistant infant behavior. The great majority of parentally maltreated children fit the disorganized/disoriented category (Main, 1991; Main, Kaplan, & Cassidy, 1985). In line with these findings, Schore (1994) argues that all early psychopathology constitutes disorders of attachment and is manifested as failures of interactive regulation and/or self-regulation of nonverbal, presymbolic affect.

In terms of the mechanisms involved in this process, Main et al. (1985) suggest that when an established attachment behavioral system receives potentially disruptive signals it counters these by actively deploying perceptual and behavioral control mechanisms. The authors conclude, albeit tentatively, that IWMs deriving from insecure attachment are resistant to modification and updating because error-correcting information is being defensively and selectively excluded from consciousness. A classical psychoanalytic approach would make the assumption that defense mechanisms such as repression, denial, projection, displacement, and idealization have been evoked in response to signal anxiety with the purpose of maintaining psychic equilibrium.

The authors suggest that the difficulty in processing attachment-related information may affect maternal sensitivity as the need to exclude, restrict, or reorganize such information may result in an inability on the part of the mother to perceive and accurately appraise the infant's attachment behavior cues. Indeed, it is proposed that because of issues stemming from her own attachment history, the mother may experience an active need to alter or inhibit the signals being expressed by the infant (Main et al., 1985). This hypothesis would seem to have been confirmed by subsequent research by

Lyons-Ruth & Block (1996) and Lyons-Ruth et al. (2005), as discussed in Chapter 3. In line with the ideas of narrative theory and concepts of metacognition and self-reflexivity, Main and her colleagues (1985) hypothesize that the coherent integration and organization of information relevant to attachment may play a determining role in the creation of security in adulthood.

Disorganized Attachment and Doll-Play Story Completion Research

Following Main et al.'s findings (1985), Liotti (1992, 1999) contends that disorganized attachment is reflected in the construction of a multiple, incoherent representational model which becomes subject to dissociation. This contention would seem to have been confirmed by research with 6-year-old children using a doll–play story completion task (Solomon, George, & De Jong, 1995). Using separation and reunion scenarios in the presence of a stranger while the children's mothers were being interviewed separately created sufficient stress to activate the children's representational models of attachment.

The authors found that children classified as secure were able to transform their fears of separation during fantasy play by inventing stories with happy endings by the end of reunion. These stories required the use of fairly sophisticated cognitive strategies that allowed them to integrate their fears with a successful resolution. In contrast, disorganized/controlling children were unable either to resolve or defend against separation anxiety. Rather, these fears either markedly inhibited playful exploration or disrupted their doll–play by flooding the content in a chaotic and primitive way. The disorganized children's stories demonstrated that fears about the caregiver or the self were out of control and potentially destructive. Dangerous events were unresolved and led to chaos and disintegration of the self and the family, and the children depicted the parents as frightening and abusive and themselves as helpless to get assistance from others to control their behavior or the events around them. Catastrophes arose without warning and dangerous people and events could not be vanquished, but resurfaced again and again (Solomon et al., 1995). The reunions of these children were marked by "role-reversal" and a punitive, controlling response towards the mother.

The stories of children classified as avoidant had a markedly different quality from those of secure or disorganized children. Fears about separation were not expressed directly but were evident in the form of avoidance of both separation and reunion. The self in the story characteristically appeared to deny the experience of separation anxiety by negating, cancelling, or "undoing" separation itself. For example, the child doll tried to accompany the parents on their trip, the child or babysitter called the parents while they were away, or the parents called to deliver a message. These events were inserted casually into the story, without explanation. The reunions of these children were characterized by non-integration of the family members. Typically the child's self-doll watched TV or went to bed just before or immediately upon the parents' return. The impression given was one of casual disinterest in the parents' return. Some of the stories had an empty, affectless quality.

The stories of children classified as anxious-ambivalent also differed greatly from those of the secure or disorganized children. Like avoidant children, fears about separation were not expressed directly. In these scenarios however, fears and other negative feelings were reversed or displaced onto characters other than the self, for example, the baby of the family, other siblings, pets, or inanimate objects. The stories featured parties or other fun activities, and caregiving, comforting responses to physical injury. The overall quality of the stories was one of busy activity and a happy mood. The reunion stories in this group were characterized by delay and distraction. In some cases, family integration was begun but never thoroughly completed because of obsessive and often irrelevant actions of the child or other characters. In other cases, the initial family greeting and reunion were delayed. The authors describe the narrative structure of these stories as digressive. The story line, if one could be detected, was constantly interrupted by distracting, time-consuming, or irrelevant activities. For example, the children or babysitter would arrange dishes and food on the dinner table, sweep, hum, or sing or prepare with endless detail for a birthday party.

While the secure, avoidant, and anxious-ambivalent children had developed an organized strategy for coping with the stress of separation, the disorganized children had no coherent means of dealing with their fears. Solomon and her colleagues conclude that the non-adaptive quality of these children's doll–play suggests that disorganized attachment behavior may emerge when feelings about the mother that normally are unintegrated become activated on reunion. The authors see controlling behavior at age 6 as a brittle behavioral strategy on the part of the child to control the parent who is the source of these unintegrated fears and thereby to regulate his or her own internal state and behavior.

Disorganization at the representational level, then, is consistent with mental models of segregated or dissociated systems of representation whereby a system which is parallel and dissociated from consciousness suddenly becomes disinhibited (Bowlby, 1988). Thus, the disorganized, non-adaptive quality of the doll–play of the frightened children would suggest that disorganized attachment behavior may reemerge in stressful situations involving fear of separation, loss, and threat to the self and the attachment figure (Solomon et al., 1995). These processes are explored in Chapters 9 and 10, which address the important social issue of intimate violence in adult relationships. In these chapters, I suggest that, in the absence of the buffering protection of a secure attachment relationship, the disorganized/controlling 6-year-old may develop into a controlling, violent man in his adult intimate relationships.

In exploring relational violence in Chapter 9, I cite adult attachment research using a variation of Hazan and Shaver's (1987) self-report measure. This is a relatively simple self-classification questionnaire; responses are systematically related to mental models of self-and-partner, beliefs about romantic love, and memories of childhood relationships with parents. The measure identifies and classifies the individual's adult attachment style (secure, anxious, or avoidant) on a dimensional continuum with discomfort with closeness and emotional intimacy lying at one end of the continuum and anxiety about abandonment and rejection lying at the other end. Thus, it may be seen that attachment research encompasses two main lines of investigation: Research utilizing the Strange Situation procedure and the AAI focuses on the intergenerational transmission of attachment patterns; by contrast, research employing self-report questionnaires is designed to reveal the social-cognitive dynamics affecting feelings and behavior in romantic relationships (Shaver & Mikulincer, 2004). Mentalization, as discussed below, may be seen as a key concept in both of these areas of research.

From an attachment theory perspective, the individual constructs mental representations of relationships during the course of development. These representations consist of expectations about the self and others derived from lived experience and nonconscious emotional procedures or strategies for processing attachment-related information and memories. As Cortina and Liotti (2007) observe, such preverbal and presymbolic experiences are encoded and stored in implicit memory, and, though not available for conscious recall, are still alive, being carried forward into adulthood in the form of expectations regarding the availability and responsiveness of others. Representational models do not simply mirror experience, they also reveal attachment phenomena, as expressed in the individual's emotional procedures for processing relational information (Slade, 2004). Although these models cannot be accessed directly, they can be inferred from observed behavior and the expression of thoughts (Solomon et al., 1995). As we have seen, disorganized attachment behavior corresponds to the construction of a representational model of self and attachment figure that is multiple and incoherent, as opposed to singular and coherent (Main & Hesse, 1990). This predisposes the person to enter a state of dissociation in the face of further traumatic experiences (Liotti, 1992, 1999; Lyons-Ruth & Block, 1996; Lyons-Ruth et al., 2005).

Mentalization and the Intergenerational Transmission of Attachment

Fonagy and his colleagues at University College London and the Anna Freud Center have developed Main's concepts of metacognition and self-reflexivity. They use the term *mentalization*. As noted in Chapter 3, this psychological concept describes the capacity to interpret the actions and behaviors of oneself and others as meaningful on the basis of intentional mental states such as personal needs, desires, feelings, beliefs, and purposes (Bateman & Fonagy, 2004). Mentalization involves both a self-reflective and an interpersonal component which, in combination "provide the child with a capacity to distinguish inner from outer reality, intrapersonal mental and emotional processes from interpersonal communications" (Fonagy et al., 2004, p. 4). The concept emerged in the psychoanalytic literature in the 1960s, but in recent years has been applied to developmental psychology by Fonagy and his colleagues in the context of disordered attachment. Research indicates that the individual's attachment history impacts on the development of the ability to mentalize. Securely attached individuals tend to have had high mentalizing primary caregivers, and thus develop robust capacities to represent their own and others' states of mind. In contrast, insecure/disorganized attachment and exposure to cumulative development trauma or dramatic abuse in a context of low mentalizing caregivers compromises the individual's mentalizing capacities (Fonagy, 2008; Fonagy et al., 2004). Such individuals have difficulty in recognizing that their own and others' mental states are representations "which may be fallible and may change because they are based on but one of a range of possible perspectives" (Fonagy et al., 2004, p. 264).

The terms *reflective functioning* and *mentalization* are often used interchangeably. Reflective functioning refers to a scale devised by Fonagy and his colleagues that operationalizes the concept of mentalization for research purposes (Fonagy et al., 1998). Recent research suggests that mentalization is not a unitary capacity but one that may fluctuate within the individual across different relational contexts. Indeed, there is increasing evidence that mentalization is a multifaceted and variable process. Moreover, even when mentalization is reasonably well-established, particular emotions may have been defensively excluded. However, it is generally agreed that the capacity to mentalize crucially depends on the infant's earliest emotional exchanges with the primary caregiver (Fonagy et al., 2004; Target, 2008). In this context, Fonagy (2008) points to the vicious cycle created by attachment trauma in hyper-activating the attachment system and shutting down mentalization. As noted in Chapter 3, as a consequence of being unable to mentalize the traumatic experience, the child relives it in the mode of psychic equivalence instead of in the "as if" or pretend mode (Fonagy, 2008; Fonagy et al., 2004; Fonagy & Target, 1996). Thus, defensive strategies and implicit procedures developed in infancy in response to attachment trauma and misattuned caregiving become aspects of character and relating that persist precisely because they are automatic and outside awareness. Stressful interpersonal contexts in later life may activate maladaptive representational models and again compromise the capacity to mentalize (Fonagy, 2008; Renn, 2003, 2006).

Interestingly, Slade's research with parents and children in psychotherapy draws a distinction between parental reflective functioning, that is the caregiver's capacity to reflect upon the current mental state of the child and upon her own mental states as these pertain to her relationship with her child on the one hand, and her capacity to reflect upon her childhood relationships with her own parents, as classified by the Adult Attachment Interview, on the other hand (Slade, 2008). Slade's research suggests that parental reflective functioning is more influential than parental attachment organization in terms of predicting positive outcomes, such as secure attachment in the child. This is thought to account for the so-called "transmission gap" noted by van Ijzendoorn (1995). He pointed out that researchers have consistently failed to clearly document that maternal sensitivity and responsiveness is what links adult and infant attachment. This led him to suggest that the mechanisms underlying such intergenerational processes of transmission have yet to be understood. It is thought that reflective functioning, as described by Grienenberger, Kelly, and Slade (2005), Fonagy (2008), Fonagy et al. (2004), and Slade (2008), helps to explain this transmission gap.

Although attachment security in the first year of life is predicted primarily by the security of the mother's attachment organization and level of reflective functioning, Steele and Steele's (2008) longitudinal study at University College London found that the father's level of reflective functioning was significantly related to a number of interpersonal and personality factors in boys in middle childhood. Such factors include self-esteem, identity formation, affect regulation, and delinquency and also the son's ability to give a coherent account of himself and others at age 11. Steele and Steele (2008) conclude that attachment is "relationship specific," with representational models of mother and father developing separately rather than as one overarching model of attachment. This fits in with Main et al.'s (1985) earlier finding showing that a child may be disorganized with one parent but not with the other. It would also seem to confirm the emerging relational concept of multiplicity—that our sense of self is represented by multiple states of mind (Bromberg, 1998; Davies & Frawley, 1994).

Attachment research, then, indicates that parents' cognitive-affective IWMs of attachment are transmitted to the growing child via patterns of interaction and processes of interactive regulation. These processes powerfully influence the development of the child's own representational models of self–other relationships. The internalization of these mental models mediate the person's subjective experience of all subsequent relationships, particularly those forged with intimate sexual partners in adulthood (Bowlby, 1979, 1988). Research also shows that older children and adults continue to monitor the accessibility and emotional responsiveness of those with whom they have formed a meaningful emotional attachment. The person seeks to maintain an optimal degree of proximity to his or her attachment figure throughout the life cycle in order to sustain feelings of security. The nonconscious procedures employed are mediated by discrete patterns of secure or insecure attachment, as represented in IWMs. As noted above, on a dimensional continuum, these representational models influence the person's "discomfort with closeness" and "anxiety over abandonment," and thus mediate the emotional quality of romantic relationships and how separations and reunions are managed in everyday life (Roberts & Noller, 1998; Shaver & Mikulincer, 2004).

Choice of adult romantic partners is one of the most significant mechanisms by which attachment patterns and early affectional ties are externalized and maintained, particularly in instances of unmourned loss (Bowlby, 1979, 1988). This contention is supported by clinical experience and observation, most directly in work with couples, which I discuss in Chapter 9. Here, a certain fit or match may be discerned in the respective partners' early insecure attachment histories with implicitly encoded maladaptive representational models being externalized and destructively enacted in their current emotional and sexual relationships. From an attachment/trauma perspective, the person's symptoms, destructive, and self-destructive behaviors are understood as expressing unprocessed traumatic experience encoded in implicit/procedural memories as represented in confused, unstable self–other representational models (Renn, 2003, 2006, 2008a).

Indeed, preliminary findings provide compelling evidence that attachment strategies and implicitly encoded procedures formed in infancy influence the playing out of the sexual system in adult romantic relationships. Hyperactive strategies include preoccupied, intrusive, and coercive attempts to persuade a partner to have sex. The preoccupied person is hypervigilant of a partner's signs of arousal, attraction, and rejection, coupled with heightened anxiety about his or her own ability to gratify and hold on to a partner. By contrast, deactivating strategies are characterized by inhibition of sexual desire and avoidance of sexual contact, or by a shallow cynical approach that divorces sex from kindness and intimacy and disparages the partner. Thus, in broad terms, secure attachment tilts sexuality towards more successful, less conflictual solutions, while anxious ambivalent attachment and avoidant/dismissing strategies tilt the patterns of sexuality towards less successful, more conflictual solutions (Lichtenberg, 2007).

DANIEL STERN'S FORM OF INTERSUBJECTIVITY

Developmental studies indicate that from the very start of life the infant is involved in numerous interactions with others, both responding to their initiatives and actively initiating interaction themselves. These findings challenge the proposal of Mahler et al. (1985) that the earliest stage of development is characterized by a state of symbiosis, an undifferentiated state that the authors implicate in the development of autism in children. In contrast, Stern's (1985) synthesis of research findings indicates that all the perceptual systems of the infant are functional at birth. For example, the infant is compelled and stimulated by the sound of the human voice and the sight of the human face. From this data, Stern (1985) concludes that the infant's states of consciousness are socially negotiated during the course of differing kinds of relationships.

This proposal mirrors Tronick, Als, Adams, Wise, and Brazelton's (1978) aphorism: "I interact, therefore I am." The authors' statement reflects the findings of the so-called "still face" situation in which the mother, after a period of normal interaction, adopts an immobile posture and mask-like expression when sitting face-to-face with her baby. The effect on the infant is dramatic and distressing in that after repeated unsuccessful attempts to elicit the expected interactional response from the mother, the baby collapses into a detached, self-protective state (Brazelton & Cramer, 1991). Tronick et al. (1978) conclude that the micro-repair of the breakdown of attunement or misaligned interaction is probably at the heart of the establishment of a viable human relationship.

This premise is supported by research using the time series regression model which films the split-second world of interaction between the mother and the infant not visible to the naked eye (Gottman, 1981). Micro-analysis of research using this technique has demonstrated the bidirectional influence in communicative processes between the mother–infant dyad in terms of the timing, tracking, and matching of vocal exchanges (Jaffe et al., 1991) and the duration of "movements" and "holds" in the changes of facial expression and direction of gaze (Beebe, Jaffe, & Lachmann, 1992). Beebe et al. (1992) cite research findings, including those of Main et al. (1985) and Trevarthan (1979), demonstrating that variations in early social interactions are predictive of cognitive development and discrete patterns of attachment at 1 and 2 years of age.

Measures used in these various research projects include mutual gazing, mutual smiling, and social play in the first 4 months of life and the mother's capacity to respond contingently to the infant's signals in the first 6 months of life. For example, maternal sensitivity during feeding at 4 weeks, in terms of rhythmic holding and the facilitation of infant activity, was found to predict secure attachment at 1 year of age. The authors argue that a dyadic symmetry is in operation, with each partner's behavior being predictable from that of the other and employed for the specific purpose of regulating the exchange. Moreover, they suggest that interaction structures are represented internally over the early months of life and play a major role in the emerging symbolic forms of self- and object representations (Beebe et al., 1992; Beebe & Lachmann, 1994). From an attachment theory perspective, the dyadic communicative process is conceptualized in terms of mutual responsiveness to attachment behavior signals.

Beebe et al. (1992) conceptualize misattunement as the loss of mutual influence or contingent responsivity. Research indicates that the infant may come to associate lack of contingency with negative affects and escalating arousal. This, in turn, may interfere with the infant's optimal regulation of his or her arousal. The authors suggest that prolonged and severe states of withdrawal to accomplish re-regulation of arousal in the face of misattuned caregiving may compromise the infant's attention and information processing capacities. They argue that an infant who typically uses inhibition of responsivity alters his or her capacity to stay alert and be fully attentive and responsive to the environment.

Daniel Stern's thinking complements a relational/attachment understanding of the inner world (Stern, 1998). He argues that repeated patterns of interaction constitute the basic building blocks of psychic formation and structures the infant's representational world. These patterns, in turn, build the perceptual, affective, and cognitive schemas used to organize and construct subsequent life experience (Fosshage, 1992). A schema is said to consist of a procedural memory. The latter consists of nonconscious, nonreflective emotional and impressionistic information derived from, and arising out of, a dynamic series of micro-events. Micro-events refer to processes of mutual influence between the mother and the infant and constitute what Stern (1998) calls the relational mode, that is "a-way-of-being-with" or "a style of relating." As noted above, mutual influence takes the form of the timing, tracking, and matching of vocal exchanges with these interactive behaviors being employed for the specific purpose of regulating the exchange (Beebe et al., 1992).

Consonant with neuroscience research in respect of implicit/procedural memory (Schacter, 1996), Stern (1985) argues that procedural memories are internalized and represented as patterns of interactive behaviors that become generalized. Findings indicate that such interactive patterns are the means by which affect is communicated and, moreover, provide a behavioral basis for the mother and infant to perceive and enter into the temporal and feeling state of the other (Beebe et al., 1992).

On theorizing about the development of self, Stern (1985) places the focus firmly on the infant's inner subjective experience and his or her interpersonal context. He adopts and operationalizes Trevarthan and Hubley's (1978) definition of intersubjectivity, namely, a deliberately sought sharing of experiences about events and things. Stern (1985) proposes four senses of the self—emergent, core, subjective, and verbal—suggesting that each emergent sense of self defines a new domain, that is, a sphere of influence or activity of social relatedness. He views the initial formation of a domain as constituting a sensitive period of development, arguing that each domain will hold predominance during that time. However, he points out that once all domains of relatedness are available to the infant, no one domain will necessarily claim preponderance during any particular age period.

Stern (1998) further suggests that the infant's newly developed senses of self provide the arena within which clinical issues are played out. Such issues include autonomy, orality, symbiosis, mastery, control, trust, dependence, independence, attachment, and separation. However, Stern (1998) argues that clinical issues are not merely age- or phase-specific, but life-course issues. He therefore contends that although these issues may take different forms during different developmental epochs, they are continually being worked on, negotiated, and reorganized in dyadic interaction across the life cycle.

For Stern (1985), then, each sense of self and each domain of social relatedness is a form of self-experience and social interaction. He therefore proposes that a sense of self with other grows alongside a sense of self and a sense of the other. Along similar lines to Winnicott (1988), Stern (1985) suggests that the mother's task is to maintain an internal line of continuity as this provides the child with a coherent sense of self and, thereby, the capacity to cope with temporary separations without recourse to maladaptive defenses. He argues that such coherence is achieved through a process of "affect attunement," a subtle process of interaction during which the mother mirrors and marks her infant's moods and behavior, either directly or by using different sensory modalities to match the shape, intensity, and timing of her infant's activity. This form of attuned, cross-modal responsiveness by the mother is thought to resonate with the child's experience, thereby creating a matching of affective inner states between the mother and the infant.

Schore (1994), too, emphasizes the nonverbal, emotion-transacting mechanisms inherent in the caregiver-infant relationship. He argues that this process takes place at pre-conscious/unconscious levels and is represented by communications between the dyad's respective right brain hemispheres that are tuned in to receive such communications. Schore contends that this communicative process facilitates a dyadic matching of psychobiological states and hence an interactive regulation of affect. In line with this hypothesis, he suggests that empathy may best be understood as nonverbal psychobiological attunement. The recent discovery of the mirror neuron system, which is activated when we observe the other's actions, intentions and emotions, taking the form of "embodied simulation," is thought to be the neural substrate of the capacity for empathy (Gallese, 2009). I discuss the mirror neuron system in greater detail in Chapter 8.

While a bidirectional model of influence points up the importance of the dyad in the organization of individual behavior, Beebe et al. (1992) emphasize that this model incorporates and integrates the crucial contribution of the individual's own self-regulatory capacities, a point also made by Schore (1994). Stern (1985, 1998) construes the mother–infant relationship as a subtle process of intersubjectivity during which states of consciousness, in terms of affect, attention, and intention, come to be shared. The self is viewed as developing through this intersubjective process and as being composed of patterns of procedural memories of interactive regulations that are developed in the context of relations with others. Psychopathology is seen as arising out of an accumulation of implicitly encoded maladaptive interactive patterns that result in character and personality types and disorders.

From Stern's (1985) perspective, the effect on the infant of the caregiver who characteristically inhibits or defensively excludes from consciousness attachment behavior signals (Main et al., 1985) is a lack of attunement and a resultant mismatch in their affective states. Mahler et al. (1985) would construe such parent–child interaction as meeting the mother's symbiotic needs instead of the infant's needs for phase-appropriate autonomy. Winnicott (1988) might well have described the situation as representing a failure of the facilitating maternal environment which, if characteristic of the relationship, would impinge on the child's inherited disposition and lead to the development of a conformistic, over-adapted false self. Bion (1984), for his part, may have viewed the mother as lacking the capacity to enter a state of reverie and contain and modify her infant's inchoate experience and projected terror, leading to an inner world characterized by "nameless dread." Bollas (1994) is likely to perceive the mother's idiomatic logical paradigm of intersubjective "being and relating" as acting to forestall the infant from attaining a sense of authentic experience. Beebe et al. (1992), Tyson and Tyson (1990) and Schore (1994), would, respectively, tend to view such misaligned interaction as compromising the infant's capacity to self-regulate nonverbal, presymbolic affect during heightened states of emotional arousal.

Stern (1985) acknowledges that the concepts he and his colleagues have developed are, in part, derived from Bowlby's theorizing about attachment and the infant research to which this has given rise. Here, as we have seen, it is postulated that patterns of interaction gradually structure and organize the child's inner world. Relational experience is internalized in the form of representational models and stored and encoded in implicit memory. These models consist of the relations the child has with primary caregivers, as well as of the child's own sense of self and of himself or herself in interaction with these significant others. It is assumed that repeated failure by the caregiver to respond in a contingent and congruent way to the infant's attachment cues and signals, and to mirror and mark the child's psychological states, leads to the breakdown of secure affectional bonds and to the organization in the inner world of insecure patterns of attachment, together with concomitant difficulties in integrating attachment relevant information and reflecting on one's own and the other's mental states (Fonagy et al., 2004; Main et al., 1985).

Disorganized attachment, in particular, is associated with a compromised capacity for mentalization. Fonagy and his colleagues (2004) note that whereas abused and traumatized individuals are able to mentalize in the context of ordinary social relationships, "they inevitably become conflicted and entangled once a relationship becomes emotionally intense, organized by mental structures that are involved in attachment relationships" (p. 13). This leaves the individual with an internal reality that is dominated by psychic equivalence. As a consequence, the nonconscious, procedural expectations that organize all relationships take on the "full force of reality and there is no sense of alternative perspective" (p. 13). This is an important clinical issue to bear in mind, both in the transference relationship and in understanding aggression and destructiveness in intimate relationships in everyday life, as discussed in Chapters 9 and 10.

As noted above, although representational models tend to reinforce a basic sense of continuity to the infant's personality or sense of self, it is thought that they remain open to elaboration, modification, and change, thereby shaping the developing child's new experience (Main et al., 1985; Sroufe, 1988). Indeed, research suggests that the mind can continue to develop throughout the lifespan via changes in representational models (Siegal, 2001). Such findings are supported by neuroscience, which increasingly recognizes that the brain retains plasticity throughout life, adapting to changes in environmental challenges and demands (Cozolino, 2002; Edelman, 1987; Mancia, 2006; Rose, 2003; Schacter, 1996; Siegal, 2001). One such challenge is provided by the process of therapy with new neural connections being reflected in updated representational models and the attainment of emotional resilience and "earned security" (Cozolino, 2002; Fonagy, 1999b; Fonagy & Target, 1996; Hesse, 1999; Main, 1991). The development of representational models is discussed in more detail in Chapter 8, and the therapeutic process of modifying non optimal models is addressed in Chapter 11.

An Observation of Mother–Infant Interactive Regulation

The following extract may put some clinical flesh on the theoretical bones of how a relational perspective informed by attachment theory, infant research, and intersubjectivity conceptualizes the development of the infant's representational world. It is taken from an 18-month observation of an infant,

Imogen, and her mother, Bernie. Imogen was 6½ months old at the time of the observation and I had been seeing her once a week since her birth.

Bernie opened the front door to me with Imogen in her arms. Imogen smiled at me in response to my greeting, but seemed unusually wary. I recalled that she had cried on seeing me last week. Although this had occurred in the context of noise, commotion, and decorators being in the house, I wondered if Imogen was experiencing a degree of stranger anxiety in respect of me.

We sat on the couch in the sitting room with Bernie on my left. She sat Imogen on her lap sideways on so that she was facing me. My supposition about Imogen's wariness appeared to be confirmed by her behavior at this point, in that she would look at me, smile briefly, but then turn away to look up at Bernie's face before looking at me again. Imogen did this two or three times, seemingly using Bernie's expressive behavioral display to gauge whether or not it was safe to interact with me. Each time Imogen looked at Bernie's face, she (Bernie) smiled and vocalized and then looked at me. Imogen followed Bernie's gaze back to me and I then smiled, vocalized and "talked" to her, uttering phrases in a musical way such as, "You know me, don't you?" and "You're not going to cry, are you?"

Observing Imogen's social referencing behavior led me to infer that she and Bernie had established a shared focus of attention. I concluded that Imogen's backwards looks up at Bernie were being made to validate the achievement of joint attention, and to confirm that they were focusing on the same target of attention, that is on me, with the intention of apprais-ing whether it was safe to engage in social interaction with me. After a few such exchanges, Bernie stood Imogen up between us, gently impelling her towards me. I took over her support by holding her under her arms, but I sensed that bringing her on to my lap at that point may have caused her distress, being experienced as an impingement or intrusion. Indeed, while stood in "no-man's land," or the transitional space between Bernie and me, Imogen glanced back to her once or twice. Bernie responded by again looking at me, imperceptibly inclining her head in my direction while, ever so slightly, ushering Imogen towards me and asking with a smile, "Are you going then?" I experienced Bernie's rhetorical question as a cue to me as much as to Imogen, and I responded by gently lifting Imogen to stand on my lap. As I did so, Bernie stood up and, on seeing Imogen beginning to engage in social play with me, went to the kitchen to make coffee.

This was the first occasion that I had observed Imogen employ social ref-erencing to attain a shared focus of attention and intention, or mutual states of inter-attentionality and inter-intentionality. Observing this newfound interpersonal capacity led me to infer that she was beginning to develop a sense of a subjective self, together with a capacity to share subjective expe-riences with significant others in an intersubjective domain of relatedness. From Imogen's response to my initiating behavior at the beginning of this day's observation, I surmised that she was feeling uncertain, if not actually fearful, about engaging with me, in that, despite her having smiled at me, she clearly felt the need to check back to Bernie several times before deciding whether it was safe enough to allow the social engagement with me to intensify. Bernie's positive expressive display appeared to signal to Imogen that it was, indeed, safe to do so.

From my observations of these subtle interactions, I inferred that Bernie and Imogen were, in some intangible way, able to read each other's feeling states from their overt behavioral display, with the latter constituting both a shared framework of meaning and a means of communication, right brain to right brain and via the activation of the mirror neuron system. Moreover, their capacity to communicate by such means would seem to indicate that procedural memories of repeated micro-events had become internalized, being represented as generalized patterns of interactive behaviors.

Having successfully read Bernie's positive affective state from her cross-modal attunement behavior, Imogen seemed able to bring her own wary feeling state into alignment with that of Bernie's. Thus, it would appear that Imogen's state of consciousness had been socially negotiated at the level of intersubjective relatedness, with Bernie's emotions being transmitted to Imogen, thereby supplying the tone and contours of her internal state at this particular moment. The intersubjective relatedness or emotional connectedness of this exchange seemed to have been achieved through a mutual process of affect attunement, with Bernie first reading and then mirroring and marking Imogen's uncertain mood and wary behavior. Attunement or inter-affectivity was accomplished cross-modally by Bernie sensitively matching the shape, intensity, and timing of Imogen's behavior during her approach/withdrawal activity in relation to me. From my observations, it seemed that the primary modalities that Bernie had brought into play during this intuitive and mutual interactive process were gaze, facial expressions, vocalizations, posture, and gesture. Bernie's attuned, contingent cross-modal responsiveness appeared to resonate with Imogen's subjective experience, thereby creating a match between her own and Imogen's inner affective states.

I concluded, therefore, that Bernie's emotional understanding (reflective functioning) and interactive regulation of Imogen's emotional state of mind, and also her availability for use as a social referent/safe haven, enabled Imogen to self-regulate her anxious, wary state, and, in turn, to organize and restructure her subjective experience in relation to Bernie and, by extension, to me, since I was the precipitating cause of her anxiety in the first place. As a result of this process of interactive regulation and contingent mutual reciprocal influence, Imogen seemed to feel sufficiently safe and secure to separate from Bernie, using her as a secure base from which to engage in social, exploratory play with me. Moreover, she was able to sustain playful interaction even after Bernie had left the room. I therefore surmised that the intersubjective process of cross-modal affect attunement and interactive regulation that had occurred during this particular encounter or "being with" experience had facilitated Imogen's sense of agency and coherence as a developing subjective self. As a consequence, she was able to self-regulate her affective state and subjective experience with regard to clinical issues of trust, separation, exploration, and autonomy. In line with Daniel Stern and Beatrice Beebe and their respective colleagues, I would argue that the observation of the micro-processes that characterize optimal mother–infant interactive regulation can be used to understand the therapeutic process and thus helpfully inform clinical work with adult patients. I illustrate these processes in a clinical vignette in Chapter 8.

Theoretical Integration?

From the foregoing discussion on attachment theory and intersubjectivity, it will be noted that the philosophical position informing these approaches with respect to the mind–body problem is that of psychophysical interactionism. As we saw in Chapter 5, this is also the position informing Kleinian and other relational and interpersonal perspectives. The latter approaches, however, tend to develop theory about the infant's state of mind retrospectively via phenomena gleaned from clinical work with adults. This notwithstanding, it would appear that theoretical assumptions drawn from clinical experience have much in common with empirical research supporting attachment and intersubjective perspectives. Indeed, Holmes (1996) argues that a truly interpersonal/intersubjective psychoanalytic psychotherapy is evolving out of the work of Klein, Bowlby, Bion, Winnicott, Kohut, and, more recently, that of Benjamin and Mitchell. To this may be added the ideas emanating from Stern and Beebe and their respective colleagues.

The extent to which this integrative process is happening is a matter of debate. In the meantime, it would seem clear that theoretical assumptions are of central importance to any discussion of the inner world, as the very purpose of psychological theory is to provide a conceptual framework for the understanding of mental functioning. Bowlby, himself, makes a similar point by quoting Kurt Lewin's dictum that: "There is nothing as practical as a good theory" (Bowlby, 1988, p. 37). What follows is my own attempt to integrate the main concepts emanating from relational psychoanalysis, attachment theory, developmental and cognitive psychology, and cognitive neuroscience.

THE THERAPEUTIC PROCESS USING AN INTEGRATED ATTACHMENT, RELATIONAL, INTERSUBJECTIVE, AND NEUROSCIENCE APPROACH

Before training as a psychoanalytic psychotherapist I worked in a forensic setting with violent people, predominantly men, some of whom had raped or killed a partner, child, or sexual rival, all of whom had histories of loss, abuse, neglect, and trauma—a toxic admixture of cumulative developmental trauma and dramatic abuse. The civil, nonforensic aspect of my work involved working with people in the throes of separation and divorce who were in dispute about the post-divorce arrangements for their children in terms of contact and residence. I found attachment theory and Minuchin's (1974) structural family therapy invaluable in informing this work. Although I now solely work in private practice, my previous experience and way of working with people who had committed grave crimes and with parents and children in distress has undoubtedly influenced my current practice and the therapeutic model that I have developed in working with traumatized people.

In discussions with colleagues over the years, many have argued that there is a need to modify psychoanalytic technique in order to work efficaciously with patients in general, and with traumatized, hard-to-reach patients in particular. I would agree and suggest that some of the most important modifications are to work face-to-face, to acknowledge the "real relationship" that develops between therapist and patient, to acknowledge our own contributions to enacted ruptures to the therapeutic relationship, to not couch everything in transference/countertransference terms, to desist from transference interpretations, and interpretations generally, in the early stages of the therapy, and to not privilege conscious, verbalizable knowledge over nonverbal "implicit relational knowing." In line with the ideas emanating from the Boston Change Process Study Group that I discuss in Chapter 8, I would suggest that implicit/enactive encounters form the basis of intersubjective relatedness and the establishment of a secure-enough base from which to explore, express, and elaborate new forms of agency and shared experiences (Bruschweiler-Stern et al., 2002, 2007; Lyons-Ruth et al., 1998).

Another radical departure from psychoanalytic technique in my practice is that, once the patient has explained his or her reasons for wanting to commence a therapy, I take an attachment, trauma, and relationship history during the initial consultation. I have found this invaluable in helping to contextualize the patient's current difficulties in living and to understand his or her nonverbal, implicit/enactive relational patterns, and habitual emotional procedures. Moreover, in my experience, people come to therapy wanting to tell their stories and needing to know that we can bear to hear them. Inviting the patient to tell his or her story at the outset in a matter of fact, but sensitively attuned way, sets the tone for the whole therapy and provides a containing/holding environment. Not doing so for fear of retraumatizing the patient may unwittingly convey the message that the therapist is too anxious, fragile, and vulnerable to hear and engage with the patient's trauma. This may lead to a subtle inversion of the relationship in which the patient cares for the therapist, thereby reenacting aspects of his or her early relationships with parents (Bowlby, 1988). This form of avoidance may also reflect the activation of the therapist's representational model or emotion schema. As Wallin (2007) and Bucci (2011) respectively point out, therapist and patient each bring their own internal working models or emotion schemas to the therapeutic encounter. The way in which the therapist's and the patient's implicitly encoded representational models or dissociated emotion schemas interact is inherently unpredictable and will emerge in the enactive or subsymbolic interpersonal domain.

Not infrequently patients will ask at the initial consultation how therapy can help them to change. I think we need to be prepared to answer such questions in an informed, honest, and open way. More generally, I also think that there is a place for sharing with our patients the theories we use in our work and the research findings that underpin such theories. I would not necessarily see this in terms of psycho-education, but rather as a form of collaborative working, and of relating to the patient in an ethical way and with mutuality and respect. I might point out to a patient that the sessions themselves merely kick-start a therapeutic process and that change requires him or her to work assiduously in between sessions so as to become increasingly adept at recognizing the activation of archaic representational models and concomitant procedural way of "remembering" via repetitive enactments in their everyday lives. To this end, I encourage the patient to note the relational context in which such enactments or procedural patterns of behavior emerge and to try to name the dissociated emotions that are motivating such behavior so that focal attention can be brought to bear on the experience. The goal is to enhance the patient's affect regulation and mentalizing capacities so that he or she can make the transition from a non-optimal, nonreflective representational model to one that is reflective and more adaptive to the given interpersonal context. I might also explain that over time new ways of thinking and feeling become encoded in implicit/procedural memory as second order representational models are established, and therefore that the hard work of having to be consciously aware of how he or she is interacting with others lessens as new, more optimal ways of being and relating gradually emerge.

To this end, not only do I suggest to new patients that they keep a "dream book" on hand to note down any significant dreams which, as we know, can be vivid at one moment and elusive at the next, flying from memory; I also suggest that they keep a "snag book" to record any momentary thoughts, feelings, or interpersonal encounters in their everyday lives that in some way created a "snag" for them, but which they quickly and habitually evacuated from consciousness. So often in the early stages of a therapy, patients come to a session feeling empty and reporting that nothing new has really happened since the last session. This is a pronounced feature in people who have developed an avoidant/dismissing state of mind with respect to attachment, as reflected in their discrete discourse style and general fear of feelings. A sense of curiosity and exploration of both their external relations and the relationship they have with themselves is markedly impoverished and severely circumscribed. Helping such patients to feel safe enough to begin to be curious and explore their internal milieu of thoughts, feelings, wishes, beliefs, and fantasies, as well as to recognize repetitive relational patterns in their everyday relationships, is at the heart of the early phase of the therapy. Achieving this often involves something of a mutual struggle, but one that can be fruitful in deepening a sense of meaningful emotional connection. It also conveys to the patient that I am interested in, and wanting to understand, the complexity of his or her difficulties in living.

My emphasis on the patient's interpersonal context is consonant with Wachtel's (2008) cyclical-contextual paradigm. Wachtel critiques relational psychoanalysis for being exclusively concerned with what goes on in the consulting room between patient and therapist and for paying too little attention to the patient's life outside of the office. For Wachtel, the patient's enduring psychological structures need to be understood in the context of his or her everyday life. Indeed, he argues that inner processes cannot adequately be understood unless they are contextualized in terms of the patient's continuing transactions and interactions with the key figures in his or her life. Wachtel contends that in order to help patients change the patterns and psychic structures that are severely limiting their lives, the therapist needs to understand and illuminate how patients unconsciously recruit others as "accomplices" in the perpetuation of their life patterns. From Wachtel's cyclical psychodynamic model, the therapeutic process requires a detailed examination of the patient's "repetitive *sequences* that characterize his interactions with other people" (p. 105, emphasis in original). A crucial part of the therapist's task is to bring into focal awareness the mutual eliciting of pattern-maintaining responses that occur in the patient's everyday relationships. For Wachtel then, the goal is to make conscious the patient's behavior—his or her repetitive actions and interactions with others that constitute his everyday life and personality.

Over and above this particular aspect of therapeutic action, which I discuss more fully in Chapter 11, developmental studies show that we are all born with an innate capacity to seek companionable shared experiences, first and foremost in the implicit domain of being and relating. I have found that even in cases of the most appalling trauma, this capacity survives and constitutes a basic form of human resilience that can be harnessed in the service of developing a therapeutic alliance. The silent witnessing of the other's trauma is not, in my view, sufficient in and of itself to bring this about. If we accept that the relationship itself is the main vehicle for change, we need to feel secure enough in our role as therapists to use our own idiomatic selves as therapeutic tools. Thus, in a particular given context we may, in a spontaneous and creative way, feel drawn to play, improvise, flirt, disclose, be outrageous, take risks, and use humor in order to establish on each reunion and to re-establish after every separation, a state of emotional connectedness or intersubjective relatedness. In addition to developmental considerations, this aspect of the therapeutic relationship may be couched in terms of the "analytic third"—a unique property that emerges in each and every therapeutic dyad (Aron, 2008; Benjamin, 2004; Ogden, 2004). As Roth and Fonagy (1996) found, although there is a need for good knowledge of technique in order to lay a foundation for effective practice, there is also a need to be able to use technical recommendations flexibly, and to deviate and go beyond them at times when the clinical situation seems to require this. This view is also expounded by Maroda (2010) in her enlightened book on psychodynamic techniques. I discuss these aspects of the therapeutic process in more detail in Chapter 7 from a relational/ developmental perspective.

With these various caveats in mind, I now summarize the different systems of ideas that I have loosely integrated into my own idiosyncratic therapeutic model. These theories not only speak to me personally, but also seem to be meaningful to my patients and thus helpful in bringing about the changes in their lives and intimate relationships that they so desperately desire.

An Integrated Therapeutic Model

Attachment theory and infant research demonstrate that psychological organization is an adaptation aimed at preserving critical, life-sustaining relationships. As Slade (2004) points out, attachment classifications used for research purposes are simply ways of describing and organizing implicitly encoded attachment phenomena. These silent phenomena and the invisible processes and relational procedures they represent are the focus of clinical work, not the classifications per se. A basic understanding of attachment theory and research sensitizes the therapist to the nature and functioning of the attachment system and aids in the observation and recognition of attachment phenomena, as revealed in the patient's speech and behavior (Slade, 2004).

The initial interview provides an ideal opportunity to begin to listen for attachment phenomena as manifested in the patient's talk about his or her relationships with parents, partners, and children. I provide a clinical example of this in Chapter 8. In my experience, many people commence therapy on becoming parents because they have become aware of repeating with their children the negative aspects of the relationship they had with their own parents. Despite this cognitive awareness, they seem unable to change the way they relate to their children in emotional and procedural terms (Renn, 2008a). Familiarity with adult attachment research will help guide the therapist to listen to the fluency, coherence, affectivity, and flexibility in the patient's narrative descriptions of early childhood attachment experiences. This provides the means of identifying the patient's particular ways of regulating and defending against implicitly encoded attachment-related memories and feelings (Slade, 2004).

Attachment research also alerts the therapist to listen for themes of attachment trauma in the form of loss, neglect, rejection, abandonment, and abuse in the patient's narrative. Such narratives, and the discrete discourse style in which they are communicated, can tell the therapist a great deal about the patient's capacity to hold and reflect upon their own and the other's mental states in making sense of behavior and relationship patterns. By extension, the patient's narrative also informs us about his or her early intersubjective experience and cumulative developmental trauma. These stories, and the discourse style in which they are related, also offer an opportunity to evaluate the patient's attributions of the other—the nature and affective qualities of his or her inner world representations of the other, and the way in which these relational dynamics are being played out in their everyday lives (Eagle, 2003; Renn, 2006, 2008b; Slade, 2004; Wachtel, 2008).

Adults who have developed a dismissing attachment state of mind avoid intimacy and the exploration of painful thoughts and feelings. By contrast, those whose early relationships have created a preoccupied attachment state of mind are angrily enmeshed with their past and current attachment figures. Adults with an unresolved state of mind in respect of trauma cannot maintain affective continuity in their inner worlds and become disorganized and disoriented when re-experiencing a traumatic event. As we have seen, these contrasting attachment patterns and states of mind are captured in attachment research utilizing the Strange Situation procedure, the doll–play story completion task, and the Adult Attachment Interview. By inducing a degree of stress, these research methodologies tap into procedural memories at the level of representation. Findings show that while the avoidant child and dismissing adult develop a state of mind that values emotional self-reliance and separateness, the ambivalent-resistant child and preoccupied adult develop a state of mind that is angry, frightened, and anxious about being separate and autonomous. The disorganized child and unresolved adult dissociate from the immediate environment and develop either a helpless or hostile/controlling state of mind (Lyons-Ruth et al., 1999; Lyons-Ruth et al., 2005). These states of mind, then, give rise to nonconscious attachment procedures and phenomena that are communicated, in part, via the patient's particular discourse style and interaction with the therapist and with key others in everyday life (Renn, 2006, 2008b; Wachtel, 2008). Being aware of our own predominant attachment state of mind and implicit procedures may help us, as therapists, to recognize and understand the enactments that we inescapably get drawn into with our patients, and inform how best to repair such inevitable ruptures to the attachment relationship or therapeutic alliance (Schore, 2011; Wallin, 2007).

In clinical practice, then, attachment theory and research are used to conceptualize the developmental antecedents and interpersonal features of the patient's difficulties in living, particularly his or her implicitly encoded procedures for managing closeness and distance and separations and reunions in intimate relationships, and the influence of these phenomena on the formation of the therapeutic alliance (Lopez & Brennan 2000). Attachment theory and research provide both a particular way of listening to the patient's story and of understanding the clinical process (Slade 1999). An aspect of this process involves identifying similarities in the complex dynamic interplay between the patient's early relational matrix and his or her current intimate relationships, including that with the therapist (Renn, 2003, 2006, 2008b; Wachtel, 2008). This facilitates an understanding of the way in which archaic, nonconscious, cognitive-affective mental models are being perpetuated in the here and now, actively mediating and distorting the person's attachment-related thoughts, feelings, and behavior, particularly at times of heightened emotional stress—how the silent relational past lives on in invisible ways in the interpersonal present (Renn, 2008b). These attachment dynamics and defensive processes are most immediately apparent in couple therapy (Shimmerlik, 2008).

From a relational perspective informed by the literature on attachment, trauma, and neuroscience, the patient's somatic symptoms and destructive and self-destructive behaviors are understood as expressing unprocessed traumatic experience encoded in implicit/procedural memories, as represented in confused, unstable self-other representational models (Renn, 2006, 2007). These nonconscious, state-dependent memories and patterns of expectancies organize experience and emerge in the relational system or intersubjective field, being communicated directly to the therapist via the patient's discourse style and expressive behavioral display. This, in turn, activates a matching countertransferential or psychophysiological response in the therapist (activates the mirror neuron system), enabling the therapist to participate in the subjective experience of the patient in terms of shared attentional, intentional, and affectional states of mind (Gallese, 2009; Mancia, 2006; Schore, 1994; Stern, 1985).

The developing attachment relationship with the therapist, then, provides a good enough safe haven and secure base from which the patient can explore and elaborate his or her self-states, as reflected in the mind of the therapist moment-by-moment, thereby unlocking the affective components of the patient's unresolved trauma (Bowlby, 1988; Holmes, 2010; Schore, 1994; Stern, 1985). In addition to the repair of inevitable ruptures to the therapeutic relationship, crucial aspects of the therapeutic process consist of the interactive regulation of heightened affective moments, the provision of new perspectives, the reorganization of maladaptive patterns of expectancies, the transformation of implicitly encoded representational models, and the promotion of reflective functioning or mentalization (Bateman &

Fonagy 2004; Beebe & Lachmann, 2002; Cozolino, 2002, 2006; Fonagy, 1999b, 2008; Mancia, 2006; Schore, 1994; Wachtel, 2008).

In terms of therapeutic action, Diamond and Kernberg's (2008) longitudinal investigation of the treatment process and outcome of borderline patients in transference-focused psychotherapy suggest that improvements in the capacity to mentalize appear to be a function of the characteristics of the therapeutic relationship, including the level of the therapist's reflective functioning about the particular patient's emotional states. This aspect of the therapeutic relationship is emphasized by Wallin (2007), who argues that the therapist's own internal world is transmitted to the patient, influencing the development of his or her internal working models. Indeed, he asserts that no factor influences our effectiveness as therapists more than our own attachment states of mind.

With regard to clinical practice, these various findings emphasize that an emotionally meaningful therapeutic relationship facilitates a collaborative coconstruction of the patient's dissociated traumatic experience and promotes the recognition of the mental states that motivate human behavior in various relational contexts (Davies & Frawley, 1994; Fonagy et al., 2004). More specifically, the process of interactive regulation of affect facilitates the recognition, labeling, and evaluation of emotional and intentional states in the self and in others (Bateman & Fonagy, 2004; Fonagy, 2008; Fonagy et al., 2004; Grienenberger et al., 2005; Slade 2008). This, in turn, engenders a coherent, secure, and agentic sense of self as archaic representational models are revised and updated and second order models develop (Bowlby, 1988; Fonagy, 1999b; Knox, 2003; Peterfreund, 1983). This, together with the patient's growing realization that he or she can contingently influence the therapist and, by extension, others in everyday life, engenders a secure enough sense of self and recognition of other people as separate, differentiated subjects who can be related to in noncoercive and nondestructive ways (Benjamin, 1995; Wachtel, 2008). As Herman (1992) points out, the antidote to the helplessness characteristic of trauma is the ability to exercise control and self-agency.

The enhancement of the patient's ability gradually to organize and integrate error-correcting information consists, in significant degree, of the moment-to-moment micro-repair of misattunement or misaligned interaction—an intersubjective process operating at the level of implicit relational knowing (Beebe & Lachmann, 2002; Bruschweiler-Stern et al., 2002, 2007; Lyons-Ruth et al., 1998; Stern et al., 1998a, 1998b; Tronick et al., 1978). The therapeutic process is informed by the tracking and matching of subtle and dramatic shifts in the patient's mood-state while narrating his or her story (Schore, 1994). This interactive process leads, in turn, to the recognition of the existence of the therapist as a separate person available to be used and related to intersubjectively within a shared subjective reality (Benjamin, 1995).

By these means, the therapist's facilitating behaviors combine with the patient's capacity for attachment. Though operating largely out of conscious awareness, this process of mutual reciprocal influence or contingent reciprocity engenders a sense of safety and security and thus the development of an attachment relationship that facilitates a collaborative exploration and elaboration of painful, unresolved clinical issues and dissociated traumatic self-states underlying the patient's difficulties in living. Key aspects of this intersubjective and reparative process are the dyadic regulation of dreaded states of mind charged with intense negative affect and the co-construction of a coherent narrative imbued with personal meaning.

Optimally, the therapist becomes a new developmental object, the relationship with whom provides a corrective emotional experience, thereby disconfirming the patient's transference expectations (Alexander & French, 1946; Eagle, 2003; Fonagy & Target, 1998; Hurry, 1998; Mitchell, 1988, 1993, 2000; Wachtel, 2008). This process enhances the patient's capacities for affect regulation and mentalization, and also his or her sense of self-agency (Knox 2003). This, in turn, strengthens the insecure/unresolved patient's ability to activate alternative self–other representational models, enhances the capacity to empathize with others, and so make more reasoned choices, and reduces the tendency to deploy mental defenses of perceptual distortion, defensive exclusion, and selective attention in stressful situations that generate a sense of endangerment to the self and a concomitant increase in the risk of destructive and self-destructive forms of behavior (Holmes, 1996; Renn, 2006). As a consequence of these changes, the patient is less constrained to unconsciously recruit "accomplices" with whom to elicit the expected negative responses that maintain cyclical sequences of interaction in their everyday lives (Wachtel, 2008).

From a neurobiological perspective, the process of affect regulation, so central to attachment theory and research, links nonverbal and verbal representational domains of the brain. This process facilitates the transfer of implicit-procedural information in the right hemisphere to explicit or declarative systems in the left. Thus, body-based, visceral-somatic experience is symbolically transformed into emotional and intentional states of mind that then become available for reflection and regulation (Damasio, 1999; Schore, 1994). Again, this aspect of the therapeutic process reflects the philosophical position of psychophysical interactionism—that the workings of the brain are expressed in terms of subjective personal experience and that personal experience influences the workings of the brain. Moreover, recognition of the interaction between mind and body may be seen as a further example of the integration of a scientific, empirical methodology with a hermeneutic, phenomenological approach in order better to understand and give meaning to the inner world of subjective experience.

CONCLUSION

From the foregoing, it may be seen that in many respects the good enough caregiver–infant relationship constitutes the prototype of a therapeutic model in work with adults and that the analytic process is redolent of the subtle intersubjective, communicative, and regulatory processes that take place between mother and child. From a relational perspective, the internal world is viewed as developing through these mutual, reciprocal influences and the mind as composed of relational configurations developed in the context of interaction with others. In consequence, the therapeutic process is perceived as being inherently interactive and thus as requiring the active participation of both therapist and patient (Mitchell, 1993).

Aspects of the various ideas, concepts, processes, and research findings discussed in this chapter reflect theoretical and philosophical assumptions derived from systems theory, interactionism, phenomenology, and social constructionism. Systems theory holds that the observer ineluctably becomes an interrelated and interconnected participant in the system as a whole, both influencing and being influenced by the mutual interactions of the system and its environment. Interactionism, phenomcnology, and social constructionism emphasize, in their respective ways, the sociability of subjective experience and behavior; the situated, context-bound nature of human existence; and the socially constructed nature of knowledge and the self. It will, I trust, be readily apparent from the foregoing that such theoretical and philosophical assumptions inform both contemporary developmental studies and new models of adult psychotherapy.

Chapter 7

A Contemporary Relational Model

Integrating Attachment, Trauma, and Neuroscience Research

INTRODUCTION

Contemporary relational psychoanalysis emerged in the 1980s in the United States in an attempt to integrate interpersonal psychoanalysis with British object relations. A relational perspective emphasizes the salience of early formative relationships on the development of personality and argues that the subject's primary motivation is to seek relationships with others. By contrast, classical Freudian thinking views motivation in terms of intrapsychic drives of sexuality and aggression. Stephen Mitchell was a prominent figure in the development of relational psychoanalysis and is widely acknowledged as the founder of the Relational School. He established the international journal, *Psychoanalytic Dialogues*, serving as its editor for the journal's first decade. Since Mitchell's untimely death in 2000, his work has been carried forward by a number of analysts and authors, including Lewis Aron, Jessica Benjamin, Philip Bromberg, Jody Davies, Emanuel Ghent, Adrienne Harris, Irwin Hoffman, Karen Maroda, Stuart Pizer, and Owen Renik.

Influenced by Fairbairn and Winnicott, Mitchell (1988) views psychopathology as characterized by constricted patterns of relatedness with missing needs being regarded as a function of the interactive relational field. The patient's problems are seen as stemming from his or her tie to familiar, but seriously constricted, relational patterns within which the self is experienced as false, fraudulent, and inauthentic. In essence, the patient must choose between remaining attached to fantasized images, which impart a subtle sense of safety and connection, and the possibility of attaining attachment to real others. For Mitchell, the central process of treatment is the relinquishment of adaptive, defensive ties to constricted relational patterns because this will allow the patient to experience an openness to new and richer interpersonal relations. He views the affective interaction between the analyst and the patient as characterized by warmth and spontaneity. In this context, he stresses that the analyst must at times be prepared to take risks in order to connect with the patient in a real and authentic fashion. However, he suggests that the analyst should express his or her own subjectivity not only through affective interaction but also through interpretative activity. By a combination of these means, the analyst becomes a particular sort of new object to the patient, different from his or her early parental objects. Indeed, Mitchell concludes that the analytic relationship provides the opportunity for the patient to integrate intrapsychic and interpersonal experiences in a different, more enriching and adaptive fashion than was possible in his or her family of origin.

CLINICAL ILLUSTRATION

The following clinical vignette is from Mitchell's book, *Relationality: From Attachment Theory to Intersubjectivity* (2000). The brief vignette illustrates the founding principles of relational psychoanalysis: an integrative approach that explores the way in which early traumatic experience impacts on personality development and may create difficulties in forming and sustaining mutually rewarding and enriching relationships in later life.

> "George" is a man in his mid-20s whose wife had left him because he was "unexciting and distant." The implications of George's early sexually abusive relationship with his uncle, which apparently included oral and anal penetration, bondage, and being dressed in female clothes, emerged during the course of his analysis with a female analyst. Aspects of these memories and associated dynamics were relived in the transference. This notwithstanding, George began to experiment with cross-dressing and to masturbate to sadomasochistic scenarios on the Internet. He felt in the powerful grip of the traumatic memories, which he found both degrading and stimulating. The impulse to reenact the abuse continued, despite his having developed an emotionally and sexually satisfying relationship with a woman. On saying goodbye to his girlfriend after an intimate weekend together, George was plagued with what he considered to be perverse, ego-alien impulses to engage in kinky masturbatory experiences and sadomasochistic activities instead of savoring the intimate pleasures of the weekend with his girlfriend.

As Mitchell points out, there are many possible ways of understanding this sequence. He details how Fairbairn might have thought about the case material from an object relations perspective. From this perspective, Mitchell suggests that George's internal object relation with his uncle

> provided some of the most intense, passionate moments of his childhood. The excitement, the sense of drama, mystery, the forbidden that characterized his uncle's experience also became George's experience. George's lustful impulses were not just vehicles to tie him *to* his uncle; they also *were* his uncle, and, through the boundary-permeable affective intensity

of those moments, they were George *himself,* at his most excited, most adventurous, most alive. (p. 114, emphasis in original)

In thinking about George's adhesive, seemingly addictive attachment to the internalized relation to the abusive uncle, Mitchell cites van der Kolk's (1994) neurobiological findings, as noted in Chapter 4, observing that there is a physiology of attachment to early objects. Thus, George's seemingly addictive propensity repeatedly to forge interpersonal relationships redolent of ties to early objects, even when these were traumatic and ego-dystonic, may reflect neurochemical as well as psychological derivatives. In the light of van der Kolk's findings, Mitchell concludes that "Early experiences are addictive, not just because of their psychological salience but also because of their neurochemical concomitants" (p. 115). Liotti's (1999) motivational conceptual framework may be used to supplement Mitchell's Fairbairnian and neurobiological understanding of the depicted sequence, in the context of George's early interpersonal experiences. Writing from an attachment and trauma perspective, Liotti argues that in order to avoid the painful, confusing experience of dissociation to which a contradictory, multiple self-representation developed in childhood is linked, the person may defensively inhibit the attachment motivational system by choosing, consciously or unconsciously, to activate a competing motivational system.

Liotti posits the existence of three basic motivational systems that compete with the attachment system: the agonistic, caregiving, and sexual systems. The activation of the agonistic motivational system leads the person to experience a high level of rage and aggression, while the defensive activation of the caregiving system may lead to a form of compulsive, controlling, caregiving behavior. Alternatively, the person may choose to interact with other people on the basis of his or her sexual motivational system. The activation of this system creates "the basis for promiscuity and for the construction of any significant relationships according to the roles of seducer and the seduced" (p. 771). Liotti argues that the choice of the sexual motivational system is facilitated if the person has been sexually abused by an attachment figure. He contends that the three patterns of interpersonal relationships, based on the abnormal activation of the agonistic, caregiving, and sexual motivational systems, are selected in the service of avoiding painful attachment experiences. He suggests that these nonoptimal systems may readily be observed in clinical practice in the treatment of people suffering from dissociative processes.

As Mitchell (2000) notes, "contemporary interpersonalists and theorists of intersubjectivity have contributed to our understanding of the ways in which the vicissitudes of early attachment experiences play themselves out in current relationships, including the transference–countertransference relationship with the analyst" (p. 101). Employing an integrated model, in the context of George's early traumatic experience of sexual abuse, the separation from his girlfriend after their pleasurable weekend together may be seen as a stressful event. For patients with a traumatic history such as George's, even a relatively minor stressor may trigger a disproportionate, fearful reaction which cannot readily be terminated (Perry et al., 1995; Schore, 2001). George's excessive reaction may itself be seen as indicating that implicitly encoded traumatic memories associated with his unresolved childhood trauma had been activated, leading to a concomitant release of stress-related neurochemicals, as discussed in Chapter 4. In consequence, the secure, coherent representational model that was available to George while he was in the reassuring and comforting presence of his girlfriend was overwhelmed, and the multiple, disorganized mental model in relation to the abusing uncle was activated in a context of separation and temporary loss. I have found that exploring with my patients in minute detail the relational context in which such shifts in representational models, object relations, or self-states occur to be a crucial aspect of the therapeutic process. Such shifts and nuances of attachment phenomena (Slade, 2004) are motivated by dissociated memories and manifested as emotional procedures in the nonverbal, implicit/enactive domain of relating and experiencing (Bruschweiler-Stern et al., 2002, 2007; Lyons-Ruth et al., 1998; Stern et al., 1998a, 1998b).

As George lacked a coherent strategy to deal with the stress of separation, the experience was dissociated or defensively excluded from consciousness. Thus, George "chose" to inhibit the attachment motivational system in order to avoid experiencing painful affect associated with his girlfriend leaving and instead activated the sexual motivational system (Liotti, 1999). Being unable to reflect upon and organize this mildly stressful attachment-related event, it would seem that George experienced it in the mode of psychic equivalence (Fonagy et al., 2004). This mode of functioning reflects the difficulty that George has in differentiating inner reality from external reality in stressful interpersonal contexts. Thus, when left alone after the pleasurable weekend with his girlfriend, George was unable to mentalize the experience and so succumbed to the impulse to seek comfort and solace in masturbatory fantasies and sadomasochistic activities with strangers on the Internet as a maladaptive form of affect regulation (Schore, 1994). Moreover, as Mitchell (2000) points out, George's adhesive attachment to the internalized uncle, as manifested in repetitive reenactments of the sexual abuse, would seem to be maintained by neurochemical as well as psychological derivatives.

Given this, I would argue that George's addictive attachment is as much to a psychobiological state as to an actual person. In this sense, his relationship to the other predominantly serves as a vehicle to re-experience a familiar, albeit traumatic, state of mind. An intimate, emotionally meaningful relationship with a real other does not carry this valence for George and thus is unlikely to be sustained, as appears to have been the case in his marriage. The description of George as being "unexciting and distant" in the relationship with his wife would indicate that he had developed an avoidant/dismissing state of mind in respect of attachment and therefore employs deactivating strategies and distancing procedures to regulate his discomfort with emotional intimacy. In terms of Ferenczi's (1933) concept of identification with the aggressor, as an abused, helpless child, it is likely that George became oblivious of himself, passively gratifying the desires of his abusive uncle. In negating himself in this way, George was transformed into the image that his uncle had of him—as an object to be abused. Ferenczi's theory may partly account for the passive aspects of George's personality and behavior. The more active part of George, in the form of physical and emotional withdrawal from others, may partly be understood by reference to Anna Freud's (1993) later formulation of identification with the aggressor. In this instance, George may be seen as identifying with a caregiver who routinely turned away from him, leaving him too alone. In contrast to Ferenczi, Anna Freud views identification with the aggressor as a defensive process whereby the individual transforms himself "from the person threatened into the person who makes the threat" (p. 113). For Anna Freud, the change from the passive role to the active role is a means of assimilating "dissociated" traumatic experience which is turned into "an active assault on the outside world" (p. 116). As Frankel (2002) notes, both forms of identification with the aggressor may be in operation simultaneously, being used to adapt to a threatening external reality as well as to cope with disturbing inner feelings that arise as a result of a threat to the self.

Mitchell (2000) does not provide any details of George's developmental history other than the sexual abuse by his uncle, as the main purpose of the vignette is to illustrate Fairbairn's thinking in respect of impulses and guilt. It may, nevertheless, be accepted that this traumatic experience alone set George on a developmental trajectory characterized by insecurity and difficulty in sustaining an emotionally enriching intimate relationship. However, as I point out in Chapter 3, trauma and abuse occur within a relational context. This being so, George's attachment history and the characteristic intersubjective/attachment system within which he experienced the trauma may be as salient to his personality development and adult psychopathology as the abuse itself. In the absence of more details about the quality of George's early and current relationships with his parents, ex-wife, and girlfriend, as well as his discrete discourse style in interaction with his analyst, my conjecture from an attachment perspective, as set out above, must remain just that, conjecture. While not wanting to minimize the traumatic impact on George of the sexual abuse by his uncle, I would agree with Mitchell (2000) that we need to take account of the broader developmental picture, too, in terms of cumulative attachment trauma, in understanding the quality of our adult patients' intersubjective relationships.

CLINICAL IMPLICATIONS OF A
DEVELOPMENTAL PERSPECTIVE

Mitchell's (2000) case vignette of George illustrates the way in which implicit/procedural memory creates a bridge between early childhood experiences and psychopathology in adulthood. The case also shows how a neurobiological and developmental perspective may be integrated with a relational model in clinical work with adults. Indeed, writers such as Emde (1980), Hurry (1998), and Schore (1994) emphasize that developmental factors play a role in all analyses and are an important aspect of the therapeutic process. Moreover, that developmental work is rooted in the individual personalities of the patient and therapist and in their spontaneous interactions. This being so, developmental work requires the therapist to bring his or her own emotions and subjectivity more explicitly into the therapeutic encounter, as advocated by Mitchell (1988). Indeed, Tähkä (1993) emphasizes the therapist's legitimate experience of parent-like feelings of pleasure and pain as part of an appropriate developmental relationship with the patient. However, it needs to be acknowledged that there is a heightened countertransferential risk in developmental work of the therapist using the patient variously as a source of narcissistic gratification, to relieve guilt, to overcome feelings of helplessness or to gratify his or her own infantile needs (Tähkä, 1993). Hurry (1998) stresses that these risks demand ongoing self-reflective monitoring of the countertransference.

The spontaneous features of developmental work also highlight the importance of the "fit" or "match" between patient and therapist. Kantrowitz (1995), in her long term follow-up study on this very issue, found that patient–analyst match was the major factor relevant to successful outcome, a point also emphasized by Maroda (2010). Developmental aspects of the therapeutic relationship may also be seen as reflecting what is often referred to as the "real relationship," as compared with the transference relationship. On discussing this clinical issue, Ogden (2004) observes that the quality of intimacy developed between therapist and patient will include feelings of camaraderie, playfulness, compassion, healthy flirtatiousness, charm, and enlivening humor. With regard to the latter, it is often overlooked that humor constitutes a shared, intersubjective experience that has significant therapeutic benefit (Lemma, 2000).

As discussed in Chapter 6, developmental studies suggest that the capacity for intersubjectivity develops in tandem with a subjective sense of self in the preverbal domain of intersubjective relatedness (Stern, 1985), and in the context of an ongoing attachment relationship. Findings indicate that the developmental achievement of mentalization or reflective functioning is seriously compromised by attachment trauma. For the child who has been abused or consistently negated, there may be a defensive avoidance of knowing the thoughts and feelings in the mind of the other. This is because the child, and later the adult, expects to discover there a hostile and malevolent intent, and a reflection of the self as bad, shameful, and perhaps even worse, as not existing at all (Fonagy, 2008; Fonagy et al., 2004; Fonagy & Target, 1996). In the light of these findings, understanding the adult patient's traumatic experience from a developmental perspective is, I would argue, crucial to informing the therapeutic relationship and process of change, and to enhancing his or her mentalizing capacity and sense of self-agency (Bateman & Fonagy, 2004; Diamond & Kernberg, 2008; Holmes, 2010; Knox, 1999, 2001, 2003).

In the service of enhancing self-reflexivity and intersubjectivity, Aron (1996) advocates asking patients to describe anything that they might have observed about the therapist and to speculate or fantasize about what he or she might be thinking or feeling in relation to the patient. He argues that this form of openness and curiosity facilitates the patient's perception of the analyst as a separate subject. However, in acknowledging the limitations of our own self-awareness, Aron points to the risk both of imposing our subjectivity onto the patient and also of presuming to know whether or not we are "validating" or "confirming" our patients' perceptions of us.

In my clinical experience, there are significant therapeutic gains to be made not only from inviting patients to think about what is in the therapist's mind, as advocated by Aron, but also from encouraging them to explore and appraise what is in the minds of the people they interact with in their everyday lives. I would suggest that this constitutes a more fully systemic way of working, as described by Wachtel (2008). So often patients seem confused about what motivates the behavior and actions of their nearest and dearest, and use the therapist in a rather passive way to try to give meaning to the intentions of others. By engaging the patient in an active process of mentalization, linked to an exploration and elaboration of the emotions associated with any given interpersonal context, he or she may be helped to shift out of an habitual nonreflective mode into an intersubjective state of being-and-relating, which understands and takes into account the other person's motivations and perspectives. As Aron (1996) points out, this intersubjective aspect of the therapeutic process may protect the patient from passively complying with, and submitting to, the therapist's power and authority in a way that reprises Winnicott's (1960) concept of the "false self."

Benjamin (1995), however, questions to what extent any aspect of subjectivity may be privileged as the truer, authentic part in relation to which other parts are false or inauthentic. Influenced, nevertheless, by Winnicott (1949, 1960, 1971), she amplifies Mahler et al.'s (1985) theory of separation-individuation, stressing the role that aggression plays in the development of intersubjectivity. Benjamin argues that mutual recognition and intersubjective relatedness are not inevitable aspects of infant development, but rather are developmental achievements linked to the quality of the mother–infant relationship, which may either be oppressive and controlling or facilitating and liberating. The struggle for recognition brings forth aggression and thus separation. This fosters a symbolic space between mother and child. The mother's task is to balance the constant tension between assertion of the self and recognition of the other. Benjamin sees this developmental process as the necessary basis for noncoercive intersubjectivity. Informed by developmental studies, she notes that relatedness is characterized not by continuous harmony, but by a continuous process of disruption and repair (Beebe & Lachmann, 1992). When the process of mutual recognition breaks down because of conflict in the mother–infant relationship, experience is organized predominantly intrapsychically rather than intersubjectively, the upshot of which is a struggle for power (Benjamin, 1995). Such unresolved developmental issues are likely to emerge in the transference/countertransference matrix.

Milgram (1974) explores the issue of power from a social psychology perspective. He draws a distinction between an autonomous, self-agentic mode of functioning in which the person views himself or herself as acting out of his or her own purposes, and an agentic state wherein the person comes to see himself or herself as an agent for executing the wishes of another person. His controversial study on obedience to authority found that for the majority of subjects the shift from self-agency to the agentic state is triggered by the act of defining a person of higher social status as part of an authority system of relevance to the subject. An authority system consists of a minimum of two persons sharing the expectation that one of them has the right to prescribe behavior for the other. Milgram found that there is a transition from the moment when the person stands outside an authority system to the moment when he or she is inside it. This may include crossing a physical threshold into the authority figure's domain. There is a sense that the authority figure "owns" the space and that the subjects must comply and conduct themselves fittingly. Importantly, entry into the authority figure's realm of authority is undertaken voluntarily. The psychological consequence of this is that it creates a sense of commitment and obligation which binds the subject to his or her role in the process. There is general agreement not only that the authority figure can influence behavior, but that he or she *ought* to be able to do so. Thus, power comes about in some degree through the consent of the person over whom the authority figure presides. As Milgram emphasizes, once the subject grants this consent, its withdrawal proceeds at great social cost. In the light of these findings, it may be accepted that the potential for the abuse of power in the therapeutic relationship is substantial.

KNOWLEDGE AS AN ASPECT OF POWER

The asymmetry of power in the therapeutic relationship has been a concern of relational psychoanalysis since its inception. As we saw in Chapter 5, the paradigm shift from a classical model to a relational model has emphasized concepts of mutual influence, discontinuity, multiplicity, and coconstruction of subjective experience in clinical work. This shift has changed the role of the therapist from an objective observer who is free from the patient's direct influence, and who provides interpretations from a detached, neutral perspective, to a two-person process in which mutual influence is ubiquitous and what the therapist knows is inevitably altered by his or her participation in the intersubjective field (Gabbard, 1996).

A relational/intersubjective perspective, then, recognizes that there are two subjectivities in operation in the analytic enterprise and emphasizes the way in which the therapist initiates behaviors and affects, as well as reacting to what the patient does in the therapy (Natterson, 1991). Moreover, there is no singular truth to be revealed, rather the patient's subjective experience and difficulties in living may be understood and coconstructed in a multiplicity of ways (Mitchell, 1993). However, as Aron (1996) and Benjamin (1992) respectively point out, an awareness of the way in which our own subjectivities and theoretical orientations influence and limit such multiple possibilities merely raise new problems of power in terms of a tension between mutuality and asymmetry as well as thorny questions about what the analyst knows and does not know.

In discussing "knowledge as power," Benjamin (1992) cautions against idealizing a stance of "not knowing" in reaction to the old classical ideal of analytic certitude. Indeed, Winnicott (1974) contends that the therapist can hold up the patient's progress "because of genuinely not knowing" (p. 177). As noted in Chapter 2, he argues that the patient's phenomenological experience of "primitive agonies" and concomitant "clinical fear" of a future breakdown is, in fact, the fear of a breakdown that has already happened, but which has "not yet been remembered" (p. 177). He suggests that patients need to be told about this crucial aspect of their lived experience for which they have no memory.

In this context, Frankel (2006) acknowledges the reluctance in contemporary psychoanalytic circles to diagnose the patient out of fear that this kind of "knowing" may objectify the patient, thereby negating or obliterating his or her subjective experience. This notwithstanding, he argues that diagnosis is an idea that cannot easily be given up because people do have distinctive personality characteristics and limitations that endure over time. Moreover, he contends that no technique can eliminate the inherent power differential in the therapeutic relationship, or the therapist's unconscious use of this relationship for good or for ill. In an attempt to overcome this dilemma and move away from a diagnostic medical model, Frankel (2002) proposes a relational model that includes the concept of diagnosis-of-the-moment: an interactive process that informs how the therapist responds moment-by-moment to the patient's changing self-states and multiple ways of organizing subjective experience. Similarly, Davies (2004) argues that in work with survivors of childhood sexual abuse, the therapist is required to make multiple shifting diagnoses in response both to the vicissitudes of the patient's self-states and to the different roles that the therapist is drawn into enacting in the transference/countertransference matrix. I outline these relational dynamics in more detail below. In this overall context, it needs to be kept in mind that powerlessness is a key feature of developmental trauma and that dissociation in reaction to trauma walls off access to self-experience and emotional connection with others (Bromberg, 1998).

Aron (1998) eschews diagnosis, emphasizing instead that what the therapist knows is partly informed by his or her observations of the patient's body in terms of gesture, facial expression, and posture. This clinical stance is consonant with the recent discovery of the mirror neuron system (Gallese, 2009), which I discuss in Chapter 8. Orbach (1995, 1999, 2004), too, highlights the use of the therapist's body countertransference to register and understand the patient's implicit affective states and communication of unconscious material. From a relational perspective, it is assumed that these processes are mutual and that the patient will change the therapist as part of a continuous process of bidirectional or mutual influence in the intersubjective field (Aron, 1996). This conceptualization of the therapeutic process is consonant with the findings of developmental studies (Beebe & Lachmann, 1992, 2002) and challenges the view of countertransference as a static, intermittent event occurring in reaction to the patient's transference. Mutual influence, however, does not imply *equal* influence in that the relationship can be mutual without being symmetrical (Aron, 1996). The therapist's struggle to understand and recover from 'mistakes' and enactments without becoming defensive or inauthentic is seen as a central aspect of the therapeutic relationship leading to mutual recognition and change (Aron, 1996; Benjamin, 1995; Frankel, 2002; Mitchell, 2000). Again, this aspect of the therapeutic process is consonant with attachment research which shows that secure attachment is facilitated when ruptures to the parent–child attachment bond are repaired in a contingent and predictable way. It follows that the process of disruption and repair in clinical work with adults promotes a sense of felt security and thus the capacity to experience new information and relationship transformations in the implicit/enactive domain (Beebe et al., 2000; Lyons-Ruth et al., 1998).

We see, then, that relational psychoanalysis is in an ongoing process of integrating the empirical findings from attachment research and developmental studies. Mitchell (1988), however, strikes a note of caution, observing a certain tendency in developmental work to view the patient as an infantile self encapsulated in an adult body—the so-called "child within" (Balint, 1968; Miller, 1991). He terms this tendency the "developmental tilt." Here, adult relational needs are collapsed into infantile neediness stemming from unsatisfied developmental needs. From this perspective, psychopathology is variously perceived in terms of frozen development, unresolved regressive residues from early life, or infantile fixations, and the patient is portrayed as a passive, inactive victim of a depriving environment. This way of thinking may be seen in Balint's (1968) formulation of the "basic fault," which reflects the lack of care and nurturance available to the individual in early development. For Balint (1968), the therapeutic process should avoid conflict and facilitate a "benign regression." By contrast, Mitchell (1988) suggests that casting the analytic enterprise as regressive seriously distorts the nature of the analytic experience by collapsing relational needs into the kinds of interaction characterized by the relationship between the small child and the mother. He argues that using the metaphor of the self as baby in such a concrete, reified fashion assumes that the clinical material reflects universal infantile needs, actual memory traces, and an underlying structural dimension to the patient's experience.

Somewhat paradoxically, and as noted in Chapter 6, in his later writings Mitchell (1993) contends that in many respects the good enough caregiver–infant relationship constitutes the prototype of a therapeutic model in work with adults, and that the analytic process is redolent of the subtle intersubjective, communicative, and regulatory processes that take place between mother and child. His change of emphasis may reflect more recent findings in the field of attachment and developmental studies. As we have seen, these show that the internal world develops through an active and mutual process of reciprocal influence, and that the mind is composed of self–other representational models developed in the context of interaction with others. I discuss the complex, intersubjective processes involved in the development of representational models in more detail in Chapter 8.

ETHICS AND IATROGENIA

From time to time, I hear colleagues rail against ethical codes of practice, arguing that the rigid, unreflective implementation of such codes may unwittingly militate against good clinical practice, particularly when working with patients with specific difficulties in living, for example those with dissociative identity disorder (DID) or learning disabilities. Central to the questions raised by those arguing for a relaxation of ethical codes is how professional bodies define abuse and the scope of boundary violations (Feltham, 2007). Are these set too rigidly, to the extent that they may constitute unethical practice? Is there a need for greater flexibility, particularly in respect of individual patients with specific needs and difficulties? The counterargument questions whether the relaxation of the therapeutic frame might unwittingly put vulnerable patients, such as those described in the literature on DID and learning disabilities, at greater risk of abuse. These ethical issues have important implications not only for these specific patient groups, but also in clinical work with patients in general; on a continuum, these issues and dilemmas apply to all therapists involved in a therapeutic relationship. Moreover, such dilemmas may be seen as being particularly pertinent to therapists who employ a relational/developmental model in their clinical work, with its emphasis on spontaneous interaction and the "real relationship."

It is generally acknowledged that ethical guidelines, limit-setting, and the maintenance of the therapeutic frame are all necessary prerequisites for undertaking therapy in a safe and boundaried environment, both for the patient and for the therapist. In this context, therapists work from the necessary injunction "do no harm." However, Feltham (2007) questions whether this might slide into a defensive mindset of "take no risks." He suggests that the therapist who plays everything by the book, employing a set of rigid prescriptions to maintain an ethical frame, á la Langs (1988), may foreclose the space to develop a humane, intersubjective relationship leaving the patient with a sense of having been abused by a too rigidly correct therapist. The "take no risks" approach may, therefore, end up breaching the "do no harm" injunction—in effect, the treatment becomes iatrogenic, that is, actively harmful. A significant factor influencing therapists to adopt an overly rigid style of working is anxiety about becoming known by their patients. Indeed, Aron (1996) suggests that one reason why therapists "choose" the analytic profession is because we have conflicts over intimacy. In Winnicottian terms, it may be said that we have a desire to be found and known by the other and a defensive need to remain hidden and incommunicado. Such anxiety may preclude the therapist from adopting a more spontaneous, intersubjective style of working that characterizes a relational/developmental perspective, as outlined above. As Stern (2004) observes, anxiety on the part of the therapist may preclude engagement in "now moments." Thus, the opportunity for change at a key moment may be lost.

Following Feltham (2007), I think it helpful to openly acknowledge that every close relationship is potentially risky—that no therapeutic relationship can be guaranteed to be problem free. De Zulueta (2007) makes this point forcefully, stating that "any caring relationship . . . is potentially vulnerable to being abusive" (p. xi). Given this, professional regulatory bodies have a clear ethical duty to make policies and vigorously police practice to protect patients from abuse and boundary violations. How to accomplish a balance between professional hysteria and harsh policing and punishment on the one hand, and a *laissez-faire* approach that would undermine the profession on the other hand, is an ethical dilemma for the profession. The tradition of built-in supervision and membership of a peer support group are added safeguards, but where do boundary violations start and finish on a continuum of seriousness, and who decides (Feltham, 2007)?

For example, does giving a distressed patient a comforting hug at the end of a painful session constitute a boundary violation? For some therapists the answer would undoubtedly be "yes," for others I suspect that it would be a resounding "no." The theoretical orientation of the therapist may also be a pertinent consideration here, in that a body therapist may occasionally employ touch as part of his or her clinical work. All too frequently, the context is given insufficient weight. For instance, the ethical dilemma involving touch may become particularly poignant when working with a patient who is disabled and has a learning disability, as movingly described by Linington (2007). Moreover, touch, in the form of a handshake at the start and end of a session, may be a cultural formality and expectation for some patients who would be affronted if this were to be withheld. However, touch in a context of a mutual erotic attraction would be inadvisable, as it could lead to the so-called slippery slope and increase the risk of a sexual boundary violation occurring, as discussed below. As Bowlby (1988) notes:

> There are occasions when it would be inhuman not to allow a distressed patient to make some form of physical contact. . . . Yet there is always danger that physical contact can elicit sexual feelings. . . . Depending on the situation each therapist must make his own decisions and draw his own lines. The more alive to such issues a therapist is the better will he be able to avoid the pitfalls. (p. 154)

Marrone (1998), in addressing issues similar to those raised by Feltham (2007), characterizes an iatrogenic relationship as one in which the patient becomes trapped in long-term work with a therapist who adopts a cold, detached, dismissive style and who employs persecutory and stereotypical techniques as a means of defending against countertransferential feelings of vulnerability and weakness in himself or herself. Marrone (1998) details a range of persecutory techniques. These include frequent and intrusive interpretations, derogation, invalidation of subjective experience, and false neutrality. He suggests that the therapist who interacts with the patient in these ways is, in effect, identifying with the aggressor (Ferenczi, 1933; A. Freud, 1993); that is, identifying with parental qualities and characteristics as a way of defending against anxiety and guilt. Marrone (1998) contends that in so doing the therapist is reenacting in the transference/countertransference matrix unresolved aspects from past relationships with his or her own parents.

Marrone (1998), following Bowlby (1988), argues that the therapist who adopts an attachment orientation is less likely to relate to the patient in an anti-therapeutic way because a therapeutic approach informed by attachment theory emphasizes the importance of human qualities of warmth, support, sensitivity, and responsiveness. Developmental studies have demonstrated that these are the very qualities in the parent that engender a sense of security and self-agency in the child. Clearly, then, such personal qualities in the therapist are essential if a therapeutic alliance is to be established.

However, Symington (1996) takes issue with the contemporary emphasis on empathy. He critiques Kohut (1971) in this respect, arguing that the therapist who places attunement and empathy at the heart of the therapeutic process by employing the "mirror transference" may avoid engaging with his or her own and the patient's inner fears and psychic pain. In such instances, the therapist may enter into a defensive mutual collusion with the patient to avoid the experience of mental pain. In this context, Symington (1996) speaks about the therapist's need of an "inner act of moral courage" to free himself or herself and the patient from the grip of feared and menacing internalized objects. Symington's interpretation of Kohut's (1971) position on empathy and the mirror transference may be seen as being too narrow and partial, in that he appears to be referring only to the first of two stages during the course of treatment. Whereas the first stage of the mirror transference does, indeed, involve adopting an empathetic stance to overcome the patient's fear of isolation and rejection lest his narcissistic aims become known, the heart of the second stage involves the mirroring, and thus the revelation, of the patient's defenses and grandiose fantasies. It may, therefore, be argued that there is an iron fist aspect to Kohut's velvet glove formulation of the mirror transference.

But to return to Marrone's (1998) argument that the therapist may at times adopt the defense of identification with the aggressor, Frankel (2002) holds the view that this particular defense is, indeed, a widespread phenomenon and one that is by no means restricted to people who have suffered dramatic trauma. He concludes that "some degree or element of trauma has played an important role in the lives of many people in whose histories trauma does not appear prominent" (p. 117). I would contend that Frankel's astute observation reflects the prevalence in the clinical population of subtle developmental trauma in the form of insecure/disorganized attachment. In agreement with Marrone, I would also suggest that Frankel's observation may be as pertinent to therapists as to patients. Indeed, Racker (1991) argues that the capacity for adequate countertransference experience depends primarily and decisively on the degree of the analyst's own integration, and the degree to which the analyst is able to divide his or her ego into an irrational part that experiences and a rational part that observes the irrational part. In cases where the analyst's attitude towards the patient is influenced by his or her own neurotic countertransference, the patient will be faced once again (and now within the analysis itself) with a reality that coincides in part with his or her neurotic inner reality.

Aron and Hirsch (1992) address similar ethical concerns in proposing that money is the last taboo in psychoanalysis. Indeed, they suggest that the analyst is faced with repeated personal and professional dilemmas concerning money matters. Specifically, the authors argue that the analyst may prolong an unproductive treatment for reasons of greed or economic dependency upon the patient. For the same reasons, the analyst may "fail to confront, challenge, or raise certain issues for fear that the patient may leave" (p. 244). Expanding on this issue, Aron and Hirsch suggest that the analyst, not wishing to have weaknesses exposed, may attempt to hide his or her personal relationship to money. The patient, on becoming aware of this vulnerability, may be drawn into helping the analyst perpetuate self-deception about this issue. The authors argue that this form of protection or collusion may result in the patient remaining "sick" or, if better, staying in treatment for longer than is necessary. Following Searles (1973), Aron and Hirsch (1992) contend that in such a situation the patient is, in effect, acting as a therapist to the analyst. They see similarities between this relational dynamic and the way in which children help their troubled parents by reversing roles and becoming a "parental child" (Bowlby, 1988). As with Bowlby (1988), the authors view this kind of interaction as a primary cause of psychopathology in children. Aron and Hirsch therefore conclude that, like a good enough parent, the analyst must be prepared to sacrifice loss of emotional and economic dependence upon the patient. They argue that unless these issues are openly addressed in the transference/countertransference relationship, the analyst may become enmeshed in the inner world of the patient and thus interminably repeat early and current unresolved internalized relational patterns. In so doing, the analyst fulfills the patient's implicitly encoded expectations, becoming a familiar toxic transference object rather than a new developmental object (Hurry, 1998).

ENACTMENTS AND BOUNDARY VIOLATIONS

The situation described by Aron and Hirsch (1992) that focuses on money matters may be conceptualized as a mutual enactment with both therapist and patient contributing to the therapeutic impasse. The same may be said of Marrone's (1998) description of a patient "trapped" in a long-term relationship with an emotionally detached therapist. Something is going on between therapist and patient that is not being understood, talked about, and repaired.

Jacobs (1986) was one of the first to use the term *enactment* in an analytic context. He conceptualized enactment as a subtle interlocking of the transference and countertransference that operates outside of conscious awareness, often through nonverbal means. More recently, he suggests that the root of enactments lies in mutually regulating and self-regulating behaviors (Jacobs, 2005). Enactments may also be understood in terms of Sandler's (1976) theory of role-responsiveness as noted in Chapter 2. Elaborating on Sandler's theory, Gabbard (1996) contends that counter-transference enactments represent a joint creation that involves contributions from both the therapist and the patient. Whereas the patient may actualize an internal scenario within the therapeutic relationship resulting in the therapist playing a role scripted by the patient's internal world, the dimensions of the role enacted by the therapist will be colored by his or her own subjectivity. This reflects the fact that therapists bring their own wishes, needs, and desires to the therapeutic situation.

On discussing countertransference enactments, Mitchell (1993) compares a relational/intersubjective model to that employed by Freud (1905b) in his brief analysis of Dora. As noted in Chapter 1, Mitchell argues that Freud's focus on intrapsychic neurotic conflict invalidated Dora's subjective experience of trauma and abuse, and perpetuated, in the countertransference, her victimization by the men in her life. Thus, Mitchell (1997) cautions us to guard against enacting or reenacting in the transference/ countertransference matrix aspects of the patient's original traumatic experience or abusive relationships by blaming, victimizing or, indeed, seducing him or her. Seductive behavior by the therapist may include a countertransferential wish to rescue or parent the patient, thereby encouraging a regressive dependency (Blum, 1994; Herman, 1992). Mitchell emphasizes that awareness of countertransference tendencies of these kinds requires continual self-reflective responsiveness to the material being presented.

Although we may well heed Mitchell's cautionary words about being drawn into enactments with our patients because doing so is likely to interfere with the development of a good working relationship, Davies and Frawley (1994) argue that traumatic transference/countertransference enactments are inevitable. Evolving out of their work with adult survivors of childhood sexual abuse, the authors delineate eight positions as expressed within four relational matrices. In a similar way to Sandler's (1976) theory of role-responsiveness, these positions, roles, or self-states may alternately be enacted by the therapist and patient in the transference/countertransference matrix. They include the uninvolved non-abusing parent and the neglected child; the sadistic abuser and the helpless, impotently enraged victim; the idealized, omnipotent rescuer and the entitled child who demands to be rescued; and the seducer and the seduced. Davies and Frawley suggest that mutually dissociated traumatic experience is particularly susceptible to being enacted in the intensity of the therapeutic relationship.

This view is endorsed by Herman (1992). Writing from a traumatology perspective, she describes the traumatic or vicarious countertransference, suggesting that the patient's dissociated trauma may overwhelm the therapist. One among several reactions to this situation is the therapist's need to defend against unbearable feelings of helplessness. Thus, therapists who ordinarily are scrupulous in observing the limits of the therapeutic frame may find themselves violating the bounds of the therapy relationship and assuming the role of a rescuer, thereby disempowering the patient. Under the intense pressures of the traumatic transference/countertransference, the therapist may take on an advocacy role for the patient, feel obliged to extend the limits of therapy sessions, allow frequent emergency contacts between sessions, and answer phone calls late at night or when on vacation. Herman points out that the therapist's defense against feelings of helplessness may lead to a stance of grandiose special-ness or omnipotence, with the attendant risk of extreme boundary violations up to and including sexual intimacy. Such violations are frequently rationalized on the basis of the patient's desperate need for rescue and the therapist's extraordinary gifts as a rescuer.

Paradoxically, as the relational literature shows, nonabusive enactments may lead to profound therapeutic change (Stern, 2010), enhancing a sense of felt security and the capacities for affect regulation and reflective functioning or mentalization (Fonagy, 2008). Indeed, there is a broad consensus that countertransference enactments are not only ubiquitous but also potentially useful (Aron, 1990; Chused, 1991; Renik, 1993). As we have seen, a relational perspective, informed by developmental studies, holds that the adequate repair of nonabusive ruptures constitutes therapeutic action with the consequent gain of a constructive outcome (Beebe & Lachmann, 1994, 2002; Benjamin, 1995; Fonagy, 1998; Roth & Fonagy, 1996). Similarly, Chused (1991) argues that the benefit for the therapy is not the enactment itself, but rather the eventual understanding that derives from the enactments. Crucially, then, the outcome depends on how the enactment is worked within the therapeutic relationship—can it be contained and collaboratively explored, validating the patient's subjective reality and, thereby, provide a shared, coconstructed emotional experience as the rupture to the working alliance is repaired, or will it replicate past abusive relationships and thus risk retraumatizing the patient? In this context, Gabbard (1996) strikes a note of caution, stating: "Integral to the notion that countertransference enactments are useful is the understanding that analysts must catch themselves in the midst of the enactment when it is manifesting itself in an *attenuated* or *partial form*" (pp. 84–85, emphasis in original).

ENACTMENTS AND SELF-DISCLOSURE

As noted in the introduction to this chapter, Mitchell (1988) argues that in order to work relationally the therapist must be prepared to take risks in the service of connecting with the patient in a real and authentic way. Thus, passionate feelings of love and hate may often arise between the analyst and patient. In this context, Mitchell (2000) observes that relationally oriented clinicians are often "portrayed as wild analysts, doing and saying anything that occurs to them in an unrestrained fashion" (p. 127). He believes that this criticism is "ill founded," arguing that relational analysts approach their clinical work with caution and responsibility (p. 127). However, Mitchell (1997) does make it quite clear that the question for the contemporary relational therapist is not *whether* to share countertransferential thoughts and feelings, but rather *when and to what extent*. In his view, selective disclosure of the countertransference may function to help the patient and therapist connect on an emotional level and, thereby, open up, vitalize and validate his or her subjective experience, providing him or her with a sense of being valued and understood. Handled insensitively, however, disclosure may close down and deaden the patient's experience. Clearly, then, the decision to disclose requires a responsible, sensitive and judicious approach by the therapist that takes full account of the need to protect the patient's personal integrity and boundaries. As Mitchell puts it, a delicate balance needs to be achieved whereby the therapist is neither excessively emotionally detached from the patient nor excessively intimate and intrusive.

Maroda (2010) defines self-disclosure as "any verbal expression of personal feelings or information on the therapist's part, whether deliberate or not" (p. 108). Self-evidently, self-disclosure can have a positive or a negative impact on the therapeutic relationship. Indeed, as noted above, Aron (1996) advocates allowing the patient access to the therapist's subjectivity in terms of disclosing his or her thoughts, feelings and fantasies. He argues that this leads to an acknowledgement by the patient of the therapist as a separate subject. This notwithstanding, in order to protect the patient, we need to ask ourselves what the therapeutic purpose is of self-disclosure, whether it would be useful, digressive, or disruptive, and what the motivation is for disclosing personal feelings or information. Moreover, as Wachtel (2008) observes, considerations about how much, when, and how to disclose require sophisticated, reflective, and patient-centered attention. In broad terms, the therapeutic benefits accruing from sensitive and responsible self-disclosure are that it may confirm the patient's sense of reality, break impasses and repair ruptures, promote new relational experiences, and facilitate shared states of mind and emotional honesty.

Although it is generally agreed that self-disclosure works best when there is a strong therapeutic alliance, both Maroda (2010) and Wachtel (2008) emphasize that we cannot always correctly appraise when disclosure will be helpful and growth-promoting and that we must, therefore, be prepared to work with the consequences of getting it wrong. These authors also stress that the interactions with the patient need to be individualized, recognizing that what is appropriate for one patient may well not be so for another. As Maroda puts it, "...therapeutic self-disclosure is a result of intuitive and artistic responses in a unique, creative moment with an individual client" (p. 113). As ever, the context needs to be taken into account in deciding whether or not to self-disclose. As Mitchell (2000) notes: "Love and hate in long-term relationships, like the analytic relationship, do not just happen. They are shaped and cultivated within contexts that are constructed slowly, over time" (p. 129).

With regard to erotic feelings in the therapeutic dyad, Mann (1997) argues that the therapist's open recognition of his or her erotic desire and subjectivity indicates a mature awareness of the differentiation between self and other which may help to preclude the sexual abuse of the patient. Indeed, Celenza (2010) argues that erotic excitement is a normal and expectable experience in the therapeutic encounter. Moreover, she suggests that "all treatments must revolve, at some level, around the question 'Why can't we be lovers?'" (p. 66). In order to avoid boundary violations, she contends that this question "... must be reckoned with and will involve the use of erotic arousal in the dyad" (p. 66). Indeed, Searles (1959) argues that successful work depends on the therapist recognizing and reciprocating the patient's transference love without acting on these feelings. Mann (1997), however, advises against the disclosure of erotic feelings to the patient, a view generally shared by Maroda (2010), who states: "I am really against disclosure of erotic countertransference, with rare exceptions" (p. 218). For his part, Mitchell (2000) states:

> Ultimately it falls to the analyst to make decisions about the constructive versus destructive implications of various affects in both participants in the analytic process, even though there is no way to make those judgments purely objectively. Part of the analyst's responsibility is to participate in and enjoy that love while it seems facilitative of the analytic process, but not to enjoy that love so much that it becomes a vehicle for the analyst's own pleasure in a way that occludes his focus on the patient's well-being. (p. 139)

Gabbard (1996), however, notes that the powerful and compelling nature of sexual and loving feelings may override the therapist's reflectiveness. Countertransference enactments of such feelings occur along a continuum from overt sexual relations between patient and therapist at one end to subtle forms of enactment involving partial transference gratifications of a verbal and nonverbal nature within the boundaries of the therapeutic frame at the other end. He states that: "In any countertransference enactment, analysts must strive to determine the relative balance of their own contributions versus the patient's contributions. A key part of that reflective process is determining which role, if any, one is playing in the patient's internal cast of characters" (p. 86).

Therapy is an inherently intense, intimate, and risky business. Trauma, like madness, is contagious; that is, it is transmitted interpersonally. Mutual or bidirectional influence, on both a conscious and unconscious level of mental functioning, is continuously in operation, for good or for ill. Therapist and patient get drawn into inevitable transference/countertransference enactments on a continuum of seriousness under the sway of nonconscious representational models, unresolved trauma, and mutual dissociation. Enactments can be a force for therapeutic change or a vehicle for abuse and retraumatization. This dichotomy is succinctly summed up by

Kernberg (1995) who, in discussing the erotic aspects of the transference/countertransference, notes: "There is probably no other area of psychoanalytic treatment in which the potentials for acting out and for growth experiences are so intimately condensed" (p. 114).

Clearly, safeguards are required! The therapeutic frame includes an adherence to ethical codes and guidelines designed to protect the patient from abuse and boundary violations. These are reinforced by regular supervision and membership of a peer support group. Maintaining the frame in a consistent and ethically boundaried way may allow the patient to feel sufficiently safe and free to develop, explore, and express erotic and aggressive feelings in relation to the therapist, thereby providing grist to the therapeutic mill. The frame, then, provides a containing structure and creates the conditions for attachment security and the symbolic elaboration of dissociated and unmentalized wishes, desires, fears, and affects deriving from unresolved trauma, loss, neglect, or abuse. Conversely, breaching the frame by, for example, adopting a position of omnipotent rescuer may unwittingly disempower the patient and foreclose on opportunities for therapeutic change.

All of this is relatively clear, but legitimate questions about the way in which ethical codes are implemented remain open to debate; namely, how rigid or flexible should ethical guidelines be, and to what extent, if at all, should they differ for different groups of patients? And: May the defensive adherence to ethical codes lead to practice that is not only unethical but also iatrogenic, particularly in respect of patients with particular individual needs and differences?

CLINICAL ILLUSTRATION

In the light of the foregoing, it may be accepted that employing a relational model and developmental sensibility may raise certain concerns about ethical dilemmas and clinical issues, such as disclosure of the countertransference, acknowledgement of the "real relationship," the asymmetry of power in the therapeutic relationship, working with enactments, and the risk of retraumatizing the patient. The clinical vignette of "Katarina" may help to illustrate some of these concerns and dilemmas.

Katarina is a 38-year-old married woman with an 8-year-old son whom I have been seeing twice a week for 4 years. At the time of writing, the therapy is ongoing. A recurrent theme in the therapy has been Katarina's ambivalence about becoming too closely attached to me because of fearing that she will lose me in some way—that I will die, get ill, change profession or retire. She also fears that she is "too much" for me and that I find the sessions with her "boring." Thus, becoming attached is experienced as dangerous because of an implicit expectation that it will lead to abandonment and loss. Such fears are repeatedly expressed in Katarina's narrative, which is characterized by the anticipation of catastrophic losses and betrayals. Paradoxically, but perhaps in an attempt to counter such fears of loss and abandonment, Katarina has attempted to extend the boundaries of the therapy, questioning, almost from the outset, why it is not possible for us to have a personal relationship. Thus, she has repeatedly expressed a wish to meet for coffee or lunch, saying that seeing me twice a week under the constraints of therapy "isn't enough."

From the details that emerged about Katarina's formative experiences growing up in Poland, her anxiety about becoming attached and concomitant expectation of loss have a basis in reality, in terms of insecure attachment to both parents, cumulative developmental trauma, and the intergenerational transmission of fearful parental states of mind linked to her parents' and grandparents' own attachment histories and traumatic experiences during the Second World War. Meaningful emotional communication in her family of origin was stilted and inhibited and has remained so in the intervening years. Katarina described her father as being emotionally distant and her mother as "living through me because she doesn't have a life of her own." Her previous therapist died unexpectedly shortly after Katarina left Poland to settle in the UK on marrying a British man she had met on holiday. Although there is no reported history of childhood sexual abuse, Katarina has engaged in sexual sadomasochism with strangers in the past.

A pronounced feature of Katarina's personality is an acute sense of dissatisfaction and disappointment with her lot in life—whatever she has is never good enough and quickly turns to dust. She also has a deep, almost paranoid, mistrust of others, believing that they are out to do her down in some way. Moreover, she can switch from a position of idealization to derogation in the blink of an eye. For example, England, the English, and everything about English culture is bad in comparison with Poland, except that when she returns to Poland to visit her family it is the same story, only in reverse, and she expresses great relief at being back in England, at least for a week or two. There is, however, a healthy part to Katarina that recognizes these other, more extreme aspects of herself. However, in attempting to understand and give meaning to her experience, both in relation to herself and to others, she tends to self-pathologize, affixing medical labels to herself, such as bipolar disorder, BPD, schizophrenia, or DID.

Despite these facets of her personality and her suspicious of therapy and therapists in general and her bitter complaints about the boundaries of the therapy, the one constant feature in our relationship has been her warm appreciation of me as her therapist. Whenever I have wondered with her whether she is putting me on a pedestal and perhaps defensively idealizing me and the therapy, she has become angry and impatient, saying, "Why can't you just accept that you're a good therapist and a genuinely nice man?" On one such occasion, and in the face of her vehemence on this point, I put up my hands in mock surrender, saying, with a playful sense of ironic self-deprecation that belied my actual words, "Okay, okay. I'm a brilliant therapist and a really, really nice man. You're incredibly lucky to have me as your therapist, aren't you?" Katarina responded by smiling wryly and allowing us to move on to talk about other matters. It may be seen, then, that from the start our relationship has been robust, characterized by a feisty struggle about boundaries, but also by emotional honesty, humor, playfulness, and irony.

Having set the scene, so to speak, I would like to now describe an encounter that occurred 2 years into the therapy. Katarina began by saying that coming to see me feels like "cheating" on her husband because she enjoys talking to me so much and can do so in ways that she can't with him. She went on to say again how disappointed and frustrated she feels in not being able to have a relationship with me outside of the sessions; that she would like to meet with me for lunch, and that she has been wondering what it would be like to have sex with me. During the weekend, Katarina had visited the historic town of York with her husband and son. Although this had been a pleasurable excursion, she had felt disconnected from her husband and child and had started to think about how much more enjoyable it would have been if she had been there with me. After relating these thoughts and desires, she fell silent and looked forlornly out of the window in a rather trancelike, dissociated way.

This was the first time that Katarina had spoken openly about sex in relation to me, and I felt in something of a dilemma as to how to respond without leaving her feeling rejected and invalidated. Whereas in the past I had dealt with her bids to have a personal relationship by emphasizing that this would destroy the therapeutic relationship together with any benefit that she might be gaining from it, on this occasion, albeit without much pre-reflective thought, I chose to respond in a different way. I said that I, too, might feel disappointed and frustrated that we can't meet for a coffee or lunch; that I, too, might have wondered what it would be like to have sex with her; that had we met under different circumstances, I, too, might have wanted to develop an intimate friendship with her. With a smile and twinkle in my eye, I ended by saying, "Although I'm old enough to be your father, the thought of spending a romantic weekend with you in York sounds very appealing. It's such a damned shame I'm your therapist, isn't it!"

Katarina turned to look at me, smiling and laughing with me as we shared the transgressive idea of a naughty weekend away together. After this, there was a perceptible shift in her state of mind—from a familiar state of disappointment, deprivation, and frustration to a more reflective state in which she could engage with me in exploring the various difficulties in living with which she is currently struggling.

Taken out of context, my response to Katarina may be viewed as egregious or, at the very least, controversial. Even when the context is taken into account, I would agree with Mitchell's (2000) contention that "All analytic writing necessarily lends itself to misreading in one direction or another...." (p. 126). I also concur with his view that it is "impossible to capture the complex texture of an analytic process in writing" (p. 89). Indeed, I find writing about the subtle, nuanced interactions between me and my patients problematic because so much of the interaction occurs in the nonverbal, implicit/enactive domain. Given this, it may be asked: How does one capture the ineffable and put it into words?

An additional problem here lies in presenting case material as if the therapist knew exactly what he or she was doing at the time. It may be argued that this position is antithetical to the chaos and unpredictability that characterizes nonlinear dynamic systems theory (Marks-Tarlow, 2011; Thelen & Smith, 1994), as well as to the concepts of "mutual influence" (Aron, 1996), and the "analytic third" (Aron, 2008; Benjamin, 2004; Ogden, 2004). The latter is seen as an emergent property that is unique to each and every therapeutic dyad. Thus, the way in which we, as therapists, "choose" to play, improvise, and self-disclose will emerge unbidden and differ markedly from patient to patient.

All of this is further complicated by the dynamic nature of memory, as discussed in Chapter 2. From a neuroscience perspective, what we remember about an encounter and subsequently put into writing may not accurately reflect the nuances of what actually happened, but consist of a recontextualization of the last time we recalled the interaction to mind. Against this, as discussed above, I think it has to be accepted that the therapist *is* consciously aware of the choices he or she makes at the time and therefore needs to take full responsibility for any decision to self-disclose (Maroda, 2010; Wachtel, 2008).

What, then, prompted my somewhat risky, improvisatory (Ringstrom, 2008) interaction with Katarina, with its playful and flirtatious "might-have-beens" and "if onlys?" And what led me to conclude that it would be safe to do so and that Katarina would hear my self-disclosure in the way that it was intended? Perhaps more to the point, why did I think that my particular response to her bid for an intimate relationship would be useful and therapeutically beneficial to her at this particular moment, when I have responded in a more formal, pragmatic way to such bids on past occasions?

First and foremost, I recall feeling immensely touched that Katarina had shared such intimate thoughts and feelings with me, leaving herself exquisitely vulnerable to a humiliating rebuff. I knew that what I said in response had to touch her in return in a way that created a meaningful emotional connection between us—that my response had to be real and heartfelt, rather than defensive or judgmental. What I actually ended up saying was an attempt to find a balance between affirming Katarina as a woman with desires on the one hand and maintaining the boundaries of the therapeutic frame on the other hand. Given the context that I set out above and the establishment of a strong therapeutic alliance, in some intangible way I knew that she knew that I knew that we were relating in the "as if" or pretend mode, and that this, in itself, made it safe to play with such highly charged material. This is not to deny that the stakes were high and that there could have been dire consequences had I got it wrong.

As to my immediate motivation in responding as I did, my main concern was both to avoid hurting or humiliating Katarina, and also to promote a new relational experience. Had I stayed silent or proffered a cogent but emotionally distancing interpretation, this would have replicated the constricted pattern of communication in her family of origin and, I suspect, left Katarina feeling crushed and shamed. In this sense, responding in such a way would, itself, have constituted an enactment. Moreover, in terms of learning from, and being changed by, the patient (Aron, 1996; Casement, 1990), Katarina had chided me in the past on my having made a particularly clumsy transference interpretation, telling me in no uncertain terms: "Paul, not everything's a bloody transference, you know!" In doing so, Katarina was reminding me that we have a real relationship, too.

From the perspective of the Boston Change Process Study Group (2008), whose ideas I discuss in the following chapter, much of the interaction between me and Katarina may be said to have taken place in the nonverbal, implicit/enactive domain. Intersubjective experience in this domain is changed by the emergence of "now moments" and "moments of meeting." I would suggest that what unfolded between me and Katarina in the session in question resulted in a now moment, culminating in a moment of meeting following my boundary setting comment: "It's such a damned shame I'm your therapist, isn't it!" Thus, while Katarina's initial experience of me in the present was shaped by implicit memories and representational models from her silent past, the moment of meeting brought our respective implicit relational knowing into a changed state of "intersubjective consciousness." This was facilitated by the verbal expression of my thoughts and fantasies which, in combination with ongoing moment-to-moment mutual regulation in the implicit domain (Beebe et al., 2005), cleared the way for her to use me as her therapist, deepened our therapeutic relationship, and, paradoxically, generated a mutual sense of trust and safety for our work together to continue.

In terms of Liotti's (1999) thinking, as discussed above with respect to Mitchell's (2000) case of George, it may be said that Katarina initially "chose" to activate the sexual motivational system in her interaction with me in this particular encounter. This served to inhibit the attachment system where her real pain lies, in terms of loss, rejection, and abandonment. More generally, I think that Katarina's cumulative attachment trauma compromised the interrelated developmental accomplishments of affect regulation and mentalization. These interlinked capacities provide the developmental basis for emotional connectedness or intersubjective relatedness. To my mind, my playful, improvisatory response to Katarina's plea for us to become intimately, even sexually, involved helped to shift the encounter from a nonreflective, essentially disconnected, style of interacting characterized by the mode of psychic equivalence, to a reflective, intersubjective form of relating characterized by creative play in the pretend mode (Fonagy et al., 2004; Fonagy & Target, 1996). Moreover, although my playful self-disclosure was risky, I think it was not only what I said but also the way that I said it that proved therapeutic. By this, I mean that my tone of voice, rhythmic cadences, and facial expression in response to my observations of Katarina's expressive display all created a cross-modal match with her psychobiological state. This, in itself, facilitated the repair to the disruption or perturbation that had occurred in our intersubjective relationship as a result of Katarina wanting something from me (a personal relationship) that I could not give to her. It may, however, be argued that, on an unconscious level, what Katarina actually wanted from me was what, happily, I provided—a new relational experience within a boundaried relationship. I would suggest that this encounter consisted of a subtle interaction between the nonverbal, implicit domain and the verbal, explicit domain, as discussed in more detail in Chapters 8 and 11.

In the intervening 2 years of therapy, there has been a marked lessening in both Katarina's fear that I will die or abandon her in some way, and in her bids for a personal relationship. As noted above, I would see these two clinical issues as being inextricably linked. As Katarina has come to trust in my emotional availability, her anxious, clingy attachment behavior has receded into the background. This would indicate that our therapeutic relationship is helping to facilitate an adaptive organization of Katarina's state of mind with respect to attachment trauma. From a neuroscience perspective, the inherent demands and challenges of the therapeutic relationship are creating new neural connections which, in attachment terms, are conceptualized as second order self–other representational models (Diamond & Kernberg, 2008; Fonagy et al., 1996; Levy et al., 2006). The development of such mental models is discussed in the chapter that follows.

Chapter 8

Intersubjectivity, Attachment, and Implicit Memory

The Development of Representational Models

INTRODUCTION

In Chapter 5, I explored the way in which the development of object relations theory challenged the view that instinctual drives are the major determinant of the nature of the representational world. As a result of this paradigmatic shift, it is increasingly accepted that external reality plays a key role in the formation of psychic structures and that what is represented internally are self–other relationships.

As we have seen, empirical research supports the view that cognitive-affective schemas or mental models deriving from actual relationships are internalized and generalized as representations of past experience (Bowlby, 1973, 1988; Bucci, 1997; Schacter, 1996; Stern, 1985). It also shows that adaptive responses to repetitive care giving patterns in early life reinforce particular neural networks that form the neurological substrate of representational models, together with sets of nonconscious expectancies about the behavior of others that are likely to be activated in later life in similar relational contexts (Grigsby & Hartlaub, 1994). Informed by these findings, contemporary psychoanalysis holds that representational models of self–other relationships are stored in implicit/procedural memory and organize interpersonal behavior largely outside of conscious awareness (Bruschweiler-Stern et al., 2002, 2007; Fonagy, 1998, 1999b; Fonagy & Target, 1998; Stern et al., 1998b). These findings have obvious clinical implications for understanding transference/countertransference enactments (Divino & Moore, 2010; Ginot, 2007; Mancia, 2006; Sandler & Sandler, 1997; Schore, 2011).

Despite the advances made by the empirical sciences in our understanding of the mind or representational world, from a philosophical perspective the term *representation* remains problematic. This is because it implies that an external object to which the representation refers can be contained and represented in our mind or brain as if it were a copy or facsimile. The problem also consists in determining which objects are used by minds to represent, and in defining the relation between representations and what they represent (Cummins, 1989). However, Damasio (1999), writing from a neurophysiological perspective, argues persuasively that the general problem of representing the object is not especially enigmatic. He contends that extensive studies of perception, learning, memory, and language have provided a workable idea of how the brain processes an object in sensory and motor terms, as well as an idea of how knowledge about an object can be committed to memory, categorized in conceptual and linguistic terms, and retrieved in recall or recognition terms.

Damasio (1999) uses the term *representation* as a synonym for mental image or as a synonym for neural pattern. Thus, rather than the object being represented as a copy or facsimile, the image we see is based on changes which occur in our organism when the physical structure of the object interacts with our body. The resultant neural patterns are constructed according to the brain's own conventions and are based on the momentary selection of neurons and circuits engaged by the interaction. The part of the neural pattern that remains in memory is built according to these same principles.

With regard to the representation of mental states or emotions, Damasio (1999) argues that representations which induce emotions and lead to subsequent feelings need not be consciously attended to, regardless of whether they signify something external to the organism or something recalled internally. His research indicates that once a particular sensory representation is formed, whether or not it is actually part of our consciousness, if the psychological and physiological context is right, an emotion will ensue. The substrate for the representation of emotions is a collection of neural dispositions in a number of brain regions located largely in subcortical nuclei of the brain stem, hypothalamus, basal forebrain, and amygdala. These representations are implicit, dormant, and not available to consciousness. However, once these neural dispositions are activated, the pattern of activation represents within the brain a particular emotion which becomes an image in the mind.

THE INTERSUBJECTIVE MOTIVATIONAL SYSTEM AND THE MIRROR NEURON SYSTEM

More generally, findings from developmental studies, cognitive neuroscience, and attachment and intersubjectivity theory show that, excepting serious birth complications, we are all born with an innate capacity to engage in collaborative and mutually regulatory social interactions. This, in turn, indicates the existence of a sophisticated intersubjective motivational system that compels us to seek companionable shared experiences (Seligman, 2009; Trevarthan, 2001, 2009). Preliminary research suggests that the neurobiological substrate for the innate capacity to read and empathically share emotions, intentions, and sensations with others is the mirror neuron circuitry, the systems of which are present at birth (Rizzolatti, Fogassi & Gallese, 2006).

It is thought that the mirror neuron system is activated when we observe the other's actions, intentions, and emotions, taking the form of what Gallese (2009) terms "embodied simulation." In essence, the same neurons fire in the brain of the person observing the actions or emotional display of another as if he or she were performing the observed action or experiencing the same feelings (Cozolino, 2002). Mirror neurons, then, permit us to participate in the other's actions without having to imitate them (BCPSG, 2008) and help to elucidate the complex process by which nonverbal emotional communication occurs (Cozolino, 2002; Divino & Moore, 2010).

Preliminary findings suggest that the capacity for neural mirroring is the neuro-physiological substrate for empathy, as well as for our ability to meaningfully appraise the actions, intentions, and emotions of others. Given this, the mirror neuron system would seem to be linked to the capacity for mentalization (Fonagy, 2008; Fonagy et al., 2004), as well as to the capacity for experiencing shared, intersubjective states of mind (Balbernie, 2007). Children diagnosed with autism have been found to lack activity of the mirror neuron system, suggesting that dysfunction of neural mirroring may be responsible for the relational deficit observed in autism (Ramachandran, 2011). However, ascertaining whether the cause of such a deficit is genetic or a result of a traumatic environment is an extremely complex and sensitive issue that requires further extensive research (Mancia, 2006).

Gallese (2009) emphasizes that our natural tendency is to experience our interpersonal relations first and foremost at the implicit level of bodily interaction. The development and maturation of neural circuitry occurs primarily in response to the infant's own interactions with the environment, the most salient factor of which is the emotional relationship with his or her caregivers (Bowlby, 1988; Edelman, 1989; Schore, 1994). Elaborating on the etiology of maladaptive ways of being and relating, Gallese argues that mirroring processes display neural plasticity and dependence upon the personal history and situated nature of the mirroring subject. He suggests that mirroring mechanisms are likely to play an important role in the constitution of the implicit memories that constantly accompany our relations with internal and external objects. In line with attachment research in general and Grigsby and Hartlaub's (1994) findings in particular, Gallese contends that the internalization of specific patterns of interpersonal relations leads to the development of characteristic attitudes toward others, and toward how we internally live and experience these relations. Mancia (2006, 2007) emphasizes the importance for psychoanalysis of implicit memory, arguing that presymbolic and preverbal experience is encoded therein. He suggests that such early experiences are not lost, even though they cannot be remembered. Moreover, he argues that they form the pillars of an early nonrepressed unconscious that conditions the emotional life of the individual across the lifespan, and that these aspects of personality are likely to emerge in the transference relationship.

The discovery of the mirror neuron system, then, may not only help us to understand the neurological substrate of empathy, but also poses intriguing questions about psychological concepts and processes such as mentalization, countertransference, projective identification, and the interpersonal transmission of fearful or traumatic states of mind (Divino & Moore, 2010; Mancia, 2006). For example, if we experience something of what the patient is experiencing viscerally, somatically, and emotionally by the mere fact of observing the nuances of his or her expressive behavioral display, it may be questionable to posit that the patient has projected a disowned aspect of him or herself onto the therapist.

This is not to say that the patient necessarily knows or understands what he or she is feeling, because of dissociation or alexithymia developed in reaction to trauma of one kind or another. This is where mentalization and the countertransference, informed by the mirror neuron system, can be crucial therapeutically. As noted above, because our observations of the patient get mapped onto equivalent representations in our own brain by the activity of the mirror neuron system, we experience the patient as if we were feeling the same feelings that he or she is expressing. The embodied aspect of what we feel would also suggest that the enteric nervous system in the gut, with its billions of neurons, plays a part in helping us to understand the patient's subjective experience via the countertransference and our capacity to mentalize the other's emotional and intentional states of mind.

Awareness of the impact of the other on the self for good or for ill is, of course, nothing new. Searles (cited in Laing, 1961) speaks of our ability to drive one another crazy, as do Laing and Esterson (1964) in their study of sanity and madness in the family. As previously noted, Herman (1992) draws attention to the traumatic or vicarious countertransference that may be experienced in working with traumatized people. Understanding these interpersonal processes of transmission from the vantage point of neuroscience in general and the mirror neuron system in particular may not only enhance our understanding of the therapeutic process, but also help protect the therapist from the risk of burnout that is attendant in our work with severely traumatized people.

THE BOSTON CHANGE PROCESS STUDY GROUP

The Boston Change Process Study Group (BCPSG, 2008) is in the vanguard of developing and promulgating many of the new ideas discussed in this book. The BCPSG was formed in the mid-1990s and consists of a group of psychoanalysts, developmentalists, and analytic theorists that includes Nadia Bruschweiler-Stern, Karlen Lyons-Ruth, Alexander Morgan, Jeremy Nahum, Louis Sander, and Daniel Stern. The BCPSG argue that findings from recent developmental studies and cognitive psychology can, when harnessed to dynamic systems theory, help us to understand and model change processes in psychodynamic treatment. Dynamic systems theory (Thelen & Smith, 1994), as applied to psychodynamic therapy, holds that relational events are unpredictable, nonlinear, and emergent properties of the particular therapeutic relationship that change over time. Therapeutic action rests on the unfolding of an emergent intersubjective process characterized by the movement towards self-organization in a context of destabilization and perturbation.

Infant researchers and practicing psychoanalysts, then, work together in the group to study the process of change as it happens in normal development and in psychoanalytic therapy. The overarching goal of the group is to explore in depth how knowledge of developmental processes may creatively inform psychodynamic therapy and to understand the process of change that occurs in treatment. A key theoretical concept in understanding the change process is "implicit relational knowing" (IRK); that is, knowledge of how to be with others. The group present IRK as a variety of procedural representation which may never become symbolically coded. Typically, IRK operates outside of focal attention and is nonverbal. This notwithstanding, it may govern intimate interactions in the implicit/enactive domain in the form of procedural memory. Indeed, Stern (2004), influenced by Edelman (1989), argues that: "Implicit regulatory memories and representations play a constant role in shaping the transference and the therapeutic relationship, in general, as well as in making up much of our lived past and symptomatic present" (p. 119). In this sense, "present experience" is largely "determined by the silent past" (p. 203).

IRK, then, assumes the existence of "active, preformed past patterns that seek expression and thus determine behavior. In this view, each successive present moment in life is a different instantiation of the past acting on the present" (Stern, 2004, p. 205). Thus, although the past is "phenomenologically silent," it is not nonexistent and, under the right conditions, reveals itself, thereby becoming an "alive past" (p. 205). However, the "clinical fact" that preformed, inflexible past patterns are often resistant to change from new present experience "runs counter to the idea that the present can easily, naturally, and rapidly change the past." As Stern notes, stuckness of this nature "supports the idea of the 'repetition compulsion'" (p. 202; see also Freud, 1920). Other key intersubjective concepts developed by the group include "now moments" and "moments of meeting" which emerge as part of a "moving along" process. "Now moments" are said to occur when two consciousnesses succeed in encountering one another. Following such "moments of meeting," disengagement takes place. The new model postulates that successful disengagement is dependent on the subject being sufficiently confident of the availability of the other. Further, disengagement creates what the group terms an "open space." Such moments of meeting bring new IRK into a state of "intersubjective consciousness." Thus, therapist and patient are able to restructure their relational systems in the light of the experience of the other's mental organization.

Change in the implicit domain deriving from now moments and moments of meeting may be progressive or sudden and dramatic, and may come about without the necessity of interpreting the experience in the explicit, "verbal-reflective domain" (BCPSG, 2008). Stern (2004) emphasizes that anxiety on the part of the therapist may preclude engagement in now moments with the result that the opportunity for change at a key moment is lost. Somewhat paradoxically, Stern argues that although the unfolding "present moment" is an implicit process; to qualify as such, the experience "must enter awareness or some kind of consciousness" (p. 122). Moreover, Stern contends that the therapeutic process "leads not only to moments of meeting, but also to moments that are propitious for interpretive work or work of verbal clarification" (p. 188). With regard to enactments, Stern argues that "they fall into a gray zone between dynamically unconscious and implicitly nonconscious" (p. 144).

The BCPSG's (2008) therapeutic model is similar to that proposed by Beebe and Lachmann (1994), which is also informed by developmental studies and systems theory. The authors describe "three principles of salience": ongoing regulations, disruption and repair, and heightened affective moments. The principles are variations on the ways in which presymbolic expectancies of social interactions, based on characteristic patterns of repeated mother–infant interactions, are organized and represented in the first year of life. Beebe and Lachmann argue that both partners jointly construct dyadic modes of regulation, which include interactive and self-regulation. The expectation and presymbolic representation of the dyadic modes of regulation as organized by the "three principles of salience" constitute the organization of the child's inner world and the criteria by which such interactions are categorized and represented beyond infancy.

Although Beebe and Lachmann's (2002) therapeutic model is consonant with the ideas of the BCPSG (2008), they emphasize the interaction between the implicit, nonverbal domain and the explicit, verbal domain, arguing that:

> A theory of interaction for psychoanalysis must ultimately address the nonverbal or 'implicit' (procedural/emotional), as well as the verbal or 'explicit' dimensions of the interaction. The nonverbal dimension is usually outside awareness, but it provides a continuous background of moment-to-moment mutual influence. The verbal system is usually in the foreground and more intermittent (speaking and listening). Simultaneously with the exchanges on the verbal level, patient and analyst are continually altering each other's timing, spatial organization, affect, and arousal on a moment-to-moment basis. This is the fundamental nature of social behavior. (p. 33)

In a paper commenting on the ideas of the BCPSG (2008), Fonagy (1998) considers it likely that "the schematic representations postulated by attachment and object relations theorists are most usefully construed as procedural memories, the function of which is to adapt social behavior to specific interpersonal contexts" (p. 348). Given this, he suggests that patterns of attachment are stored as procedural memories which themselves are organized as representational models. Consonant with neuroscientific findings relating to the mirror neuron system (Gallese, 2009), Fonagy argues that knowledge of these procedures is accessible only through behavioral performance, that is, by the direct observation of the individual's manner or style of relating. Previously, it was assumed that such knowledge was accessed through the verbal report of ideas or memories.

Fonagy (1998) contends that the therapeutic model proposed by the BCPSG (2008) adds relevance to the Strange Situation procedure (Ainsworth et al., 1978) as a method of assessing the way in which an infant's attachment behavior is developed with a specific caregiver (Main et al., 1985). This is because the classification of secure or insecure patterns of attachment taps into procedural memory (Crittenden, 1990). Further, he points out that in the case of adult attachment research (Main, 1991), attachment security is evaluated by reference to "the procedures used by the individual to create an attachment-related narrative" (p. 348). As we saw in Chapter 6, in such research the quality of the person's discourse style and the manner in which it is related is of more clinical significance than its historical content. Fonagy refers to van Ijzendoorn's (1995) meta-analysis of the predictive validity of the Adult Attachment Interview (George et al., 1985; Main & Goldwyn, 1985), concluding that the success of this heuristic instrument "speaks volumes for the promise of a procedure-oriented psychodynamic approach" (p. 348).

The suggestion here is that working with procedural memory requires an astute awareness of the multiple meanings encoded into a single verbal message by the use of stress, speech pauses and intonation, and so on. In this context, Beebe, Jaffe, Feldstein, Mays, and Alson (1985) cite evidence showing that the adult verbal communicative process, in terms of turn-taking and intrapersonal/interpersonal pauses, operates in a similar way to the nonverbal, mutual regulation process that occurs in the mother–infant dyad, as observed in developmental studies. In line with such research, the BCPSG's (2008) therapeutic model emphasizes interpersonal factors in the generation of procedural aspects of personality functioning based on the concept of "now moments" (Fonagy, 1998). Fonagy (1998) suggests that the new integrative model proposed by the BCPSG (2008) offers a clear psychological paradigm of intersubjectivity, complete with developmental roots and technical implications. With regard to the latter, these focus on the micro-processes that take place in the here-and-now of the analytic situation. Indeed, Fonagy views the interactional aspect of the therapeutic relationship as providing the key to understanding psychic change. He concludes that the effective ingredient of therapy must be contained within the relationship component because this is the only feature that the different techniques of talking cure have in common.

In a meta-analysis of successful outcomes, Roth and Fonagy (1996) found that research evidence supports "moments theory" in that it suggests that the extent to which ruptures to the therapeutic alliance are adequately addressed is predictive of the outcome of therapy. Fonagy (1998) argues that in using a similar model of relating or interacting, the therapist may become a new developmental object whose involvement with the patient permits a departure from past experience with other people. This may be seen to resonate with Alexander and French's (1946) principle of providing the patient with a "corrective emotional experience." More specifically, Fonagy et al. (2004) suggest that in many instances the goal of therapy is "the observation of patterns of interaction and the identification and correction of maladaptive models, principally through strengthening an overarching mental capacity to activate alternative models of interaction selectively...." (p. 470). The mental capacity to which the authors refer is the psychological concept of mentalization or reflective functioning. More generally, Fonagy (1998) suggests that "moments of meeting" involve the intersubjective recognition of a shared subjective reality during which therapist and patient contribute something to the interaction that is both unique and authentic.

A DEVELOPMENTAL PERSPECTIVE

As we have seen, our innate tendency from birth onward is to seek sociable engagement with others, and socio-emotional relations play a central role in organizing our personality and psychic reality. Given this, the question arises as to what occurs to interfere with such hard-wired tendencies and what processes maintain nonoptimal ways of experiencing and relating. These would seem to be particularly pertinent questions for psychoanalysis. I would argue that an understanding of the dynamic nature of memories, and of the way in which the two major memory systems operate and interact, is salient to these questions and to a concomitant understanding of the invisible process of therapeutic action (Renn, 2010). Indeed, findings from the disciplines noted above have led to a burgeoning interest in contemporary psychoanalysis into the nonverbal, implicit/enactive dimensions of the therapeutic process with individuals and couples.[*]

---

[*] See BCPSG (2008); Beebe et al. (2005); Beebe & Lachmann (2002); Bruschweiler-Stern et al. (2002, 2007); Fonagy (1999b); Lyons-Ruth et al. (1998); Reis (2009a, 2009b); Ringstrom (2008); Seligman (2009); Shimmerlik (2008); Stern et al. (1998a, 1998b); Teicholz (2009); Wilkinson (2010).

From a developmental perspective, the processes involved in the internalization, representation, and intergenerational transmission of discrete patterns of interactive regulation have been illuminated by infant research. This has demonstrated that subtle, fine-grain interactive micro-behaviors are related to intersubjectivity, attachment, and the transmission of emotion from one generation to the next. As we have seen, such micro-behaviors operate at the level of implicit relational knowing (BCPSG, 2008; Stern et al., 1998a) and include the coordination of gaze direction, vocal inflections, body posture, and facial expressions. The infant perceives and remembers the caregiver's repetitive subtle behaviors in the form of presymbolic interactional expectancies. Thus, the cumulative impact of repeated interactions that are consistently matched or mismatched creates a structuring effect on the infant, for good or for ill, who then generalizes these presymbolic representations of interactional expectancies to other interpersonal contexts (Beebe et al., 1992; Beebe & Lachmann, 1992; Knox, 1999, 2001; Peck, 2003; Stern, 1985; Teicholz, 2009). The caregiver's timing, tracking, and coordination of interactive regulations occurs in the implicit/enactive domain. Secure attachment is facilitated when the coordination is neither too low (avoidant) nor too high (enmeshed). Mid-range coordination that is contingent and predictable, yet flexible and variable, is optimal as it promotes a sense of felt security and thus the capacity to experience new information and relationship transformations (Beebe et al., 2000).

Patterns of interactive regulation, then, emerge moment-by-moment and are mediated by the caregiver's attachment state of mind and level of reflective functioning (Beebe et al., 2005; Fonagy, 2008; Fonagy & Target, 1996, 1998; Fonagy et al., 2004; Hurry, 1998; Slade, 2008). These repeated patterns of interpersonal experience are encoded in implicit/procedural memory and conceptualized as self-other representational models. A salient aspect of these mental models consists of generalized beliefs and expectations about relationships between the self and key attachment figures, not the least of which concerns one's worthiness to receive love and care (Bowlby, 1973, 1988). Research using the Strange Situation procedure (Ainsworth et al., 1978) and the Adult Attachment Interview (George et al., 1985) is designed to induce a degree of stress and thereby activate the attachment system and concomitant representational models. As noted above, in effect this research taps into implicit/procedural memory, the dynamics of which are manifested in infant attachment behavior and adult discourse style (Crittenden, 1990; Fonagy, 1998, 1999b; Goldwyn & Hugh-Jones, 2011; Slade, 2004).

From a relational/intersubjective/attachment perspective, psychopathology is seen as arising from an accumulation of nonoptimal interactive patterns that result in enduring character and personality traits and concomitant difficulties in interpersonal relationships (Bradley, 2003; Grigsby & Hartlaub, 1994; Mitchell, 1988; Spezzano, 1993; Stern, 1985, 1998). As previously noted, in neurobiological terms these findings reflect a trauma-induced deficit in the brain's right orbitofrontal systems, as a result of which affective information implicitly processed in the right hemisphere is inefficiently transmitted to the left for semantic processing (Schore, 1994, 2001). Thus, the psychological meaning of problematic emotional experience does not become organized into an explicit, coherent narrative and sense of self (Boulanger, 2007; Holmes, 1999a; Main, 1991; Main et al., 1985; Roberts, 1999; Terr, 1981; van der Kolk, 1994; van der Kolk & Fisler, 1995). The resultant representational models of the self as bad and endangered are indelibly held in mind (LeDoux et al., 1989) and may be enacted at the procedural level in subsequent interpersonal contexts that cue the retrieval of traumatic memories (Ginot, 2007; Mancia, 2006; Schacter, 1996; Schore, 2011). The triggering event may be subtle and seemingly relatively minor such as a raised voice or angry face, but the response may be excessive and disproportionate (Renn, 2003, 2006, 2010).

We see then that representational models developed in early life mediate and distort experience of actual relationships and guide and direct feelings, behavior, attention, memory, and cognition out of conscious awareness. Nonverbal, implicit processes may therefore be viewed as providing a measure of continuity from childhood to adulthood and as organizing transference expectations in everyday life, as well as in the therapeutic encounter (Beebe & Lachmann, 2002; Beebe et al., 2005; Clyman, 1991; Divino & Moore, 2010; Mancia, 2006; Sandler & Sandler, 1997; Schore, 2011). Moreover, as previously noted, early childhood experiences in the form of cumulative developmental trauma have life-long effects on our functioning at the implicit, nonverbal level of behavior, emotion, and arousal (Beebe et al., 2005; Damasio, 1999; Lyons-Ruth & Block, 1996; Lyons-Ruth et al., 2005; Mancia, 2006; Pally, 2005; Perry et al., 1995; Schore, 1994, 2001; van der Kolk & Fisler, 1995). Indeed, findings indicate that once patterns of interpersonal interaction are established, they tend to become actively self-perpetuating because potentially disruptive signals are countered by the deployment of perceptual and behavioral control mechanisms. Thus nonoptimal representational models are resistant to change because error-correcting information is being defensively and selectively excluded from consciousness (Main et al., 1985). This non-conscious process may be equated with the perceptual filtering mechanism described by Rose (2003) from a neuroscience perspective, as detailed in Chapter 2. It may also be seen to partly account for the stability of character and the perseverance of maladaptive ways of experiencing and relating that are maintained by the procedural component of implicit memory (Beebe & Lachmann, 2002; Beebe et al., 2005; Fonagy, 1999b; Grigsby & Hartlaub, 1994; Knox, 1999, 2003; Lyons-Ruth et al., 1998; Mancia, 2006; Stern et al., 1998a, 1998b; Wilkinson, 2010).

CLINICAL ILLUSTRATION

The following case vignette of the first two sessions that I had with a new patient, "Patricia," illustrates aspects of attachment research, the BCPSG's (2008) ideas, and the dialectic between the implicit, nonverbal mode and explicit, verbal mode, as noted by Beebe and Lachmann (2002).

> Patricia, an attractive single woman in her early 30s, had self-referred. During the first session, she spoke in considerable detail about her reasons for seeking therapy. She told a story of a fragmented family, losing contact with her father when she was 6 years old following her parents' separation and divorce. She had an unhappy school and home life, being bullied by a group of girls at school, and feeling excluded by the close alliance between her mother and older sister at home. She has an ongoing difficult relationship with her mother who, herself, was abandoned by her parents as a child and separated from her twin sister, whom she never saw again after being adopted.
>
> Patricia had been diagnosed with depression in her early 20s and was currently being treated with anti-depressants. She spoke of feeling emotionally dead and disconnected from herself and from others. Although in employment, everyday tasks were experienced as a huge burden weighing her down. She feared that her moods and behavior were intractable and that change would not be possible because of an imbalance in her brain chemistry. She had tried therapy once before, speaking in a dejected way of a failed short-lived therapy with a female therapist some 2 years previously. She described feeling angry, confused, and persecuted by the inconsiderate behavior of family, friends, and work colleagues who, she believed, treated her in a dismissive and unfair way. She was plagued by guilt whenever she tried to assert herself, and so, instead, would ingratiate herself with others by putting their needs before her own, despite feeling a smoldering sense of injustice. All of this made matters worse, as it left her feeling that she was over-controlling of herself and manipulative of others.
>
> A major reason for Patricia wanting therapy was a problem in sustaining intimate, sexual relationships with men. She said that she felt like a child in relation to men and that she allowed herself to be sexually used and emotionally abused by the men in her life. Despite this, she felt unable to leave the abusive relationships. More generally, Patricia spoke of feeling socially shy, inept and impulsive, physically ugly, morally prim, and sexually undesirable.

Although I trust that I have set out Patricia's many and various difficulties in living in a relatively coherent way, her discourse style in telling me her story was characterized by unfinished sentences, story lines that suddenly disappeared, only to merge with unrelated situations and expressions of hurt and injustice, and a pronounced difficulty in reflecting upon her experience in a collaborative way with me. There was an angry and excessive preoccupation with her past and present attachment relationships, with the boundaries between the two often seeming confused and diffuse. I had considerable difficulty in getting a word in edgewise to bring her back to focus on a particular aspect of her life that she had started to tell me about before she again wandered off at a tangent, starting a new thread and leaving the previous story unfinished and dangling in the air.

Patricia seemed to be reliving in the here-and-now the emotional experiences that she was relating from the past, and to have little consciousness of me as a person to be connected with. Indeed, apart from gently guiding her back to the point of her story from time to time, I felt largely superfluous. However, I noted that whenever I shifted position in my seat, she would abruptly stop the flow of her monologue. This, I think, indicated that Patricia's attachment system was in a state of hyperactivation and that she was anxiously hypervigilant, monitoring my every move. Indeed, an informal benchmark for the establishment of a sense of safety and security with some patients is when they continue to speak during any movements that I might make. Moreover, a certain body-symmetry often develops, in that the patient's and my own shifts in position tend to mirror or mimic each other's. This may indicate the operation of the mirror neuron system and reflect the establishment of a bodily form of intersubjectivity.

I think it fair to assume that at a first meeting the patient is likely to feel somewhat vulnerable and to experience a degree of stress in the presence of a stranger, no matter how well-disguised this state might appear. This very stress tends to activate an archaic representational model and a discrete discourse style that communicates implicitly stored information to the therapist about the patient's current attachment expectations, early intersubjective experiences, and developmental trauma. Although much of this could be discerned from the content of Patricia's story, the form of discourse in which she told it indicated a lack of "earned security" and an ongoing preoccupied state of mind in respect of attachment, together with a concomitant difficulty in making sense of her own and other people's behavior and mental states.

Preoccupied attachment is the adult corollary of infant ambivalent-resistant attachment organization. It indicates an under-controlled emotion regulation system, as manifested by the hyperactivation of the attachment system, by an exaggerated style of emotion regulation, and by attempts to dramatically heighten emotional experience. The person's representational model tends to be characterized by dysregulated anger and an ever-present fear of abandonment. Research indicates that this attachment state of mind develops in a relational matrix in which the preoccupied caregiver is inconsistently available and uncontingently responsive, or has an attachment need to keep the infant emotionally dependent on him or herself. Thus, the caregiver focuses on negative affect to the exclusion of helping the child to regulate his or her emotions. The failure to respond to attachment needs in ways that are consistent, contingent, and congruent with the infant's psychobiological state serves to keep the child intensely focused on the attachment relationship. This, in turn, reduces the chances of the child becoming emotionally independent of the caregiver. In such infant–caregiver dyads the child is likely to develop an ambivalent-resistant pattern of attachment organization that matches the caregiver's preoccupied state of mind, together with a style of regulating emotion that is preoccupied and under-regulated (Main et al., 1985; Peck, 2003). The initial indications were that Patricia's early attachment and intersubjective experiences had shaped and structured her inner world in these ways, as reflected in the attachment phenomena that I had observed and experienced at our first meeting.

Patricia began the second session in a vein similar to the first by listing, in a rather hopeless and desultory way, the various problems she has in her relationships. Midway through the session, she told me that she had gone out for a drink with work colleagues the previous evening. She described feeling sad and socially inept with her colleagues, hiding these feelings with a "smiley" exterior, and anxiously filling any gaps in the conversation with "empty words." In a rather heavy, defeated, and despairing way, she said, "I expect I'll do the same here, so the therapy won't work." Uncharacteristically, she left an interpersonal pause and for the first time I felt invited to engage with her in a more direct way. I said in a quiet, soft voice: "But I might choose not to respond to your 'empty words' and leave a silence instead."

Patricia looked at me sharply with an anxious, startled expression. I gazed back with bright eyes, smiled warmly, tilted my head to the left and, with a slightly quizzical, yet challenging, expression, raised my eyebrows and waited. Patricia stared back, looking a bit panicky. I held her gaze, and she started to laugh, shyly at first, covering her eyes with her left hand in embarrassment and peeping at me through her fingers. But she then seemed to surrender herself to the experience. Her laughter was prolonged and so delightful and infectious that I found myself involuntarily joining in. In between bouts of gurgling laughter she asked, "What have you done to me? I'm always the one that makes people laugh. No one ever makes me laugh. How did you do this? It's your training, isn't it?"

Patricia went on to describe a "tingling feeling" in her throat, saying, "I know this therapy is going to work, I can feel it," adding, "I haven't felt so alive in years." However, she also said that her joy and pleasure were tinged with fear and trepidation and that part of her wanted to flee from the room. In a playful tone of mock rebuke, and with bright smiling eyes, she said, "You're dangerous, you are!"

For someone like Patricia, who has been depressed for years and apparently habitually false and inauthentic in her relationships, to suddenly feel alive and emotionally connected must, indeed, have felt dangerous and alarming, the more so, perhaps, because of my gender. In terms of the BCPSG's (2008) model, Patricia and I shared a "now moment" that emerged in a rather sudden, dramatic, and unpredictable way, catching us both by surprise and leading to a "moment of meeting" in the implicit/enactive domain. Initially, the mutual experience was predominantly body-based and nonverbal and brought our implicit relational knowing into a changed state of "intersubjective consciousness."

From an attachment perspective, I would say that my implicit coordinated interactions with Patricia during the "now moment" experience were in the mid-range, that is, they were neither avoidant nor enmeshed, but contingent and congruent to her state at that particular moment. Thus, there was also a degree of flexibility and variability which, given the way the interaction developed, seemed to have promoted a good enough sense of felt security in Patricia that she could risk experiencing a relationship transformation in the here-and-now of the therapeutic encounter (Beebe et al., 2000).

The opportunity for this shared, intersubjective moment and new way of experiencing one another to emerge would, I think, have been lost had I chosen to interpret Patricia's expectation that the therapy would fail because of her "empty words." Could her very use of this phrase have implicitly influenced me to avoid using empty words of my own? No matter how clever and creative, an interpretation at that point would likely have deadened Patricia's lived experience and confirmed her expectation that spontaneous emotional connection is all but impossible for her. I think that this would also have been the case in the first session had I chosen to make a transference interpretation about her difficulty in leaving abusive relationships with men. Although I was not consciously aware of the implicit, nonverbal aspects of mutual influence occurring moment-to-moment in the first session (Beebe & Lachmann, 2002), I think that procedural/emotional aspects of the encounter paved the way for the "moment of meeting" to emerge in the second. This would seem to confirm Stern's (2004) contention that "making narratives involves not only words, but also direct experiences that are in the implicit domain" (p. 192).

On a more general point, I often find with patients like Patricia, who carry a diagnosis of depression and who tend to self-pathologize in such a way, that they are not globally depressed. Rather, their depressed state appears to be context-dependent in that it comes and goes, depending on the social situation that they are in and the representational model or self-state that emerges in a given social context. The key factor here is emotional connectedness or intersubjective relatedness. Whenever the patient feels emotionally and authentically connected with another, the depression tends to lift, however temporarily. By contrast, feeling isolated and alone in the context of the ongoing absence of a companionable, intersubjective relationship is often accompanied by feelings of low mood and depression. Helping the patient to recognize these shifts in mood, mental models, or self-states can be therapeutic, bringing a sense of hope to counter despair. In this sense, the dramatic shift in Patricia's state of mind in the second session would suggest that the "now moment" experience constituted a transition from an archaic representational model to one that is actually available to her, but which needs to be strengthened and consolidated so that it becomes a more consistent aspect of her lived experience. My thinking in this regard accords with Wachtel's (2008) suggestion that paying attention to the patient's healthier, more adaptive ways of being, and examining the contextual nature of their moods and behavior, "can greatly enhance our clinical work" (p. 73).

Chapter 9

Attachment, Trauma, and Intimate Violence

INTRODUCTION

This chapter presents a relational perspective on intimate affective violence informed by the literature on attachment, trauma, and affect regulation. This may further explicate the role that implicit memory, dissociation, and representational models play in the development and maintenance of personality traits and adult psychopathology.

A violent act may be defined as an attack upon the body of another which is committed with the explicit intention of causing physical harm and injury (Fonagy, 1999c; Mirrlees-Black, 1999; Motz, 2001; Perelberg, 1999). There is general agreement that interpersonal violence falls into two broad types of behavior: predatory or psychopathic violence, which is held to be planned and emotionless, and in which the perpetrator seeks out a victim with whom he has no attachment relationship; and defensive or affective violence, which arises in reaction to the perception that one's personal safety or sense of self is under threat, and which is preceded by heightened levels of emotional arousal (Fonagy, 1999c; Fonagy & Target, 1999; Gilligan, 2000; Meloy, 1992; Mitchell, 1993; Panksepp, 2001; Siegal et al., 1999). Despite these distinctions, both types of violence involve the experience of unbearable states of mind which cannot be regulated, reflected upon, or symbolized (Cartwright, 2002; Fonagy, 1999c).

Findings confirm that the vast majority of violent assaults between adults occur within an existing intimate relationship and fall into the defensive or affective category (Meloy, 1992; Roberts & Noller, 1998). Indeed, official statistics for England and Wales reveal that on average two women are killed by their current or former male partners or lovers each week (Hoare & Povey, 2008; Home Office, 2006/2007; Povey & Allen, 2003). Further, research shows that childhood physical and sexual abuse take place mainly within a domestic situation and are perpetrated by a member of the child's family (Cawson, Watton, Brooke, & Kelly, 2000; Crittendon & Ainsworth, 1989; Dutton, 1995; Dutton & Painter, 1981; Dutton, Saunders, Starzomski, & Bartholomew, 1994; Hoare & Povey, 2008; Home Office, 2006/2007;

Mirrlees-Black, 1999; NSPCC, 2007; West & George, 1999). In this context, it should be noted that the strength of the attachment bond is unrelated to the quality of the attachment relationship. Indeed, abused children and battered partners typically show signs of being strongly, albeit traumatically, attached to their abusive caregivers or intimate partners (de Zulueta, 1993; Dutton & Painter, 1981; Follette, Polushy, Bechtle, & Naugle, 1996). Findings also reveal, however, that domestic violence operates on a broad continuum of seriousness with homicide lying at one extreme and pushing and shoving at the other. Moreover, an increasing body of research presents a picture of inti-mate relational violence that is reciprocal and bidirectional in nature (Archer, 2000; Bartholomew, Kwong, & Hart, 2001b; Hoare & Povey, 2008; Home Office, 2006/2007; Mirrlees-Black, 1999; Roberts & Noller, 1998; Stets & Straus, 1990; Straus & Gelles, 1986). This finding appears to obtain in both opposite-sex and same-sex relationships (Mohr, 1999). Commonly, the violence is infrequent, confined within the family, and relatively "minor." Whatever the form, violence and abuse are wholly unacceptable: The acts may differ in magnitude, but not in essence (Stein, 2007).

A RELATIONAL PERSPECTIVE ON VIOLENCE AND AGGRESSION

While aggression and destructiveness are seen as biologically rooted, a rela-tional perspective views such behavior as secondary, arising in response to a perceived threat to the psychological self in an intersubjective/attach-ment matrix characterized by trauma and abuse, rather than innate, as in the death instinct (Black, 2001; Freud, 1920; Klein, 1933; Schwartz, 2001). Indeed, Mitchell (1993) argues that we all experience enough danger and threat in childhood to harbor a fair amount of destructive aggression. Given this, he suggests that it is universal to hate and to plan revenge on and the destruction of those we love when we feel endangered, betrayed, shamed, and angry. However, experiencing aggressive and destructive thoughts, feelings, and fantasies in response to a stressful interpersonal situation is one thing, the violent enactment of this experience is quite another. Furthermore, while violence is viewed by many as having reached epidemic proportions in modern society (Gilligan, 2000), in more prosaic terms it may be seen as just one of many diverse forms of psychopathologi-cal reactions to trauma.

Just why an individual should "choose" violence as the preferred way to express his or her personal psychopathology, rather than say somatization, self-harm, eating disorder, alcohol/drug misuse, depression, or psychosis is an intriguing question. A consideration of this issue would need to examine socio/cultural/historical factors and socially constructed gendered aspects of the person's experience as coconstructed in the therapeutic relationship with each unique individual. This reflects the all-important hermeneutic and social constructionist aspects of the therapeutic process that tend to get lost in general theorizing. In my view, the subjective meaning of such maladaptive behavior is to be gained by attending to the subject's phenomenological experience of unmourned loss and unresolved psychological trauma in a particular social and relational matrix (Renn, 2003, 2006). As previously noted, I consider that an understanding of the person's subjective experience and of the therapeutic process is facilitated by an approach that incorporates empiricism and hermeneutics (Renn, 2010).

Focusing on the issue of intimate violence, I contend that affective violence is rooted in the disruption of intersubjective/attachment processes and constitutes a disorganized, maladaptive reaction to a perceived threat or sense of endangerment to the self. From this perspective, attachment theory may be understood as a theory of trauma—the trauma of separation and loss in the face of overwhelming fear and helplessness. It is important to recognize that attachment needs are not outgrown with childhood but characterize intimate relationships across the life cycle. With regard to relational violence, Bowlby (1984) notes how appallingly slow psychoanalysts and psychotherapists have been in appreciating the prevalence and far-reaching consequences of violent behavior between family members. Increasingly, however, a relational/attachment perspective is being used to understand affective violence.

From this perspective, the key to understanding violence is the evolutionary function of anger. Bowlby (1973) contends that "threats of separation and other forms of rejection, are seen as arousing, in a child or adult, both anxious and angry behavior" (p. 253). Indeed, research findings indicate that angry protest is an instinctive biological response to separation from the preferred attachment figure whose physical presence and emotional availability afford the child safety, protection, and psychobiological regulation. The adaptive function of angry protest is to increase the intensity of the communication to the lost person with the set goal of achieving reunion (Bowlby, 1973, 1988). Disturbance of attachment is the outcome of a series of deviations that take the child increasingly further from adaptive functioning. Thus, the child's anger may become dysfunctional if the caregiver's response is insensitive, lacks contingency, or is actively unloving and abusive, thereby generating intense feelings of fear, shame, hate, and rage and a felt sense of threat, anxiety, and insecurity. Such individuals develop representational models of self and significant others imbued with expectations of the other's unavailability (Bowlby, 1969, 1973). These mental representations may be activated in later life in situations involving stress and a sense of threat to the self (Bowlby, 1969; Mikulincer, Florian, Cowan, & Cowan, 2002a).

Unexpressed anger in childhood, then, becomes split off into a segregated or dissociated representational system of the personality characterized by pathological mourning and profound emotional detachment (Bowlby, 1973,

1979). Child abuse and cumulative developmental trauma violate the child's sense of trust, identity, and agency and, in the absence of any resolution via subsequent positive attachment relationships, may have a pernicious and seminal influence on adult psychopathology: All too often the violated child becomes the violent adult (Bowlby, 1988; Follette et al., 1996; West & George, 1999). In this sense, violence may be seen as representing the extreme of behaviors that are all too human (Stein, 2007). Representational models deriving from implicitly encoded developmental trauma provide the templates for psychopathology in later life, which may include violent, destructive, and self-destructive forms of behavior (Schore, 1994). Such mental models interfere with the ability to consider the other's perspective and feelings and predispose the individual to expect hostile intent in ambiguous social situations (Bartholomew et al., 2001; Bowlby, 1988; Cortina & Liotti, 2007; Fonagy et al., 1997, 2004). Indeed, Fonagy and his colleagues (2004) argue that brutalization in the context of attachment relationships generates intense shame. When this is coupled with a history of neglect and a consequent weakness in mentalization, it becomes "a likely trigger for violence against the self or others, because of the intensity of the humiliation experienced when the trauma cannot be processed and attenuated via mentalization" (p. 12). From this perspective, the alien, dissociated part of the self is used as a survival strategy "to contain the image of the aggressor and the unthinkable affect generated by their abusive actions. . . ." (p. 13).

From a relational perspective, intimate violence involves disturbance of the attachment processes and is understood as the distorted and exaggerated version of attachment behavior that is potentially functional (Bowlby, 1973, 1979; de Zulueta, 1993; Fonagy et al., 1997). While a disorganized attachment state of mind does not inevitably lead to the enactment of affective violence in intimate relationships, in line with Lyons-Ruth and Jacobvitz (1999), I would argue that it constitutes a potent risk factor. Stalking or harassment, a prevalent crime in both the UK and the US may similarly be understood in terms of attachment pathology deriving from acute separation anxiety and fear of abandonment. In such cases, the insecurely attached person is ineluctably drawn to follow and seek proximity to the real or fantasized attachment figure onto whom such relational dynamics have been displaced or redirected in order to assuage overwhelming feelings of loss, shame, and isolation (Hoare & Povey, 2008; Home Office, 2006/2007; Meloy, 1992; Povey & Allen, 2003). The following case example illustrates the attachment dynamics involved in stalking behavior.

CLINICAL ILLUSTRATION

"Hardeep" embarked on a campaign of violence and harassment when his partner, "Jaswinder," ended their relationship. His violent behavior in relation to Jaswinder had brought Hardeep before the courts on several occasions and culminated in his breaking into her home one night armed with a knife and assaulting her when she phoned the police.

Hardeep was 25 at the time of the assault and is the second oldest of six children. He was born and raised in India, but the family moved to the UK when he was aged 14. Prior to leaving India, Hardeep's favorite uncle died, as did his father soon after the family had settled in Britain. Hardeep's mother was an anxious, fearful woman who related to him in an overly protective way. This took the form of a morbid preoccupation with his physical health, diet, and personal safety, fearing, for no apparent rational reason, that he would die. Because of this fear, Hardeep's mother discouraged him from leading an independent life outside the family home; instead, she kept him firmly tied to her, seemingly as a means of quelling her fear and anxiety. It would seem that she had inverted the relationship with her son, unwittingly using him as her attachment figure.

This merged, noncontingent style of relating intensified following the death of her husband. In her grief, she increasingly turned to Hardeep for comfort and emotional support, and he became her confidante and constant companion. Although he resented this imposed role, he felt trapped in it by a sense of duty and obligation, fueled by guilt and shame whenever he tried to step outside of this role. Thus, he was unable to express the anger and frustration he felt towards his mother for what he saw as her failure to "give me my freedom."

Hardeep's relationship with Jaswinder was his first intimate, sexual involvement with a woman. He continued to live with his mother throughout their intense, turbulent 2-year relationship and was unable to accept that Jaswinder wanted to lead an independent life while they were together, or that she eventually wanted to end their relationship because of his coercive and controlling behavior. He spoke of feeling lonely, distressed, frightened, and angry because of her wish to leave him and of responding by becoming ever more dependent on her. Hardeep denied the reality of the loss and, instead, perceived his affiliation with Jaswinder and her parents as "close," despite all evidence to the contrary. He made frequent intrusive telephone calls to Jaswinder, visited her and her parents' respective homes uninvited and unannounced, and kept Jaswinder under regular surveillance, frequently following her every movement. He resorted to violence in an attempt to frighten her and thereby bring her under his power and control. Prior to this situation, Hardeep was a conscientious, passive, and law-abiding citizen, who worked in the family business and saved assiduously to fulfill his mother's wish to go on holiday together to India.

I described in Chapter 6 how early, nonoptimal representational models persist into adulthood, coexisting with more appropriately adaptive ones (Bowlby, 1973, 1979). Also that Liotti (1992), building on the findings of Main (1991), posits a connection between disorganized attachment, dissociation, and the construction of a multiple, incoherent representational model with respect to the primary attachment figure. An incompatible model in respect of one and the same person generates oscillating beliefs and expectations. Thus, at times of intense emotional stress the earlier and less conscious model tends to become dominant (Bowlby, 1984, 1988). In later life, the confused, unstable representational model imbued with dysregulated rage, shame, and hate deriving from childhood fear of abandonment and dread of loneliness may be activated under circumstances of separation and loss. These affective states cannot be mentalized and thus may result in extreme behavior, including violence (Fonagy et al., 2004).

This conceptual paradigm, in conjunction with a neurobiological perspective, may be used to understand Hardeep's violent behavior in the context of Jaswinder ending their relationship. The clinical evidence, combined with Hardeep's recent forensic history, indicates that he had developed an unresolved/disorganized state of mind with respect to loss and trauma. As a consequence, his capacity to mourn loss and regulate negative affective states of anger, shame, and rage when under stress was deficient. Abandonment by Jaswinder was experienced in traumatic terms, activating a multiple, incoherent representational model characterized by confusion and fear. This, in turn, caused him to seek proximity to Jaswinder in a clinging, tearful and dependent way. When she failed to respond to his pleas and provide the comfort, security, and support he needed to alleviate his stress and deactivate his attachment system, his coping strategies and mental defenses were overwhelmed by negative affect and an unregulated cascade of stress-related neurochemicals. This, in turn, suppressed the hippocampus and enhanced amygdala activity, leading to the reemergence of trauma-related childhood memories, conceptualized as a dissociated archaic representational model.

Lacking the capacity to represent, mentalize, and organize feeling states of fear, shame, hate, and rage, Hardeep acted out his emotional distress in an escalating pattern of stalking that culminated in a violent assault on Jaswinder. By his own admission, this maladaptive behavior was, in part, a frantic attempt to control Jaswinder to ensure her continuing emotional and physical availability, thereby protecting him against disturbing feelings of loss, shame, and fear of self-annihilation. Her understandable reluctance to respond to him kept Hardeep in a protracted state of psychobiological stress, thus his fear and attachment behavioral systems remained in a state of chronic activation. Being unable to self-soothe and self-comfort, he desperately sought proximity to Jaswinder, since she had become his main attachment figure.

As a result of this unhappy situation, Hardeep was faced with an exquisitely painful and irresolvable problem: As Jaswinder was his primary attachment figure, it was to her that he instinctively turned for comfort at times of stress to deactivate the physical, emotional, and neurobiological reaction that he was experiencing; however, her understandable rejecting and abandoning behavior was the unwitting cause of his distress. Lacking a coherent strategy to deal with separation and loss, and thus the capacity to mentalize, regulate, and process his traumatic state of mind, Hardeep's behavior became increasingly obsessive and disorganized. He denied the loss and distorted his perception of the relationship, rationalizing his controlling, stalking, and violent behavior, which he cast in terms of protecting Jaswinder from others and from the excesses of her own self-destructive behavior.

Hardeep's terrified reaction to the loss of Jaswinder may, then, be seen as the reemergence of implicitly encoded, context-dependent childhood memories associated with early unresolved loss and trauma: in Winnicottian terms, the breakdown that has already happened, but which has not been "remembered." In this relational context, Hardeep's anger, stalking, and violence may be understood as motivated by fear and an urgent need to protect the self from being retraumatized. His violence and desperate attempts to maintain proximity to Jaswinder may, therefore, be viewed as a pathological form of attachment behavior—as "attachment gone wrong" (de Zulueta, 1993).

GANG VIOLENCE AND STRANGER VIOLENCE

A relational/attachment perspective may also be used to understand what motivates some young people to join gangs. This social phenomenon may be understood in the context of the young person's subjective experience of neglect, abuse, lack of parental supervision, absence of a father figure, and alienation from educational and social institutions. Lacking the security afforded by affectional bonds developed in a loving and containing family environment as well as any meaningful investment in society, the gang may function as an alternative family system within which strong bonds of loyalty and attachment are forged. Danger and threat from rival gangs in the context of territorial disputes, often involving the selling and distribution of drugs, may escalate into gang violence. Violence is supported and consensually validated by the gang members and may be used by the young people to confirm their gender or social status within the peer group (Stein, 2007).

Similarly, youngsters who arm themselves with guns and knives for self-protection may use the weapon precipitately when feeling endangered and under threat. The urban environment is perceived to be inherently unsafe. Indeed, research indicates that many perpetrators are terrified of their victims (Hoare & Povey, 2008; Home Office, 2006/2007; Stein, 2007). I would suggest that young people who are insecurely attached with disorganized inner worlds characterized by chaos, fear, and disaster are much more likely to hold such catastrophic perceptions, project the threat and menace outwards, and carry weapons for self-protection than are youngsters who are securely attached with inner worlds characterized by trust and confidence in others (Solomon et al., 1995).

Violent behavior may be displaced or redirected from the original source of hatred and hostility toward a weaker, more vulnerable target, for example, a child; or it may be motivated by a need to control the adult partner to prevent him or her from departing, as in the case of Hardeep. In many instances, homicide may be explained as the result of the perpetrator being unable to tolerate the attachment figure leaving (Bowlby, 1984, 1988). This contention would seem to be confirmed by data which show that the murder of a partner is most likely to occur in a context of rejection and physical separation and to be imbued with intense affective violence (Downey, Khoun, & Feldman, 1997; Dutton, 1995; Fonagy, 1999c; Hoare & Povey, 2008; Home Office, 2006/2007; Mirrlees-Black, 1999; NSPCC, 2007; Povey & Allen, 2003). Indeed, findings demonstrate an association between separation distress and an elevation in the secretion of the stress hormone cortisol. As noted in the case of Hardeep, in combination these factors may overwhelm the limited mentalizing and coping strategies of the insecure/disorganized individual (Bradley, 2003; Fonagy et al., 2004; Schore, 1994).

With regard to stranger violence, fear of annihilation may be projected outward and become embodied in the person of the stranger. Thus, the violent act may often have the aim of attenuating an actual or perceived threat to the person committing it (Stein, 2007). Redirection and displacement are, therefore, clinical issues that require consideration in understanding violent acts against strangers. We need to ask: "Who did the unknown hapless victim represent to the violent stranger in the particular context in which the assault occurred?" and "What dissociated relational dynamics were suddenly disinhibited and acted out in the violent attack on the stranger?" Research shows that young men are at the greatest risk of becoming victims of stranger violence and also that young men are most likely to be the perpetrators of such acts. In comparison, the risk of domestic violence and sexual assault is significantly higher for women than for men. As noted above, pregnancy constitutes an increased risk factor, with up to a third of female victims being pregnant during the violent relationship (Hoare & Povey, 2008; Home Office, 2006/2007).

THE "NORMAL" MURDERER

Comparative studies of violent male offenders reveal that many men who kill the partners they profess to love do not present with histories of dramatic trauma or abuse or as being aggressive and antisocial. Rather, they may present as model citizens whose early environments seem to have been relatively benign. In cases such as these, the violent act and accompanying affective rage appears to be sudden and inexplicable and to arise in response to little or no provocation (Cartwright, 2002; Weiss, Lamberti, & Blackman, 1960). Clinical experience indicates that in such instances the violent individual's psychological self has been violated in childhood in more subtle and covert ways than in those involving clearly dramatic trauma and abuse, as described in Chapter 3 (Fonagy & Target, 1999; Lyons-Ruth & Block, 1996; Lyons-Ruth et al., 2005). I concur with this contention and argue that the very "normality" of some violent people constitutes an aspect of a complex, but rigid, defensive organization forged in a relational/attachment system characterized by subtle developmental trauma that is cumulative in its effect and encoded in the systems of implicit/procedural memory (Renn, 2003, 2006). Under normative levels of stress and emotional arousal, the individual is able to regulate his or her affective states and may attain considerable success in career and financial terms. However, in a context of rejection and abandonment by the partner, separation from any children of the created family, and an accumulation of stressful factors such as sexual jealousy, bereavement, redundancy, and financial problems, the person's conscious coping strategies and unconscious defensive structure break down (Downey et al., 1997; Dutton et al., 1994; Cartwright, 2002; Renn, 2003, 2006).

Situations involving loss, betrayal, and abandonment activate a multiple, disorganized representational model together with a cascade of unregulated neurochemicals and the reemergence of trauma-related childhood memories (de Zulueta, 1993; Liotti, 1992; Lyons-Ruth & Jacobvitz, 1999; Mancia, 2006; Schacter, 1996; Schore, 1994; van der Kolk, 1994). This psychobiological state is experienced as posing an imminent threat to the self and fuels a maladaptive, incoherent response which overwhelms the person's regulatory and mentalizing capacities. Not infrequently, this culminates in the enactment of a dissociated, shame-driven murderous rage deriving from the original traumatizing relational matrix in which the self was felt to be endangered. The violent act may also, in part, be seen as a compulsive reenactment of dissociated personal trauma which temporarily transforms the sense of helplessness associated with the original traumatic experience into one of power and control: The person who was once the persecuted victim identifies with the aggressor and thereby is transformed into a persecutor (Ferenczi, 1933; Fonagy et al., 2004; Frankel, 2002; Freud, A., 1993; Renn, 2003, 2006; Stein, 2007; van der Kolk, 1989).

VIOLENCE AND GENDER: SIMILARITIES AND DIFFERENCES

The British Crime Survey for 2006–2007 found that in the great majority of domestic violence incidents the victims were women and the perpetrators were men. Approximately one-third of female victims of partner abuse had been pregnant at some point during the violent relationship. Also, as noted above, on average two women are killed each week in England and Wales by their intimate male partners. Furthermore, offenses recorded by the police in 2007–2008 in the "most serious sexual" category reveal that women are far more likely to be the victims of sexual violence than men. This was also the case in respect of harassment offenses. In the light of these findings, it is clear that there is an appalling incidence of violent assault on women by men (Dutton, 1995; Dutton et al. 1994).

With respect to intimate violence in the family, Home Office researchers found that self-completion questionnaires consistently reveal a relatively similar incidence of domestic violence for both men and women. The peculiar contradiction between self-report findings and those relating to face-to-face interviews is partly accounted for by the sensitivity involved in disclosing intimate violence to an interviewer (Mirrlees-Black, 1999). The picture of similar rates of domestic violence for men and women revealed by the Home Office self-report module has been replicated by attachment and social science researchers (Archer, 2000; Bartholomew, Henderson, & Dutton, 2001a; Bookwala & Zdaniuk, 1998; Magdol et al., 1997; Miga, Hare, Allen, & Manning, 2010; Roberts & Noller, 1998; Stets & Straus, 1990). However, one finding consistently moderated by gender is that women are much more likely to suffer injury than men in violent relationships. Researchers believe this may be why women are more likely than men to perceive domestic violence as a crime and to report such incidents to the police.

The National Society for the Prevention of Cruelty to Children (NSPCC, 2007) cites research showing that the most common perpetrator of childhood sexual abuse in the family is a brother or stepbrother, followed by a father and other male relatives. The killing and physical abuse of children by parents, however, are committed in roughly equal proportions by mothers and fathers. The source of the woman's violence is located in early experiences of neglect and abuse, predominantly at the hands of her own parents (Follette et al., 1996). Researchers contend that the woman perceives the child as an extension of herself, rather than as a separate subject (Motz, 2001; Welldon, 1988). Perhaps unsurprisingly, it was found that mothers who had been abused in childhood and whose capacity for reflective functioning or mentalization had, therefore, been compromised, were more likely to become abusing parents themselves than were mothers who had not been abused (Follette et al., 1996).

Research shows that, in comparison to men, women tend not to be violent outside of their intimate relationships. It is suggested that attachment insecurity underlies a woman's use of violence and that such insecurity arises in the private domain of the family as the couple struggle to manage their respective attachment conflicts concerning "discomfort with closeness" and "anxiety over abandonment" (Feeney, Noller & Hanrahan, 1994; Mikulincer & Shaver, 2007; Roberts & Noller, 1998; Simpson, 1990). From an attachment theory perspective, the psychological mechanisms underlying couple violence are thought to be similar for both genders and to occur in same-sex as well as opposite-sex relationships (Bartholomew et al., 2001a). Indeed, a review of the literature by Mohr (2008) shows that same-sex romantic relationships are attachment relationships and are influenced by the same processes and dynamics as heterosexual relationships (Mohr & Fassinger, 2003; Roisman, Clausell, Holland, Fortuna, & Elieff, 2008). This suggests that such behavior needs to be understood from within a relational, dyadic context and to be informed by attachment theory and research (Carnelley, Hepper, Hicks, & Turner, 2011; Miga et al., 2010). Specific sociocultural factors may also need to be considered in understanding relationship violence in minority ethnic communities.

With respect to people who have developed a fearful/avoidant attachment style, there is a desire for a close relationship but a countervailing fear of disapproval and rejection. This ambivalent internal conflict leads to inflexible behavioral strategies designed to avoid emotional intimacy which, in turn, create disappointment and tension within the couple relationship, thereby increasing the risk of violence (Bartholomew et al., 2001; Bond & Bond, 2004; Downey & Feldman, 1996; Dutton et al., 1994; Roberts & Noller, 1998). It should be stressed, however, that understanding violence from a relational and trauma perspective does not exculpate the male perpetrator from his individual responsibility for violence.

In terms of relationship quality, findings show that some attachment dimensions appear to be gender-specific. For females, "anxiety over abandonment" was found to be a strong correlate of relationship quality being linked with jealousy and low levels of communication, closeness, partner responsiveness, and satisfaction. For males, "discomfort with closeness" was the crucial attachment dimension of relationship quality (Feeney et al., 1994; Shaver & Hazan, 2004; Roberts & Noller, 1998; Simpson, 1990). These gender differences may reflect sex-role stereotypes whereby women are socialized to value emotional closeness and men are socialized to value self-reliance (Byng-Hall, 1999). Avoidant attachment reflects a reliance on deactivating strategies characterized by inhibition of proximity seeking and a preference for managing stressors alone. Anxious attachment indicates hyperactivating strategies manifested as strenuous attempts to attain greater proximity, support, and love combined with a fear that such love and support will not be forthcoming (Cassidy & Kobak, 1988). Research has confirmed Bowlby's (1969) assumption that the attachment system and concomitant representational models are activated when a person feels threatened or distressed (Mikulincer, Gallath, & Shaver, 2002b; Simpson, Rholes, & Nelligan, 1992; Simpson, Rholes, & Phillips, 1996).

In more general terms, research using a variation of Hazan and Shaver's (1987) self-report measure found that individuals' adult attachment styles (secure, anxious, or avoidant) were of relevance to couples' communication patterns, relationship satisfaction, and the overall quality of the love relationship (Cowan, Cowan, & Mehta, 2009; Mayseless & Scharf, 2007; McCarthy & Taylor, 1999; McCarthy & Maughan, 2010; Miga et al., 2010; Roberts & Noller, 1998). Insecure couples that had difficulty in sustaining emotionally meaningful and satisfying relationships were found to be at greater risk of resolving conflict through violent means than were securely attached couples (Dutton et al., 1994; Hamel & Nicholls, 2006). As previously noted, there is also some evidence to show that attachment strategies and emotional procedures formed in childhood influence the playing out of the caregiving, care-seeking, and sexual behavioral systems in adult intimate relationships (Lichtenberg, 2007, 2008).

Understanding couple violence in a relational context with attachment status as a key link in this process has clear implications for the choice of intervention (Bartholomew et al., 2001; Clulow, 2001; Hamel & Nicholls, 2006; Mikulincer et al., 2002). In clinical practice, I have found that in relationships involving infrequent, low-level violence in which the couple is committed to staying together and struggling to understand their abusive behavior, it may be more effective to work with them conjointly rather than separately. Furthermore, as noted above, research indicates that the similarities between opposite-sex and same-sex intimate relationships far outweigh the differences (Mohr, 1999; Mohr & Fassinger, 2003; Roisman et al., 2008). Given this, it is likely that attachment issues also underlie violence in same-sex relationships. Conjoint work using an attachment-based psychodynamic approach may, therefore, be equally appropriate and effective in working with same-sex couples.

The clinical picture is very different for women caught up in an opposite-sex battering relationship in which the violence is frequent and severe. Despite being repeatedly physically and psychologically abused, the woman may experience great difficulty in leaving the abusive man. This phenomenon may partly be explained by the development of a traumatic attachment bond. As already noted, abused children and battered spouses develop traumatic attachment bonds to their abusive caregivers or partners (de Zulueta, 1993; Dutton & Painter, 1981). Moreover, the maladaptive emotional and psychological attachment to the abuser would seem to be reinforced by neurochemical derivatives (Mitchell, 2000; van der Kolk, 1989, 1994).

The contention that the battered woman becomes traumatically attached to the perpetrator receives support from research showing that women with a history of childhood abuse are at an increased risk of marrying an abusive partner (Follette et al., 1996; Kalmuss, 1984; Motz, 2001; Welldon, 1988). In addition to the fear and social isolation induced by the man's violence and controlling behavior, the woman's difficulty in separating from her violent partner may be seen in terms of a collapse of behavioral and attentional strategies. These implicitly encoded relational dynamics, in the context of threat, danger, and coercion, indicate the activation of a disorganized/disoriented representational model developed in childhood with an unresolved or abusive caregiver who was both the source of fear and alarm and the solution to these traumatic states of mind (Lyons-Ruth & Jacobvitz, 1999; Main & Hesse, 1990).

Thus, in addition to socially constructed gendered aspects of experience which militate against women feeling entitled to fulfill their needs and desires in a context of unequal power relations, the battering relationship may be viewed as providing a maladaptive vehicle for repetitive reenactments of unresolved trauma (van der Kolk, 1989, 1994). Such reenactments consist of dissociated attachment trauma involving repeated exposure to fear without resolution (Main & Hesse, 1990). Indeed, an important motivational factor in the perpetuation of archaic attachment bonds in the here-and-now is the desire to recreate a familiar relationship pattern, however violent and self-destructive this may be, precisely because it is familiar and thus, in a paradoxical way, provides a modicum of felt security (Bowlby, 1988; Fairbairn, 1996). Couple work in cases characterized by such violent, dysfunctional, and unstable attachment dynamics is strongly contraindicated. In my view, the woman needs help to physically and emotionally separate from her battering partner, and the man should be worked with separately with the goal of resolving the attachment trauma that is likely to be motivating his violent behavior.

With respect to the relatively few women who kill their male partners in a context of loss, betrayal, and abuse, I suspect that their violent behavior is motivated in part by unresolved attachment trauma in ways not so dissimilar to the much greater number of men who murder their female partners. In addition to these psychological factors, the greater strength and fighting competency of men, the physical injuries and psychological harm received in an ongoing battering relationship, and the issue of provocation need to be kept in mind in understanding women who kill their male partners. Moreover, although the focus of this chapter is on understanding violence from a relational and trauma perspective, it is important to emphasize that a broader understanding of violence and abuse needs to take into account the social and political context of unequal power relations within which the violence occurs (Clulow, 2001).

Attachment theory, then, holds that the person's cognitive-affective representational models of early self-other relationships mediate all subsequent relationships, particularly those with intimate partners in adulthood. In object relations terms, it is argued that the failure to attain "mature dependence" reflects a persisting state of psychological merger with the early maternal love object, a state driven by insecurity and chronic separation anxiety. It is contended that love relations in adulthood conform to the pattern of the individual's early undifferentiated relationships with his or her parents. Via processes of transference and identification, later love relations assume the emotional significance of these original relationships (Fairbairn, 1996). A neurobiological perspective adds another level in understanding the seemingly addictive quality that characterizes so many traumatic and abusive intimate relationships (Mitchell, 2000; van der Kolk, 1989, 1994).

COUPLE THERAPY AND THE LINKS BETWEEN ADULT ATTACHMENT STATES OF MIND AND INTIMATE VIOLENCE

The decision whether or not to work therapeutically with a couple whose intimate relationship is characterized by violence and abuse should be informed by an assessment of risk, by relevant research findings, and by the couple's particular needs and sociocultural context. The detrimental emotional impact on any children of the family should also be assessed because research shows that witnessing violence in the home is a significant risk factor for the development of disorganized attachment in children (Lyons-Ruth & Jacobvitz, 2008). Moreover, experiencing domestic violence in childhood was found to be the best predictor, for both males and females, of becoming a victim of violence in adult couple relationships (Wekerle & Wolfe, 1999).

I think it good practice to see the couple together for an initial meeting followed by a separate interview with each partner. This may facilitate disclosure of violence and emotional abuse. It also provides the opportunity to take each partner's attachment and relationship history, explore each partner's experiences of abuse and psychological trauma, and assess the general emotional and sexual quality of the relationship and the respective adult attachment states of mind, as reflected in their discrete discourse styles. In cases where the couple disclose a low level of violence and abuse and both partners indicate their desire to freely participate in couple therapy with the initial goal of eliminating all forms of abuse, it makes good clinical sense to work on the relationship conjointly, not least because the woman is much more likely to be physically injured in a violent exchange (Bograd & Mederos, 1999).

How, then, can attachment theory and research help us to understand the contradictory relationship between violence and abuse on the one hand and love and intimacy on the other hand? To paraphrase Oscar Wilde, why do so many people hurt the ones they love?

As noted above, adult attachment can be represented by two underlying dimensions reflecting the degree to which an individual feels discomfort in intimate relationships or fears abandonment from the partner. These dimensions are labeled "discomfort with closeness" and "anxiety over abandonment" (Feeney et al., 1994; Mikulincer & Shaver, 2007; Roberts & Noller, 1998; Simpson, 1990). Adults with a dismissing attachment state of mind report more discomfort with emotional intimacy and interdependence, whereas those with a preoccupied attachment state of mind report higher levels of anxiety over abandonment and fear of rejection. Researchers have presented evidence showing that couple violence is related to the regulation of intimacy and the maintenance of proximity within the relationship (Bond & Bond, 2004; Downey et al., 1997; Dutton et al., 1994; Roberts & Noller, 1998). These findings are consonant with the contention that the main purpose of defense in attachment theory is affect regulation, and that the means of achieving this are behavioral and intrapsychic mechanisms conceptualized as distance regulation (Dozier et al., 2001; Sroufe & Waters, 1977).

Whereas a secure partner may provide a buffering effect for the behavior of an insecure individual, the pairing of two insecure individuals may prove a highly volatile combination, especially if one partner is fearful of abandonment and the other is uncomfortable with intimacy. This not uncommon combination of couples with these particular adult attachment styles or states of mind may be especially fraught and combustible because of the conflicting needs for intimacy involved. In particular, a person who is anxious over abandonment may find the withdrawal and emotional distance of a partner who is uncomfortable with closeness extremely anxiety-provoking (Cohn, Silver, Cowan, Cowan, & Pearson, 1992; Roberts & Noller, 1998). The dismissing partner's distancing behavior activates the preoccupied partner's archaic representational model, together with fearful affect and the expectation of abandonment. As the preoccupied partner escalates the appeal to have dependency needs met, this activates the dismissing partner's representational model imbued with discomfort with intimacy and sets in train procedural responses of withdrawal and emotional distancing. This leads to subsequent pursuer–distancer escalations, a relational dynamic that may be seen as a negative example of bidirectionality or mutual influence. When the closeness/distance struggle cannot be negotiated to suit both partners' intimacy needs, the conflict, fueled by chronic fear and distress, may escalate out of control and erupt into violence (Byng-Hall, 1999).

Dismissing individuals, then, tend to deactivate their attachment system and withdraw from conflict situations, presenting as overly independent, self-reliant, and emotionally detached. By contrast, preoccupied people hyperactivate their attachment system and are chronically hypervigilant and anxious about rejection and abandonment (Cassidy & Kobak, 1988). They have such excessive needs for support and reassurance that they are inevitably frustrated and disappointed in not having these needs met. They may become increasingly demanding and potentially violent when their attachment needs are not fulfilled (Bartholomew et al., 2001). Indeed, research has identified an association between couple violence and withdrawal from conflict with violence being used to protest the distance and prevent the partner from leaving the scene of conflict. Therapeutic approaches that are unfamiliar with such attachment dynamics often employ "time out" as a safety strategy. However, unless carefully thought through and managed, the time out strategy may unwittingly escalate the conflict, being miscon-strued as a defensive withdrawal, and thus place one or other partner at greater risk of a violent assault.

Individuals whose attachment histories have made them especially sus-ceptible to anxiety, rejection, separation, and loss may be most likely to appraise ambiguous behavior by a partner as rejecting and unsupportive. This is likely to be subjectively experienced as posing an imminent threat to their security and integrity as a psychological self. Sexual jealousy and fear of rejection and abandonment are common triggers of violent inci-dents in intimate relationships with the violence functioning in a wholly maladaptive way to regulate intimacy and maintain proximity to the loved one whose loss is so desperately feared (Bartholomew et al., 2001a; Hazan & Shaver, 1987; Holtzworth-Munroe, Stuart, & Hutchinson, 1997; Shaver & Mikulincer, 2004).

The "stuckness" that characterizes troubled couple relationships may be seen in terms of Wachtel's (2008) cyclical psychodynamic model as out-lined in Chapter 6 and Sandler's (1976) theory of role-responsiveness as noted in Chapters 1 and 7. These relational, systemic models are eminently adaptable to clinical work with couples, a crucial aspect of which is to bring into focal attention the way in which each partner repeatedly elicits from the other emotional responses and patterns of behavior that maintain nonconscious sets of expectancies encoded in implicit/procedural memory, conceptualized as representational models. In addition, I have found it therapeutically beneficial to help couples build into their relationship three interlinked features that keep a relationship viable and on track: safe haven/secure base functions, a process of rupture/repair, and emotionally mean-ingful communication.

The concept of the safe haven/secure base derives from attachment the-ory and is shorthand for being emotionally available, responsive, and sup-portive. This needs to be a one-way process with respect to the parent and child so as to preclude the parent inverting the relationship, thereby using the child inappropriately as his or her attachment figure (Bowlby, 1988). However, it needs to be a two-way process in adult relationships, especially in adult romantic relationships. Thus, the distressed person needs the part-ner to be his or her safe haven and to respond in ways that afford emotional understanding and psychobiological regulation. In so doing, the partner becomes a secure base, facilitating exploration and elaboration of the emo-tional states and difficulties that have emerged in a particular relational context. Ruptures to the attachment relationship or love bond will inevita-bly occur on both a micro and macro level of misattunement. If, however, the romantic relationship is characterized by rupture after rupture without adequate repair, the couple will become increasingly estranged and alien-ated from one another.

Self-evidently, both safe haven/secure base functions and the process of repairing disruptions to the attachment relationship involve good, emotionally meaningful communication. What often gets in the way of such communication is fear of feelings which, as noted above, may become so intense in intimate encounters that they erupt into a violent enactment. Therefore helping the couple to be less frightened of their own affective states and to start to take emotional risks that subjectively may feel very dangerous is a crucial aspect of therapeutic action. The context of violent enactments in the couple's everyday life frequently revolve around the emotional unavailability of the other in situations involving a stressful event, interpersonal conflict, or a separation and reunion that is unmarked. With regard to the latter, this may be something as "minor" as continuing to watch a TV program when the partner arrives home from a day at work. This may be subjectively experienced as an intense narcissistic mortification, reflecting an attachment history of being repeatedly negated, unseen, and unrecognized by the other. Not infrequently, such encounters lead to an excessive emotional response which, in itself, is an indication that an archaic representational model has been activated. I discuss such relational dynamics in more detail in Chapter 11. My emphasis here, however, is that, in clinical work with individuals or couples, building in and explicitly consolidating the three interlinked aspects of a good enough relationship discussed above is not only therapeutically beneficial, but also essential to establishing a sense of safety that is a prerequisite for effective clinical work to commence.

From the foregoing, it may be seen that instead of focusing on perpetrators and victims in isolation, a relational or systemic approach informed by attachment theory and research explores the interaction between the partners' adult attachment styles or states of mind and the nonconscious emotional procedures that they habitually employ in their intimate relationships. This shifts the focus from the individual to the dyad, and to a discussion of the relational context in which the violent behavior develops and is being maintained in the implicit/enactive domain (Mikulincer et al., 2002; Roberts & Noller, 1998). Therapeutic action consists in making explicit such procedural ways of relating and in linking the way in which emotional conflict about closeness and distance, particularly in contexts involving separations and reunions, activates dissociated, archaic self-other representational models imbued with early attachment trauma encoded in the systems of implicit memory.

Couple violence is a complex phenomenon and has both relational and individual origins. Understanding the traumas, adult attachment states of mind, and implicitly encoded representational models that people bring to their intimate relationships in the context of their early attachment histories may help us to assess whether or not, and under what specific circumstances, couple violence is more likely to occur. Violence, as a relationship trauma, corrodes and violates the couple's love bond and compromises the capacity of the relationship to serve as a secure base and safe haven for either partner (Bartholomew et al., 2001a). Following a comprehensive assessment of risk, the employment of an attachment-based psychodynamic couple therapy may enhance the partners' understanding of their mutual needs for security, love, and closeness. The overarching goals are for the couple to end the violence and abuse, soften their blaming attitudes, repair any relationship traumas, and communicate their hurts and needs in an emotionally engaged and direct way (Johnson, 2004). Optimally, the therapeutic process will help the couple to function more effectively as a source of security for one another, thereby decreasing the likelihood of violence and abuse in the future (Bartholomew et al., 2001a).

In the chapter that follows, I present an extensive case study of a violent man to further illustrate the role that implicit memory, trauma, dissociation, and representational models play in the development of personality and adult psychopathology. I use a brief, time-limited psychodynamic model to show the way in which research findings from attachment theory, developmental psychology, traumatology, and cognitive neuroscience can be integrated into an overarching relational model.

Chapter 10

Brief, Time-Limited Psychodynamic Psychotherapy

A Case of Intimate Violence from a Forensic Setting[*]

INTRODUCTION

Research findings relating to young offenders reveal a history of maltreatment and loss in up to 90% of those interviewed (Boswell, 1996; Fonagy et al., 1997). Such experiences are linked to security of attachment. In this context, a meta-analysis of more than 10,000 Adult Attachment Interviews (AAIs) found that individuals likely to engage in criminal behavior overwhelmingly have insecure states of mind on the AAI (Bakermans-Kranenberg & van Ijzendoorn, 2009). Moreover, a meta-analysis of 62 surveys of the prison population found that the prevalence of psychosis, major depression, personality disorder, and post-traumatic stress disorder was considerably higher among prisoners than in the general population (Fazel & Baillargeon, 2010). These findings accorded with my clinical experience when I worked as a probation officer with adult offenders in the community. In common with Cordess (1997), I found that those who had committed violent offenses had themselves been victims of childhood abuse and/or suffered neglect or loss experienced as traumatic and disorganizing. Indeed, the violent enactment of unresolved childhood trauma was a consistent feature in the behavior of those with whom I worked and was frequently associated with the misuse of alcohol and illicit drugs.

The case study that follows illustrates the clinical application of an integrated therapeutic model in a probation setting. It is presented as an example of the work that I undertook with violent people and to draw links between childhood trauma and subsequent violent offending. The case elucidates the way in which attachment theory may be used to explicate offending behavior and assess risk in a forensic setting. In line with Boswell's (1998) advocacy of research-minded practice, the study seeks to demonstrate the

---

[*] This chapter is an adaptation of "The Link Between Childhood Trauma and Later Violent Offending: The Application of Attachment Theory in a Probation Setting," in F. Pfäfflin and G. Adshead (Eds.), *A Matter of Security: The Application of Attachment Theory to Forensic Psychiatry and Psychotherapy* (pp. 109–144). © 2004 Jessica Kingsley Publishers. Reprinted with permission.

importance of asking offenders about their traumatic backgrounds at the point of assessment (Bowlby, 1944). The therapeutic model illustrates a brief, time-limited approach (Balint, 1972; Mander, 2000) and how the clinical application of a therapeutic model with attachment theory and infant research at its core may enhance the offender's capacity for affect regulation, mentalization, and narrative intelligibility. The improvements in these capacities reflect the integration of dissociated trauma, the development of second order representational models, and a concomitant decrease in the risk of violent behavior (Bowlby, 1988; Fonagy, 1999b).

AN ATTACHMENT THEORY PARADIGM

Attachment theory played a central part in my assessment of the offender, and I anticipated that this approach would underpin my intervention with him. As indicated above, I found attachment theory a powerful tool in explicating offending behavior and assessing risk and, furthermore, eminently adaptable to working effectively with offenders in a forensic setting. From this developmental perspective the person's inner world of subjective experience is structured, shaped, and organized by interpersonal interactions and emergent patterns of attachment conceptualized as self-other mental representations or internal working models (Bowlby, 1973, 1980, 1984).

   With regard to traumatic childhood experiences involving separation and loss, Bowlby (1969) found that when a young child is unwillingly separated from the attachment figure, he or she expresses emotional distress. In the event of the separation being prolonged necessitating the child being placed in unfamiliar surroundings, such distress is likely to become intense. Typically, the child's distress follows a sequence of protest, despair, and emotional detachment. Bowlby (1969) suggests that these phases may be linked to three types of responses: separation anxiety, grief and mourning, and defense. Further, he argues that these responses are phases of a single process—that of mourning separation and loss. The traumatic quality of the child's grief reaction is encapsulated in Bowlby's (1980) poignant observation that: "Loss of a loved person is one of the most intensely painful experiences any human being can suffer" (p. 7).

   Bowlby (1979, 1980) emphasizes that the crucial process of mourning generally takes place in the context of the family's characteristic attachment behavior toward the child. He contends that the family may either facilitate the expression of grief by responding sympathetically to the child's distress or adopt an inhibiting attitude that causes the child to suppress or avoid typical feelings of fear of abandonment, yearning, and anger. Bowlby found that a supportive and sympathetic attitude within the family may lead to a process of healthy mourning even in children as young as 2 years. The process consists of normative behavioral responses of anxiety and protest, despair, disorganization and detachment, and reorganization. By means of this process, the loss is gradually accepted by the child, whose capacity to form new attachment bonds is restored following a period of disorganization.

By contrast, in pathological mourning the child's unexpressed ambivalent feelings of yearning for, and anger with, the attachment figure are split off into segregated or dissociated systems of the personality and the loss may be disavowed. As a consequence and in the absence of a trusted substitute attachment figure, the child has little alternative but to move precipitately to a defensive condition of emotional detachment, thereby internalizing a representational model of attachment that is avoidant, ambivalent, or disorganized with respect to separation and loss. In such instances, the child's attachment behavioral system may either remain deactivated or become hyperactivated. Although expressed in different ways, the factor that these two main strategies have in common is that attachment-related information is being defensively and selectively excluded from consciousness (Bowlby, 1980, 1988).

In describing childhood pathological mourning, Bowlby (1979) makes the important point that his hypothesis is not confined to the actual death of, or separation from, the attachment figure. Indeed, he stresses that the child may experience separation and loss in numerous, less overt ways; for example, in the form of threats of abandonment, parental rejection, depression, neglect, and/or abuse as well as loss of love (Bowlby, 1979, 1988). Such a child's family situation may be said to consist of both dramatic trauma and cumulative developmental trauma. Bowlby emphasizes that the common factor in these various situations is loss by the child of a parent figure to love and to attach to. He contends that representational models shaped by childhood experiences of pathological mourning may be activated under conditions of separation and loss in adulthood, together with the expression of dysfunctional anger, shame, hatred, and violence (Bowlby, 1969, 1979, 1984, 1988). This assumption accords with my clinical experience and has been confirmed by adult attachment research (Mikulincer et al., 2002b; Simpson et al., 1992; Simpson et al., 1996).

As discussed in Chapter 6, Main, Kaplan, and Cassidy (1985) utilized the Adult Attachment Interview (George, Kaplan, & Main, 1985) in order to classify parental states of mind with respect to attachment and trauma. To briefly recap, using this research tool and Ainsworth et al.'s (1978) Strange Situation procedure, which observes and classifies the attachment status of children, Main (1991) found that the child's discrete pattern of attachment organization has, as its precursor, a characteristic pattern of caregiver–infant interaction and its own behavioral sequelae. Thus, as predicted 5 years previously, there was a significant match between the mother's and her child's attachment classifications. In the main, secure/autonomous mothers had infants who were securely attached; those with a dismissing state of mind had avoidant infants, while preoccupied mothers had ambivalent-resistant infants. There was a strong correlation between mothers whose discourse transcript in the AAI was classified as unresolved in respect of trauma and disorganized/disoriented infants. We will recall that the unresolved classification is made solely on the discussion of trauma, abuse, and loss experiences and is superimposed on one or other of the three main attachment classifications.

These findings indicate that secure, fearful, and traumatic states of mind are transmitted across generations via processes of interactive regulation, cross-modal attunement, and reflective functioning or mentalization. However, as previously noted, recent research with fathers reveals that attachment is "relationship specific," with the child's representational models of mother and father developing separately (Steele & Steele, 2008). Thus, a child may be securely attached or indeed disorganized with one parent, but not with the other. Nevertheless, there is broad agreement that malignant childhood events relevant to attachment such as separation, loss, and abuse may cause difficulty in integrating and organizing information, and that such difficulty may play a crucial role in the creation of security in adulthood.

Peterfreund (1983) suggests that different representational models are in operation during different activities and in different situations making predictive calculation and adaptive behavior possible. In advocating a "heuristic" as opposed to a "stereotypical" approach to the process of psychoanalytic psychotherapy, he stresses the significance of information processing and error-correcting feedback in this process, arguing that these are the means by which perceptually distorted representational models are modified, updated, and fine-tuned. Peterfreund's synthesizing approach reflects Bowlby's emphasis both on empirical observation of human relationships and the fact that many of the concepts underpinning attachment theory are derived from cognitive psychology and developmental psychology. Given this, attachment theory may be seen as acting as a bridge between cognitive science and psychoanalysis (Holmes, 1993).

In line with this thinking, my work with violent people in the criminal justice system was informed by findings from infant research, adult attachment research, traumatology, object relations theory, relational psychoanalysis, intersubjectivity, and neuroscience, particularly with respect to findings relating to affect regulation and the operation of the implicit memory system. These perspectives provided me with a particular way of listening to the offender's narrative and discrete discourse style and of understanding the clinical process (Slade, 1999). In accordance with this view, Stern (1998) argues that "search strategies" which explore the patient's past are an integral aspect of the therapeutic process, contending that "In good part, the treatment is the search" (p. 203). Similarly, Fosshage (2011) suggests that "The exploratory process itself contributes to new relational experience" (p. 68). As we have seen, in line with attachment theory, Stern

(1985, 1998) views psychopathology as deriving from an accumulation of maladaptive interactive patterns in childhood that result in character and personality types and disorders in adulthood.

THE OFFENDER: JOHN

Personal and Forensic History

John, the subject of this case study, has given his permission for this chapter to be published. Names have been changed, however, and personal circumstances disguised in order to protect identities. John was 48 years old at the time we met. He grew up in a large family, being one of eight children. He is the youngest of four brothers, one of whom was killed in a road traffic accident several years previously, and he has two older and two younger sisters. He spoke of his father as being "distant and always at work" and his mother as "anxious and over-protective." He recalled that she had played out an elaborate pretence with respect to his father's occupation by telling neighbors that he worked in a bank, whereas, in fact, he was a barman. John completed his secondary education at the age of 15, leaving school with no academic qualifications. By this time, he was misusing drugs and alcohol. He went on to develop a dependency on the latter. As a consequence of this problem, John's employment record is inconsistent and, in the main, comprised of manual and semi-skilled work.

John has had a series of unstable relationships with women characterized by violent, controlling behavior, possessiveness, and sexual jealousy on his part. Because of his problematic attitude to women, John consulted his general practitioner (GP) when aged 18. He was referred for psychiatric assessment, but not offered ongoing treatment. John married when aged 28, but insisted, "there never was a true love," adding, "I haven't wanted to commit myself." He avoided doing so in part by "always having relationships with two women at the same time." This situation obtained during the course of his 13-year-long marriage, which John described as an "on-off affair." He related how he would often pick fights with his wife to give himself an excuse to leave home and go on a drinking binge. The marriage was childless, but John has three children from a subsequent relationship, which, typically, was brief, intermittent, and volatile. He has had no contact with his children for several years and was unaware of their current whereabouts. At the time we met, John was largely estranged from his own family and not in an intimate relationship.

John has been involved in the criminal justice system for more than 30 years, appearing before the courts for the first time as a juvenile. Though he has convictions for traffic offenses and, when younger, burglary, the most prominent and consistent feature of his offending behavior is drink-related intimate violence. The latter commenced in adolescence and, as mentioned above, was the reason John was eventually referred for psychiatric assessment. He has convictions for grievous bodily harm, assault with intent, assaulting the police, possession of a firearm, and criminal damage. On one occasion he went to his ex-partner's home armed with an ax, which he used to break in to remonstrate with her for leaving him. John has been subject to a range of sentences including discharges, fines, probation, community service, and imprisonment. He has had numerous sojourns in rehabilitation units for his alcohol problem, but always returned to misusing drink. One of his brothers also has an alcohol problem, but John is the only member of the family to become embroiled with the law.

The index offense consisted of a serious assault on John's then partner, Sylvia. The couple had been in a relationship for 2 years, but lived separately. John came to suspect Sylvia of being sexually involved with someone else. He went to her home in a drunken state one evening and accused her of having sex with another man, calling her a "slag and a whore." When Sylvia denied John's accusation, he attacked her with his fists and feet in an uncontrollable rage, causing serious injury to her head and body, only desisting when finally she told him "what I wanted to hear." At court, the photographic evidence of Sylvia's injuries was said to be "horrific." John denied the offense when arrested, maintaining that Sylvia's injuries were self-inflicted. He was convicted following a jury trial and sentenced to 2½ years imprisonment.

First Contact and Initial Assessment

John's case was allocated to me when I transferred to the probation office in his home area. His reputation at the office was that of a perpetual client with whom everything had been tried. I wrote to John in prison to introduce myself as his new through care officer. In his reply, he alluded to the attack on Sylvia, saying: "It wasn't anger, it was alcohol talking. I'm not angry by nature." Though clearly John was distancing himself from his anger and violence in this statement, there was at least an implicit admission of his assault on Sylvia.

I met John for the first time during his temporary release from prison on home leave. He had managed to retain his local authority tenancy by subletting to a male alcoholic friend, but previously had lived alone. John was due to be released on parole a month later, and his period on license would run for 8 months. At this first meeting, I assessed John's attachment history, which included asking him about childhood experiences with respect to separation, loss, and abuse. He was clearly surprised and puzzled by the tenor of my questions as he had not been asked about such issues before. After initial hesitation, John spoke of having had frequent separations from his family from about age 5. These were the result of a series of operations for ENT problems necessitating his hospitalization. He recalled struggling with the nursing staff on one occasion as he fought to retain consciousness while being held down and given "gas." However, he did not believe that these experiences had had any adverse effect on him.

John's discourse style when discussing these experiences was brief and dismissive, indicating a deactivating attachment strategy with respect to these memories. The dismissive quality of his narrative together with his history of unstable intimate relationships and propensity for violence suggested the development of an avoidant/disorganized pattern of childhood attachment (Main, 1991; Main et al., 1985; Main & Weston, 1982). Given these clinical features, I held in mind the possibility that John might have responded to the enforced, multiple separations from his family by precipitately entering a state of emotional detachment (Bowlby, 1973, 1979). In reviewing studies linking insecurely attached children and subsequent criminal behavior, Fonagy et al. (1997) suggest that insecure attachment constitutes a distinct risk factor. Further, the authors argue that patterns of attachment operate as mechanisms of defense to help the child cope with idiosyncrasies of parental caregiving and that criminality involves disturbance of attachment processes. These findings accord with de Zulueta's (1993) proposal, based on Bowlby's (1984, 1988) thinking that "violence is attachment gone wrong" (p. 3).

It soon became clear that John's ideal view of himself was that of a passive, nonviolent man who, in his own words, "wouldn't hurt a fly." My tentative hypothesis at this point, in the context of his extensive history of violence towards women, was that John was carrying powerful, unprocessed emotional pain, that he was disowning feelings of anger, shame, and hatred and that, lacking the capacity to contain, regulate, and process such emotions, these built up in response to stressor events, generating intense internal conflict which eventually became overwhelming and compromised his tenuous capacity for mentalization (Fonagy, 1999c; Fonagy et al., 2004). At such times, John resorted to binge drinking. Under the disinhibiting effect of alcohol, it would seem that his dissociated emotional turmoil was unleashed and enacted in the form of a violent rage. This clinical picture indicated that John might be prone to experiencing a traumatic stress reaction and the reemergence of implicitly encoded childhood trauma when embroiled in an intense, emotionally-charged situation characterized by actual or expected separation and loss (de Zulueta, 1993; Herman, 1992; Lyons-Ruth & Jacobvitz, 1999; Meloy, 1992; Schacter, 1996; Schore, 1994; van der Kolk, 1989; West & George, 1999). From this perspective, traumatic affect is seen as having a disorganizing effect on mental functioning and being a significant motivating factor in the manifestation of psychopathology (Tyson & Tyson, 1990).

I harbored reservations about John's ability to engage in a therapeutic process. These misgivings centered on the fact that he was denying the violent assault on Sylvia and that his record of attending appointments when on license in the past had been far from exemplary. Further, as noted above, John was resistant to the idea that past experience might have a maladaptive effect on behavior in the present, specifically in relation to his alcohol misuse, as he had been told at a rehabilitation unit that "alcoholism is a disease." He therefore expressed a good deal of skepticism about the prospect of change, having passively accepted this fatalistic diagnosis. Nevertheless, I explained what our work together would involve, should he decide on this option, emphasizing the collaborative nature of the process. John responded by saying that he would "give it a go" as nothing else he had tried had been successful. Despite John's seemingly dismissing attachment state of mind, I felt that we had established a rapport and that the all-important "match" or "fit" prerequisite for therapeutic work to commence had emerged in this first meeting (Kantrowitz, 1995). John signed a standard medical consent form giving me permission to contact his GP in order to discuss any relevant issues.

Given the setting within which I then worked, my intervention with John would be brief and time-limited and, thus, speed in assessing the clinical issues was a major consideration. In fact, I had a total of 13 sessions with John; each session lasted a full hour. A follow-up meeting was held 6 months after his period on license had ended. I incorporated such meetings into my practice, as I saw these as serving a dual purpose of evaluating the effectiveness of my work and of providing the client with a sense of continuity and connection to a "secure base" (Bowlby, 1988), or at least to one experienced as secure-enough. In my experience, the availability of an ongoing link at this critical time helped to preclude the often noted, though anecdotal, phenomenon whereby the client reoffends towards the end of the supervisory period, seemingly in reaction to the impending loss of a relationship with an attachment figure that had become significant.

Therapeutic Intervention

The first meeting following John's release from prison was focused on helping him recognize and own disturbing thoughts and feelings. An example of this difficulty emerged when John spoke in mild terms about the friend whom he had allowed to stay at his home while he was in prison. John returned to find the place a complete tip and rent arrears of nearly $1,600 owed to the housing department. At first John spoke of feeling "a bit let down" and, later, when I questioned his passive response, of being "fucking angry," vacillating between these two attitudes. It seemed to me that John was quite confused as to how he actually felt about his friend and in two minds about how to respond, speaking in the same breath of going to reason with this person and of beating hell out of him!

This narrative appeared to provide a glimpse of the conflict and disorganization characterizing John's representational world of object relations or confused, unstable internal working models of attachment. On the one hand, he seemed to identify with the hurt, angry, disappointed child who had been let down and whose trust had been betrayed; on the other hand, to identify with a dismissing parent who deflected and perhaps even forbade the expression of difficult thoughts and painful feelings. This situation seemed to be recreated in the session in that John anxiously deflected any attempt on my part to connect with him on an emotional level. Indeed, I felt under immense pressure not to talk about meaningful issues and events, and I experienced a countertransferential sense of futility and despair.

It would have been all too easy to have succumbed to the sense of hopelessness that I was experiencing and thus to have given up on the attempt to engage John. Instead, I sought to understand his emotional state and subjective experience. In ways not too dissimilar to the stress-inducing aspect of the Strange Situation procedure (Ainsworth et al., 1978) and the Adult Attachment Interview (George et al., 1985), I viewed the emotionally heightened exchange with John as having activated an archaic representational model together with a habitual, procedural way of experiencing himself in relation to other people (Bowlby, 1969; Mikulincer et al., 2002b; Simpson et al., 1992; Simpson et al., 1996). As we have seen, such mental models take the form of nonverbal, nonconscious implicit/procedural memories. These emotional procedures were expressed in John's subtle behavioral performance, the observation of which provided a micro-behavioral basis for me to experience, share, and cross-modally match his affective state (Beebe et al., 1992; Beebe & Lachmann, 1992, 2002; Stern, 1985, 1998). In the light of recent neuroscience and developmental research, my emotional and psychophysical response to John may be conceptualized as the activation of the mirror neuron system at the level of implicit relational knowing (Bruschweiler-Stern et al., 2002; Gallese, 2009; Lyons-Ruth et al., 1998).

Despite the intensity of the interaction, my reading of John's overt behavior influenced me to stay in the affective moment, which I viewed as an unconscious communication of unmanageable feelings. I decided to share aspects of my countertransferential experience of being with him, wondering whether the powerful thoughts and feelings stimulated in me mirrored something of his own experience (Casement, 1990; Maroda, 1991). John confirmed that he had felt a mounting sense of anxiety, verging on panic, adding that he usually avoided talking about his feelings. Avoidance of this sort, particularly in men, may reflect the way in which gender, culture, and inner prohibition coalesce, resulting in a defensive splitting of thought from feeling—an enacted manifestation of the "unthought known" or of "unformulated experience" (Bollas, 1987; D. B. Stern, 1997). From a developmental/neurobiological perspective, such behavior may indicate a failure of parent-child interactive affect regulation and a concomitant incapacity to self-regulate emotional states when under stress (Beebe & Lachmann, 1992, 2002; Lyons-Ruth & Block, 1996; Schore, 1994). Research data suggests that in such instances, the lack of a contingent parental response to the child's attachment needs may, if characteristic of the relationship, come to be associated with negative affect and escalating arousal, leading to prolonged and severe states of withdrawal and the defensive exclusion of attachment cues. The internalization of such nonoptimal interactive patterns may interfere with the person's ability to regulate arousal. This may compromise the capacity to mentalize one's own and the other's emotional and intentional states of mind as well as the ability to stay attentive in order to process information in situations involving interpersonal stress (Beebe et al., 1992; Fonagy, 1999c; Fonagy & Target, 1996; Fonagy et al., 2004; Main et al. 1985). My capacity to mentalize John's states of mind and willingness to share my own thoughts and feelings appeared to enhance his mentalizing capacity in this particular therapeutic encounter (Diamond & Kernberg, 2008).

Disclosure of Childhood Trauma

Somewhat paradoxically, John appeared relieved by the dawning realization that inner emotions may be recognized, shared, and understood (Benjamin, 1995). Seemingly as a consequence of this intersubjective experience of interactive regulation, a more reflective mood and positive affective state prevailed. This exchange, in turn, appeared to evoke in John memories of a traumatic event that had taken place when he was 8 years old. Tentatively, John related how he and his then best friend, Ricky, had been playing near a fast-flowing river. John's memories of the event were somewhat vague and hazy, but he recalled that Ricky had slipped on the moss-covered embankment into the river and drowned. John came to believe that people suspected him of having pushed his friend into the river. Indeed, I found myself silently questioning whether John might have had a hand in Ricky's death. Again, I observed the nuances of his facial expressions, direction of gaze, vocal inflections, bodily orientation, and gesture when relating this traumatic event, as well as monitoring my own affective and bodily responses. I detected nothing in John's overt behavior at that time, or subsequently, to indicate that his narrative was anything other than authentic in regard to this matter. I therefore concluded that Ricky's death had, indeed, been a tragic accident.

In addition to feeling blamed and accused, John came to view himself as a "bad" person because his attempts to save Ricky had failed. John went on to speak of having confused and intangible memories of being in court in the aftermath of Ricky's death and of growing up feeling burdened by "guilt." The court in John's memory was probably that of the coroner who carried out the inquest into the circumstances of Ricky's death. It seemed likely that, in a similar way to those who live through a major disaster, John experienced a deep sense of guilt at having survived when Ricky had died (de Zulueta, 1993; Herman, 1992), and that this whole situation had been exacerbated by his having to appear at the coroner's court.

I wondered whether the trauma of Ricky's drowning had activated John's earlier trauma, that of being separated from his family and held down and "gassed" in hospital—drowning in gas, as it were. This observation seemed to resonate with John's subjective experience. He became deeply thoughtful and reflective, sitting in silence for a considerable time. He looked sad and forlorn, and his eyes brimmed with tears. When he surfaced from this pensive mood he appeared to recognize aspects of himself as if for the first time. He spoke about persistent feelings of sadness, anxiety, and watchfulness, and questioned whether these could be linked to his disturbing childhood experiences. It seemed that the recollection of these state-dependent memories had started the process of unlocking the affective components of John's unresolved trauma (Stern, 1985). Despite the similarity in our ages, my primary countertransference at this point was that of a benign, concerned parent seeking to understand and ameliorate a child's confused state and emotional distress.

Although the session had been challenging and intense, John seemed buoyed up and expressed the hope that ghosts could finally be laid to rest. His positive affective response and disclosure of unresolved childhood trauma suggested that a secure-enough therapeutic alliance had been speedily established. To my mind, my challenging yet contingent interaction with John managed to be neither avoidant nor enmeshed but midrange and thus engendered a sufficient sense of felt security for him to risk a somewhat new way of experiencing himself in interaction with me (Beebe et al., 2000). This, in turn, appeared to facilitate the process of exploring dissociated thoughts and feelings associated with his unresolved trauma. I would argue that the gradual modification of nonoptimal representational models initially hinges on such micro-processes of interactive regulation in the nonverbal, implicit/enactive domain, but that such interactions need then to be explored and elaborated over time in the verbal, explicit domain.

Repetition of the Trauma

During subsequent sessions, John and I tried to give meaning to what, in symbolic terms, he might be enacting unconsciously via his offending behavior. It seemed to me, at least in part, that he was reenacting a destructive and self-destructive pattern of behavior in identification with the "bad," traumatized 8-year-old child who had been unable to mourn Ricky's death, and who was left carrying a tremendous burden of shame and guilt. My tentative hypothesis was that an aspect of this reenactment involved John being drawn compulsively and repetitively to stand accused in the dock of a court, thereby reliving the trauma and, at the same time, confirming his negative core belief or implicitly encoded fantasy of himself as a bad, guilty person (van der Kolk, 1989). Moreover, I wondered whether the repetitive experience of being adjudged guilty and sentenced to a period of incarceration had the temporary effect of assuaging John's deep and pervasive sense of guilt and shame. This hypothesis rang true for John and became a "key therapeutic metaphor" in our work together (Stern, 1985). Further, the coconstruction of significant events in John's childhood seemed to go some way towards filling gaps in his personal history by beginning to provide his fragmented experience with coherent narrative meaning (Holmes, 1996; Main, 1991; Main et al., 1985; Roberts, 1999). John elaborated on these thoughts, saying that he felt safe and secure in prison, whereas on the outside he was continually assailed by feelings of panic, anxiety, and an impending sense of danger, as if something dreadful were about to happen. As discussed in Chapter 2, in phenomenological terms, it would seem that John's sense of "nameless dread" and "primitive agonies" linked to his unresolved trauma were experienced as "a fear of a breakdown that has already happened" but which has not been "experienced" and thus is prone to being repeated at an unconscious level of mental functioning (Bion, 1984; van der Kolk, 1989; Winnicott, 1974, p. 104).

Continuous Assessment and Ongoing Intervention

At this point in my work with John my assessment had crystallized. Keeping relevant research findings in mind, I based my assessment of John's psychopathological behavior on the theoretical premise that cognitive-affective states associated with his traumatic experiences had been subject to perceptual distortion, defensive exclusion, and selective inattention, becoming encapsulated in a segregated or dissociated, disorganized, and multiple representational model (Bowlby, 1980; Liotti, 1992, 1999; Main et al., 1985). In line with Herman (1992), I surmised that the lack of an appropriate response to John's trauma had left him with a pervasive sense of alienation and disconnection in his relationships. I concluded that the main therapeutic tasks were to facilitate a process of mourning by assisting him to make connections between dissociated thoughts and feelings associated with the traumatic events he had described (Bowlby, 1973, 1979, 1988; Spezzano, 1993), and to modify nonoptimal, implicit/procedural representational models (Bowlby, 1988; Fonagy, 1999b). This work had, of course, already commenced to some extent during the assessment process, reflecting Stern's (1998) contention, alluded to above, that the search process is, in itself, therapeutic.

By this stage, John seemed committed to working on these unresolved issues and he stuck doggedly to the task, appearing to have an active need to tell his story and create a coherent narrative. He admitted to being desperate for a drink after the previous session, but told me that instead he had made a conscious effort to think about what we had discussed. In line with Main's (1991) research into metacognitive monitoring, I had enjoined John in quite a directive way to bring focal attention to bear on what he was experiencing in any given moment and to develop a dialogue with himself. This involved the employment of the consciousness system—using thought and his mind in a new and novel way so as to contain, explore, and assimilate raw psychic pain, and of stepping outside of himself in order to closely observe and monitor his thoughts, feelings, and behavior. Following Fonagy et al.'s (1997) development of Main's (1991) research on metacognitive monitoring, these therapeutic strategies were designed to enhance John's reflective functioning, thereby increasing his capacity to contemplate and understand (mentalize) both his own and others' emotional and intentional states in a coherent way. The overarching therapeutic goal was to assist John better to regulate his emotional anguish and visceral-somatic bodily states without becoming overwhelmed to the extent that he misused alcohol as a maladaptive form of self-regulation with the attendant risk of his violently enacting his unresolved trauma in his intimate relationships. As we have seen, an important aspect of the therapeutic process involved the evocation of key traumatic experiences encoded and stored in the systems of implicit/procedural memory, as conceptualized as self–other representational models, and of making these models consciously available for dyadic regulation and ideational elaboration (Bowlby, 1988; Fonagy, 1999b; Fonagy & Target, 1998; Schore, 1994; Spezzano, 1993; Stern, 1985).

As the weeks went by, John reported that he was keeping his drinking within sensible limits and had tidied up and decorated his flat. He looked healthier with clear eyes and a better color to his complexion, and he seemed more at ease with himself. The impression of John being less anxious and conflicted was quite pronounced and he related how, prior to this improvement, the mere act of leaving home to catch a bus to the town center would engender anxiety, panic, and a sense of danger which he would quell with drink. John also noted changes in the way he was responding to others and they to him, acknowledging that in the past he would often deal with his aggressive impulses by provoking aggression in others, thereby giving himself a ready excuse to be violent and resort to alcohol misuse. He went on to recall feeling acutely persecuted and paranoid as a child following Ricky's death, saying that he lived in a state of fear and anxiety about the prospect of being attacked by Ricky's family because "they thought I'd killed Ricky."

Such fears may well have been realistic but, in my opinion, were also likely to have been fueled by fantasies of retaliation which flourished in the absence of an affectively attuned, containing parental response in a family system that was cumulatively traumatizing. It seemed to me that John's later violent behavior reflected research by Greenberg, Speltz, and DeKlyen

(1993) and Solomon et al. (1995) which reveal that disorganized children develop representational models characterized by chaos, fear, helplessness, and hostility. Having no coherent strategy to deal with experiences of separation and loss, the child relates to others in a coercive and controlling way. As noted above, Main et al.'s (1985) longitudinal research supports the proposition that representational models developed in childhood tend to persist over time. Moreover, as we have seen, neuroscience research indicates that such implicitly encoded models may be activated in situations that reprise the original trauma, leading to the reemergence of childhood trauma and an unregulated release of negative neurochemicals, thereby increasing the risk of the traumatic experience being violently enacted in the person's current intimate relationship (Perry et al., 1995; Schacter, 1999; Siegal et al., 1999; van der Kolk, 1989, 1994).

Certainly, lack of trust and controlling behavior became major issues for John as he developed into adolescence and adulthood, together with clinical issues of affect regulation, mentalization, autonomy, dependence, intimacy, attachment, separation, and loss. He spoke of his surprise at being able to talk to me about personal and painful matters, and he went on to risk rejection by asking if he could contact me after his parole license had ended, should a crisis arise. I agreed to this request, viewing it in terms of an adult relational need rather than the gratification of an infantile desire (Mitchell, 1993). Also, as previously mentioned, I told John that I would like to have a follow-up meeting with him in any event. This exchange seemed to indicate that he was internalizing his relationship with me in the form of a secure-enough base from which to explore and elaborate his traumatic experiences, but that he still needed to feel there would be the opportunity for direct proximity-seeking should something untoward occur (Bowlby, 1980, 1988). I was encouraged by the fact that John was beginning to make links between his traumatic childhood experiences and the anxiety, panic, and aggression manifested in later years. He seemed increasingly able to appraise the significance and meaning of these distressing affects (Schore, 1994), and to use the working alliance or developing attachment relationship to negotiate and reorganize unresolved clinical issues (Stern, 1985).

Childhood Amnesia/Dissociation

Some confirmation of this progress emerged towards the end of the session. John related that when aged 28 and on the point of marrying, "my mother told me I'd changed when I was 8." Apparently, she had offered no explanation as to why this should have happened. Significantly, John went on to say that to this day no one in his family has ever alluded to Ricky's death, adding that he had suffered "amnesia" between the ages of 8 and 11. It seemed likely that, lacking the emotional and cognitive capacities to assimilate the traumatic event unaided, John's only option was to resort to a form of dissociation, that is, an altered, detached state of consciousness (de Zulueta, 1993; Herman, 1992). For whatever reason, it would appear that John's parents were insensitive to his needs and unable to help him deal with the aftermath of the tragedy, perhaps misguidedly believing that ignoring the event was for the best. Indeed, there was nothing to suggest they were intentionally cruel or malign, but that for reasons stemming from their own attachment histories, they were defensively excluding from consciousness John's attachment needs as a means of avoiding vicarious distress (Lyons-Ruth & Block, 1996; Main et al., 1985).

The information provided by John, when listened to with relevant research findings in mind, led me to tentatively surmise that his parents had been unable to respond to his distress because of the fear this evoked in themselves (Lyons-Ruth & Jacobovitz, 1999; Lyons-Ruth et al., 2005; Schore, 1994). In this event, it seemed likely that John came to perceive his parents' dismissing, nonreflective response to his fear as both frightening and frightened and thus to experience his own state of arousal as a danger signal for abandonment (Main & Hesse, 1990). In consequence of the family's disorganized caregiving-attachment system and the fear and insecurity to which this relational matrix gave rise, it would appear that John's attentional strategies were compromised and that he developed an exquisite vulnerability to trauma and dissociation (Liotti, 1992, 1999; Lyons-Ruth & Jacobovitz, 1999). His subsequent behavior suggests that he adapted to this unhappy situation by inhibiting his mentalizing capacity, becoming increasingly emotionally detached from his parents as well as from aspects of his own subjective experience, particularly affective states of anxiety, fear, shame, and rage (Fonagy, 1999c; Fonagy et al., 2004). Thus, although John's mother was physically present, she appears to have been inaccessible psychologically and emotionally and, therefore, unavailable to help John develop the capacities to regulate, reflect upon, and process negative affect and traumatic states of mind. His subsequent misuse of addictive substances may be seen as having its etiology in these very incapacities with first drugs and then alcohol being used to suppress dreaded psychobiological states and hence restore a semblance of affect regulation (Schore, 1994). In this context, it would seem reasonable to hypothesize that John's childhood attachment to his parents was characterized by what Settlage et al. (1990) and Schore (1994) term "proximal separations."

Discussion

John's clinical material brought to mind research that addresses the etiology of cognitive-affective disturbance in children. I have outlined some of this data in previous chapters, but in the context of this case study and John's experience of both dramatic and cumulative developmental trauma, this may be worth reiterating as these findings would seem to be particularly relevant to the clinical features of this case.

For example, Solomon et al. (1995) have shown how the disorganized child resorts to controlling, aggressive behavior in the absence of a coherent strategy to cope with the trauma of separation and loss. Liotti (1992), following Main (1991), posits a connection between disorganized/disoriented attachment and dissociative disorders. As we have seen, according to Liotti's hypothesis, the child's disorganized/disoriented attachment behavior corresponds to the construction of an internal working model of self and attachment figure that is multiple and incoherent, as opposed to singular and coherent. Liotti (1992) suggests that a multiple internal working model of this kind may predispose the child to enter a state of dissociation in the face of further traumatic experiences. Similarly, Davies and Frawley (1994), in their work with adult survivors of childhood sexual abuse, view dissociation as existing on a continuum with multiple personality disorder or dissociative identity disorder (MPD/DID) representing the most extreme form of mental defense against severe, protracted trauma. This opinion is shared by Mollon (1996) who questions whether MPD/DID should be conceptualized as part of a broad grouping of trauma-based psychiatric disorders or as a unique form of personality organization deriving from dissociative and post-traumatic factors.

From a social constructionist perspective, D. B. Stern (1997) views cognition as an amalgam of thought and feeling and an integral aspect of a continuous phenomenological process operating within the interpersonal field. Under optimal conditions, this process functions to organize, structure, and unify subjective experience, thereby providing the individual with a sense of coherence and meaning. However, Stern argues that experience may be split for defensive reasons in reaction to trauma and result in the isolation of emotion from mentation. Van der Kolk & Fisler (1995) found that, in effect, the traumatized subject is left in a state of "speechless terror." Lacking the words to describe the traumatic event and construct a coherent personal narrative, the individual experiences great difficulty in regulating internal states. Moreover, the authors' findings show that subjects traumatized in childhood experience more pervasive biological dysregulation than those first traumatized in adulthood. In both instances, however, the traumatic incident is initially "remembered" in the form of fragmented somatosensory experiences (van der Kolk, 1994). Similarly, McDougall (1985, 1989) argues that cumulative trauma consequent on a mother's insensitive way of handling and interacting with her infant may, during the course of development, lead to a split between word-presentations and affect-laden experiences. McDougall (1985, 1989) adopts Nemiah's (1978) and Sifneos' (1973) concept of alexithymia, that is the inability to recognize and describe discrete emotional states. She postulates that affective reactions associated with the traumatizing caregiving process are either avoided or rapidly ejected from consciousness. As a result of this developmental failure, the individual may be susceptible to psychosomatic symptoms in later life.

As outlined in Chapter 6, Fonagy et al. (1997, 2004) posit that the child's capacity to explore the mind of the other and develop as a thinking and feeling being arises within the matrix of a secure attachment relationship. Insecurity of attachment, on the other hand, undermines the child's capacity to reflect on and integrate mental experience. The authors argue that such individuals lack insight into the representational basis of human interaction and intentionality. This being so, they resort to concrete solutions to intrapsychic and interpersonal problems, attempting to control their subjective states and self-cohesion through physical experiences such as substance misuse, physical violence, and crime.

Van der Kolk (1989), in reviewing studies pointing to the underlying physiology of attachment, posits that endorphin releasers are laid down in the early months of life within the context of attachment to caregivers with different styles of caregiving. He concludes that affectively intense experiences are accompanied by the release of these neurochemicals and that this psychobiological process comes to be associated both to states of security and trauma. With these findings in mind, Mitchell (2000) comments on the seemingly addictive propensity to repeatedly forge intimate adult relationships redolent of ties to early objects, even when these are traumatic. He suggests that such behavior may reflect neurochemical, as well as psychological and emotional derivatives.

Much of the aforementioned theory and research is derived from Bowlby (1988), who presented a paper in 1979 entitled "On Knowing What You Are not Supposed to Know and Feeling What You Are not Supposed to Feel." Here, Bowlby cites findings by Cain and Fast (1972) to show how distorted communications between parent and child, which disconfirms the child's thoughts and feelings of real events, may engender intense guilt. Cognitive dissonance or intrapsychic conflict of this kind may lead the child to develop a chronic distrust of other people and of his or her own senses, together with a tendency to find everything unreal.

The response of John's parents (though he spoke only of his mother in this context) would seem to suggest that emotional states were characteristically dismissed and deflected. Moreover, as we have learned from John, his mother appears to have entered prolonged periods of denial during his childhood, seemingly prompted by feelings of shame and social embarrassment as evinced by her refusal to openly acknowledge the reality of her husband's actual employment status. As noted above, research has demonstrated a significant link between such parental characteristics, in terms of a dismissing discourse style on the one hand and insecure-avoidant attachment behavior in children on the other (Main, 1991; Main et al., 1985; Main & Weston, 1982). Further, as previously pointed out, children with an avoidant pattern of attachment have been found to show a marked lack of empathy towards peers in distress. Indeed, Main and Weston (1982) observed a distinct tendency in such insecurely attached children to behave in an aggressive and hostile way, as did Grossman and Grossman (1991). In John's case, as with so many men who suffer unresolved childhood trauma, substance misuse and violent behavior followed. The links between these factors were, again, highly reminiscent of the work on trauma by de Zulueta (1993) and Herman (1992). They also accord with findings cited by West and George (1999). These show that male perpetrators of adult relational violence report a high incidence of childhood histories of severe abuse and trauma (Downey et al., 1997; Herman & van der Kolk, 1987; Kalmuss, 1984).

Later Sessions

Session 8: Gender Identity

During the eighth meeting with John issues surrounding sexuality and gender emerged. Given the avoidant/disorganized attachment behavior characterizing John's adult intimate relationships, I silently questioned the security of his masculine identity. Despite being a stocky, powerfully built and somewhat gruff and macho man, John was sporting a ponytail hairstyle. Moreover, as already noted, he generally adopted a passive, non-aggressive stance, seemingly disowning authentic thoughts and feelings in a way reminiscent of Winnicott's (1988) concept of the false self. John's style of relating at this point elicited feelings within me of inauthenticity and emotional disconnection. Thus prompted, I asked myself whether he might be employing a feminine identification in his interpersonal relationships as a defense against being overwhelmed by anger and rage deriving from archaic ambivalent feelings of separation from and engulfment by the symbiotic mother (Khan, 1979; Mahler et al., 1985; Stoller, 1986; Stubrin, 1994).

On discussing the way in which men and women may incorporate both masculine and feminine attributes, John's emotional and behavioral responses were initially averse. His reaction put me in mind of the fact that heterosexual men not infrequently form temporary homosexual liaisons when imprisoned for any length of time. On discussing this delicate subject, I keenly observed John's behavior for any signs of intrusiveness or persecution as I sought to establish a sense of emotional connection or intersubjective relatedness with him (Stern, 1985, 1998). Again, I felt rather parental in the countertransference as though fulfilling functions that were containing emotionally as well as informative on a cognitive level. The relational aspect of the therapeutic process, and the salience of interactive regulation, would seem to confirm the importance of utilizing a developmental model in clinical work with offenders, given the high incidence of unresolved childhood trauma in the offender population.

Following these exchanges, John was able to elaborate on the experiences he had had while in prison. More generally, we explored how heterosexual men with a confused sense of gender identity may manifest homosexual panic and deal with feelings of shame and anger by denying aspects of their sexuality that create anxiety and, instead, project these into others by means of projective identification. A dialogue developed exploring the way in which defensive behavior of this kind, allied to a morbid fear of the other, may act as a touchstone for violence that targets minority groups; for example, "gay bashing" and racist attacks. Although the latter appeared not to be features of John's pattern of offending behavior, this discussion seemed further to enhance his reflective functioning or mentalizing capacity. He appeared more able gradually to recognize others as separate from himself and as having distinct feelings, intentions and desires (Fonagy et al., 1997, 2004).

Session 9: Relapse and Transference Issues

Before the ninth session, John attended the funeral of a family friend. During this session, John volunteered the information that he had consumed about six pints of beer at the wake. We discussed this in the context of what the death of his friend had evoked in John. He said that his predominant feelings were of anxiety and guilt. John linked these feelings directly to a fearful anticipation that I would "misjudge" him for drinking. I wondered whether this dynamic again constituted a transference reenactment connected with John's childhood trauma, particularly the unmourned loss of Ricky. At that time, whether in reality or in fantasy, John did indeed feel misjudged and blamed for Ricky's death. Further, as we have seen, it would appear that his parents' response lacked empathy and was dismissive of his emotional pain and distress. On an unconscious level, therefore, John may well have been expecting a similar response from me, as it would seem that I was being attributed an archaic parental role in the transference (Sandler & Sandler, 1998). His relapse provided the opportunity to explore some of these issues in that it enabled him to re-experience his traumatic attachment to a dismissing, emotionally unavailable parent in a way that was bearable (Holmes, 1996). My task at such times was to survive John's omnipotent destructive fantasies without collapsing or retaliating (Winnicott, 1988). This "holding" response appeared to help John recognize my existence as a separate person available to be used and related to intersubjectively (Benjamin, 1995). Moreover, by relating to John in this unfamiliar way, I became a new developmental object, different from the original pathogenic object that he expected to encounter in transferential reenactments (Fonagy, 1998; Hurry, 1998; Schore, 1994). It may also be accepted that the therapeutic relationship was providing John with a "corrective emotional experience" (Alexander & French, 1946).

Session 10: The Etiology of John's Violent Behavior

John opened the 10th session by saying he felt on an "even keel," adding that he was continuing to spend a good deal of time thinking about past experiences as well as monitoring his thoughts and feelings in the here-and-now, particularly when in an emotionally disturbed mood. At such times, in line with my suggestion, he would try to trace the immediate trigger of the affective distress and then make links between the past and the present. The therapeutic purpose of setting John this "homework" was to encourage him to stay with the dreaded lived experience long enough to reflect on and attempt to self-regulate primitive, unintegrated affective states, and to recognize when an archaic representational model had been activated, leading him to expect some dreaded outcome. These problematic experiences would then be brought to sessions for collaborative exploration and coconstruction of their etiology and meaning. My expectation was that this therapeutic intervention would gradually assist John to develop the capacity to elaborate and transform disturbing somatic experiences into a coherent narrative (Schore, 1994; Spezzano, 1993; Stern, 1998). With regard to this process, Schore (1994) emphasizes that the therapist's own tolerance of affects will critically determine the range and types of emotion that may be explored or disavowed in the transference–countertransference relationship. It may be accepted that this consideration is of particular relevance in a forensic setting because the practitioner is often starkly confronted with the bleaker aspects of human experience and the darker side of human behavior. However, I would suggest that this consideration may pertain equally in private practice with non-forensic patients.

The current session focused in a direct way on John's violence to women. This issue had been a delicate subject up until this point because his violent behavior, especially in regard to women, jarred with his ideal self, leaving him feeling deeply shamed. At our first meeting John had displayed a pronounced tendency to minimize his culpability and blame Sylvia. Indeed, we will recall that he had completely denied the offense initially and was convicted following a jury trial. John's capacity for denial brought to mind his mother who, as we have seen, appeared to have deployed the self-same defense mechanism with equal conviction. In this context, I have learned from hard experience that working precipitately with denial is clinically sterile and counterproductive, generating intense mutual feelings of frustration and rage in the participants as early parent–child roles and patterns of interaction get reenacted in the transference–countertransference matrix. Fortunately, by this stage in my relationship with John, a secure enough working alliance had been forged, and thus the time seemed ripe for us to explore this form of defensive behavior. As we did so, John's dissociated affect of shame and anger became increasingly available for interactive regulation. This process facilitated his gradual acceptance and active responsibility for his violent behavior, an enhancement in his ability to empathize with Sylvia, and an acknowledgment that her perspective may have differed markedly from his own.

My thinking with respect to John's violence was that states of anger, hate, rage, and shame as well as pining for the lost object had been dissociated as a child, primarily in relation to his mother. This adaptive defense was needed because separations from her and the family had been managed insensitively as had the later trauma in respect of Ricky, reflecting the family's disorganized caregiving–attachment system (Lyons-Ruth & Block, 1996; Lyons-Ruth & Jacobovitz, 1999). As noted above, the effects of these events and relational patterns tend to become frozen in time (Herman, 1992), being preserved and represented internally as nonreflective, nonverbal procedural memories in the form of presymbolic interaction structures and representational models. It would seem that these unmodified mental models were, in turn, activated and expressed in violent behavioral enactments in John's relationships, particularly at times of intense interpersonal stress (Beebe et al., 1992; Bowlby, 1969; Fonagy et al., 1997, 2004; Main et al., 1985; Mikulincer et al., 2002b; Schore, 1994; Simpson et al., 1992; Simpson et al., 1996; Stern, 1985, 1998; West & George, 1999). Such repetitive reenactments of his unresolved trauma were supported by neurochemical as well as psychological derivatives (Mancia, 2006; Mitchell, 2000; Perry et al., 1995; Siegal, 2001; van der Kolk, 1994). This hypothesis received some confirmation when John went on to speak of becoming angry with a man who had recently battered his wife. On discussing the incident, it became clear that much of the anger generated in John was not solely because of the man's physical abuse of the woman. His feelings were also inflamed because this person had subsequently flatly denied that the assault had taken place, even though all his acquaintances knew full well that it had.

This scenario appeared to have powerful associations and resonances with John's childhood, in that in a similar way everyone had known that Ricky had drowned. As we have seen, despite the reality of this traumatic event, John's emotional and cognitive experience had been denied or, at best, unacknowledged, with Ricky's death becoming, in effect, a well kept "family secret" (Pincus & Dare, 1990). Thus, John's capacity for metacognitive monitoring or mentalization was fatally compromised since the information he was receiving about the traumatic event was contradictory and distorted. This, in turn, seems to have led to the development of a multiple, incoherent representational model with respect to his attachment to his mother, and a concomitant state of disorganization and dissociation, together with the implicit expectation that his attachment figure would abandon him (Liotti, 1992; Main, 1991).

As Solomon and George (1996) and Solomon et al. (1995) found, disorganized attachment is characterized by controlling behavior toward the attachment figure in the context of the child feeling frightened, abandoned, helpless, and vulnerable. This fraught situation is likely to have been exacerbated in John's case by the separations he had experienced at a younger age when hospitalized and subjected to surgical intervention. The clinical evidence in the here-and-now attested to these factors having contributed to the development of a predominantly avoidant pattern of attachment organization which, in line with Fonagy et al. (1997), I viewed as an adaptive defense mustered in the face of unattuned caregiving. Moreover, the overall clinical picture suggested that insecurity stemming from separation anxiety had interfered with John's capacity to differentiate himself psychologically from his attachment figure and, thereby, attain a state of "mature dependence" (Fairbairn, 1996). In this context, it is of interest to note that West and George (1999) suggest that psychological merging may explain the conflict between engulfment and abandonment that appears to be so characteristic of the physically abusive male. The volatile shifts between such states of mind would again suggest the development of disorganized/disoriented attachment in a context of unresolved trauma (Liotti, 1992; Main & Hesse, 1990).

As we have seen, Bowlby (1973) emphasizes that anger with an attachment figure who fails to provide the expected comfort at times of stress is a normal and integral aspect of the attachment system. It would appear that this safety valve was not available to John because he lacked both external and internal permission to experience disturbing negative affect (Spezzano, 1993). He had little option, therefore, but to develop a defensive organization against anger and rage, in part, identifying with the dismissing, non-reflective qualities and characteristics of his relationship with his mother as a way of defending against feelings of guilt and anxiety (Ferenczi, 1933; Fonagy et al., 1997; A. Freud, 1968). When these mental defenses were overwhelmed in his adult relationships because of actual or predicted abandonment, a disorganized, multiple representational model was activated, together with the reemergence of his childhood trauma, which was enacted with the violent, destructive force of an adult (Bowlby, 1969; Mikulincer et al., 2002b; Simpson et al., 1992; Simpson et al., 1996). From the perspective of Liotti's (1999) motivational conceptual framework, John habitually "chose" to inhibit the attachment motivational system and, instead, to activate the "agonistic" motivational system, characterized by aggression and rage, in order to avoid experiencing dissociation and unresolved attachment trauma.

In the latest incident of this repetitive pattern, this internal dynamic was externalized, being displaced or redirected from John's original primary attachment figure (his mother) and projected into Sylvia who, at the point of the break-up of their relationship, he perceived as untrustworthy, rejecting, and abandoning. Indeed, John's "theory of mind" appears to have led him to expect betrayal and shame at the hands of Sylvia (Fonagy et al., 1997; Schore, 1994; West & George, 1999). Thus, she became a vehicle for his intolerable and persecutory self-states, that is, for the internalized aspects of his relationship with his mother that he experienced as alien, frightening, and unmanageable (Fonagy, 1999c; Fonagy et al., 2004). Further, aggression, rather than love, seems to have become an emotionally "rewarding" way for John to express his ambivalent world of object relations (Dicks, 1993).

Fear of abandonment, then, seems to have been the primary affect that led to the sudden activation of John's attachment system and maladaptive representational model of the relationship with his mother. As already noted, a salient feature of this mental model was John's expectation that his primary attachment figure would not be available or accessible at times of affective stress to provide comfort and protection (Bowlby, 1969; Schore, 1994; West & George, 1999). The clinical evidence, combined with John's forensic history, indicated that his mentalizing capacity was prone to becoming compromised and disorganized by intense separation anxiety and dysregulated fear, shame, hatred, and rage when he felt threatened by the loss of a female partner with whom he had formed an intimate attachment.

The theoretical model of male violence proposed here converges with that delineated by West and George (1999). These authors contend that intimate adult relational violence is rooted in attachment disorganization, viewing this pattern as inextricably linked to unresolved trauma and to a segregated representational system characterized by dysregulated affect and pathological mourning. West and George (1999) suggest that the perpetrator's defensive and tightly controlled regulation of his attachment system breaks down at the moment of the assault as a consequence of his becoming flooded with negative affect and distorted perceptions deriving from his personal trauma.

With regard to the index offense, the significance for John of Sylvia's perceived sexual infidelity lay, in part, in the fact that it represented her independence of mind and psychological separateness. In my opinion, any move by her towards a separate, independent existence would have conflicted with the explicit and implicit role expectations that John had brought to the relationship, being construed as a threat to his sense of security (Dicks, 1993). Thus, John's violence was, in part, a frantic attempt to control Sylvia in order to ensure her continued availability, both to protect him against infantile loneliness and immature dependence (Dicks, 1993; Fairbairn, 1996), and to carry the alien, persecutory parts of himself (Fonagy, 1999c; Fonagy et al., 2004). The thought of abandonment by Sylvia instilled terror in John because loss was experienced as a retraumatization and, therefore, as a threat to the coherence and stability of his very sense of self (de Zulueta, 1993; Fonagy, 1999c; Herman, 1992).

I was struck, moreover, by the fact that John's vicious assault on Sylvia had been triggered at the very point that she denied having sexually betrayed him and that John continued to beat her mercilessly until she told him the "truth." Again, I silently wondered to what extent this ghastly episode was a recreation in the present of unresolved aspects of John's childhood relationship with his mother who, throughout his life, adamantly denied and invalidated the reality of his traumatic experience (van der Kolk, 1989, 1994). Thus, it would appear that John's violence not only had the effect of making him feel coherent and real, but also of eliciting the response from Sylvia he so desperately needed to hear—a voice that validated the "truth" of his subjective experience (Fonagy, 1999c). Clearly, John's violent behavior could easily have escalated out of control and led to a charge of murder or manslaughter, as in the case of so many other insecurely attached men who had responded with extreme violence when their female partners had ended the relationship. Sharing these thoughts with John seemed to have a sobering effect on him and again engendered a state of deep, prolonged and silent reflection.

Session 12: Indications of Change

At the twelfth session, John announced with great confidence that he no longer thought of himself as an alcoholic. I was surprised to see that he had had his hair cut short. I silently wondered whether this dramatic change in his personal appearance was emblematic of a firmer sense of masculine identity together with a concomitant lessening of his need to defend against feelings of anger and aggression. In terms of Mahler et al.'s (1985) process of separation–individuation, I asked myself whether John's apparent sense of a more secure male identity indicated the achievement of a higher level of psychological differentiation from the internalized symbiotic mother.

Be this as it may, John again spoke of feeling more at peace with himself, seeing this as manifested in his ability to entertain more positive thoughts and feelings about himself and others, and by the fact that he had effected a reconciliation of sorts with his family and had got himself a job. He then drew a creative analogy with a childhood situation, telling me that he had underachieved educationally because he had gone deaf in one ear as a result of his ENT problems. Having been seated at the rear of the classroom, John had been unable to hear with clarity what the teacher was saying, and his schoolwork suffered accordingly. Once this problem had been identified, John was brought forward to a front row desk and subsequently came top of the class. With a twinkle in his eye, John said that now the problem of his unresolved trauma had been recognized he could move to the top of the class in terms of his emotional and psychological development.

Though clearly there were elements of affectionate teasing and idealization in this comment, it seemed to me that his narrative competence had markedly improved in that he now appeared able to speak in a coherent, concise, and plausible way about painful childhood events. This newfound autobiographical capacity seemed to indicate that John had begun to mourn and, thereby, integrate previously unassimilated traumatic experiences (Holmes, 1996), and thus was developing a sense of "earned security" (Hesse, 1999). Thus, from an attachment theory perspective, the positive therapeutic change reported by John and observed by me indicated that maladaptive representational models of himself in relation to others, as well as to the traumatic event of Ricky's death, had begun to be modified and updated. In addition to the improvement in John's narrative intelligibility, change was manifested in his enhanced sense of felt security and reflective capacity.

The Final Session

At the final meeting, John reiterated his belief that a "weight" had been lifted from him. Specifically, he spoke of no longer feeling persistently anxious, paranoid, and persecuted or of experiencing a deep and pervasive sense of dread, sadness, and depression. The abatement of these symptoms indicated that an enhancement had occurred in his capacity to use thought and language to transform dysregulated somatic experiences into subjective states of consciousness that could be thought about and reflected upon (Schore, 1994). John was still in employment and managing his drinking. I confirmed that I would contact him in 6 months time and that he could telephone me in between times should the need arise. He expressed a sense of loss and frustration at not having had this kind of help years ago. He also questioned why, in more than 30 years of being involved in the criminal justice system, no one had thought to talk with him about his early traumatic experiences, saying he felt that much of his life had been "wasted" as a result. This situation emphasizes again the importance of obtaining relevant information about the client's formative experiences and developmental history as part of a process of effective assessment, particularly in brief, time-limited work. I thought that John's feelings of loss were being conflated with sadness at the ending of our relationship. I acknowledged the paradox he seemed to be highlighting—that even positive change involves loss of one form or another. On a positive note, I concluded that John's newfound ability to express attachment-related affective experiences was, in itself, evidence of the progress he had accomplished during the past 8 months.

The Therapeutic Process

The progress made by John was dependent on his ability to gradually organize and integrate error-correcting information received as an ongoing aspect of the therapeutic process (Bowlby, 1980, 1988; Main et al., 1985; Peterfreund, 1983). A significant aspect of the process of change was John's enhanced capacity to mentalize his own and others psychological states (Bateman & Fonagy, 2004; Diamond & Kernberg, 2008).

Following Tronick et al. (1978), I viewed this process as consisting, in significant degree, of the moment-to-moment micro-repair of attunement or misaligned interaction—an intersubjective process operating at the level of implicit relational knowing (Bruschweiler-Stern et al., 2002; Lyons-Ruth et al., 1998; Stern et al., 1998a, 1998b).

This process was informed by the tracking and matching of subtle and dramatic shifts in John's mood-state as he narrated his story (Schore, 1994). This interactive process led, in turn, to the recognition of a shared subjective reality (Fonagy, 1998). By these means, my facilitating behaviors combined with John's capacity for attachment. Though operating largely out of conscious awareness, this mutual, reciprocal process permitted the development of a working alliance or attachment relationship (Schore, 1994) that was secure enough to facilitate a collaborative exploration of painful, unresolved clinical issues linked to his misuse of alcohol and violent offending behavior. As we have seen, key aspects of this intersubjective and reparative process were the interactive regulation of dreaded states charged with intense negative affect (Schore, 1994) and the coconstruction of a coherent narrative (Holmes, 1996). Thus, I became a new developmental object, the relationship with whom provided a corrective emotional experience by disconfirming John's pathogenic transference expectations as stored in implicit/procedural representational models. This overall process also enhanced John's mentalizing capacity (Alexander & French, 1946; Fonagy, 1998, 1999b; Hurry, 1998; Schore, 1994). Moreover, following Schore (1994), I assumed that the interactive process involved in regulating John's emotional states had facilitated a connection between his nonverbal and verbal representational domains, resulting in the transfer of implicit information in the right brain to declarative systems in the left hemisphere.

As agreed, I contacted John for a follow-up discussion 6 months later. His progress had been sustained; he was still in work, keeping his consumption of alcohol within sensible limits, and had not re-offended. Prior to the ending of John's period on license, I had liaised with his GP who, in consultation with John, agreed to refer him to the local mental health resource center. John attended an assessment session there with a clinical psychologist. It was mutually agreed that no further work was needed at that stage.

CONCLUSION

Given the wide incidence of intimate violence in Western society, understanding the clinical issues underlying such behavior and developing an effective therapeutic model to address the problem is a pressing social concern. An important consideration in this context is the traumatic effect on children who repeatedly witness scenes of abusive male violence in the home (Cawson et al., 2000; Lyons-Ruth & Jacobvitz, 2008; Werkerle & Wolfe, 1999). I would argue that an integrated relational model, centered on attachment theory and research as outlined in this study, has a significant contribution to make in this area of work.

With regard to my brief intervention with John, it remains to be seen whether this will prove to be effective in the long term. I was keenly aware that far more could have been achieved therapeutically, not least on consolidating the progress he had made in regulating his somatic and affective states without resorting to alcohol misuse. This, however, was not a viable option, given the constraints of time and resources obtaining within the probation service and the limited period of his parole license. Nevertheless, I consider that the brief, time-limited work undertaken with John helped modify his nonoptimal representational models and to resolve, in some degree, the childhood trauma underlying his adult violent offending behavior. This, in turn, enhanced his sense of security and capacity for narrative competence and mentalization, thereby strengthening his ability to activate second-order representational models and consider other peoples' perspectives (Fonagy, 1999b). These interlinking positive therapeutic changes should fuel the potential for further personal growth and so provide John with a greater ability to empathize with others and make more reasoned choices in the future (Fonagy & Target, 1998; Holmes, 1996). That said, John had not developed an intimate relationship during the period that we were working together. Any progress he had made would, in my opinion, be sorely tested in such a relationship. Despite his evident progress, I would harbor grave concerns for the safety of any future female partner, particularly in a context of separation and loss.

More generally, I consider that this case study illustrates that it is not the traumatic childhood event in and of itself that is salient in personality development and adult psychopathology, but rather the characteristic caregiving-attachment system within which the child experiences the trauma. As previously described, research has demonstrated that the securely attached child develops the capacity to stay attentive and responsive to the environment and to use error-correcting information to construct a coherent narrative when presented with scenarios involving separation and loss (Main, 1991; Main & Hesse, 1990; Main et al., 1985; Solomon et al., 1995). As already noted, it would seem reasonable to hypothesize that the secure/autonomous adult has developed the mental capacity to process information more readily in the aftermath of a traumatic event than the insecure, disorganized subject whose ability to regulate states of arousal at moments of stress was compromised during early development. As Bowlby (1973, 1979) has observed, the quality of the emotional bond between the child and the caregiver will vitally influence whether mourning proceeds along a healthy path or takes a pathological course. He also emphasizes the therapeutic benefit of modifying the patient's internal working models (Bowlby, 1988). From an attachment theory perspective, therefore, the overarching therapeutic task in my work with John was to help him to express and mentalize dissociated thoughts and feelings linked to the trauma of unmourned childhood loss and to modify maladaptive representational models so that he could begin to experience himself in relation to others in new and more enriching ways (Bowlby, 1979, 1988; Fonagy, 1999b; Fonagy & Target, 1997, 1998; Fonagy et al., 2004).

In a meta-analysis of outcome studies, Roth & Fonagy (1996) found that the extent to which ruptures to the working alliance were adequately addressed during the course of the therapy was predictive of the efficacy of the intervention. The authors conclude that the relationship component is the common effective ingredient in positive outcomes. Their findings accorded with my clinical experience in applying attachment theory in my work with violent people and would seem to confirm the respective findings of Schore (1994) and Stern et al. (1998) that the interactive emotion-transacting aspect of the therapeutic encounter is the main mechanism of intrapsychic change.

Chapter 11

The Role of Explicit and Implicit Memory in Therapeutic Action

In Chapter 6, I set out the complex and multifaceted nature of the process of therapeutic change using an integrated therapeutic model. The purpose of this chapter is to focus on one, albeit salient, aspect of therapeutic action—the role that memory plays in both the maintenance and modification of self-other representational models.

If we accept that the internal world of subjective experience is encoded and stored in the systems of implicit/procedural memory (Fonagy, 1999b; Fonagy & Target, 1997; Pally, 2000, 2005; Schacter, 1996) as conceptualized as relational configurations; self-states; object relations; emotion schemas; or self–other representational models (Bowlby, 1973, 1988; Bromberg, 1998; Bucci, 1997, 2011; Davies & Frawley, 1994; Fonagy, 1999b), it may be argued that implicit modes of interaction, particularly as these relate to verbal and nonverbal emotional communication, become a central focus of the therapeutic process. This is particularly the case if we also accept that such nonconscious experience is enacted in our most intimate relationships and is most readily accessed in the context of those relationships (Fonagy 1998; Renn, 2010; Ringstrom, 2008; Shimmerlik 2008; Stern et al., 1998a; Wachtel, 2008). Given this, it follows that what we communicate to others and register from others, both in everyday life and in the therapeutic encounter, often occurs out of awareness and in an enactive mode of relating. This emphasizes the fact that emotional communication is complex and, at times, highly ambiguous and that our experience is mediated by implicit, nonverbal representational models (Bowlby, 1973, 1988; Fonagy, 1999b; Fonagy & Target, 1997; Shimmerlik, 2008). Therefore, accessing and making explicit invisible procedural ways of experiencing and relating so that implicit memories can be subtly changed and encoded within modified representational models becomes a crucial aspect of therapeutic action. In this conceptual framework, presymbolic, implicit/enactive encounters form the basis of intersubjective relatedness and promote the establishment of a secure-enough base from which to explore, express, and elaborate new forms of agency and shared experiences (Lyons-Ruth et al., 1998; Stern et al., 1998b). In this sense, psychoanalysis may be seen as the active coconstruction of a new way of experiencing self with other (Fonagy, 1999b; Fonagy & Target, 1998; Wachtel, 2008) and as identifying problematic patterns of organization (Fosshage, 2011; Wachtel, 2008).

This perspective contrasts sharply with classical psychoanalysis which, as noted in earlier chapters, is more concerned with the verbal, symbolic aspects of the therapeutic encounter than with the nonverbal, implicit/enactive elements. From a traditional perspective, interpretation, the lifting of repression, and the recovery of dynamically repressed childhood memories are key aspects of therapeutic action (Chused, 1996; Fonagy & Target, 1997). While psychoanalytic therapy of all persuasions encourages the patient to tell his or her story, and therefore to talk about childhood memories, a contemporary approach argues that therapeutic action is largely unrelated to the actual recovery of such memories because in most cases these will have occurred too early to be consciously and accurately remembered. Given this, the events that have led to deeply pathological ways of experiencing and relating to the other are likely to antedate the development of the explicit memory system. Therefore, working only with the verbalized element of therapy fails to take into account core developmental and intersubjective aspects of personality embedded in representational models and enacted at the implicit level in the transference/countertransference matrix, as well as in everyday life (Beebe et al., 2005; Chused, 1996; Emde, 1990; Fonagy & Target, 1997, 1998; Ginot, 2007; Hurry, 1998; Pally, 2005; Teicholz, 2009; Wachtel, 2008). As Bucci (1997) notes, the struggle to symbolize the implicit/enactive level of interaction in adult dyadic life is one of the major goals of psychoanalysis. This is made all the more difficult because of the invisible nature of implicit/procedural memory (Schacter, 1996). In the light of these factors, Fonagy and Target (1997) argue that the lifting of repression in order to recover previously unavailable memories needs to be reconceptualized as a process that facilitates change in the way the patient understands and feels in relation to a childhood experience. This conceptualization of therapeutic action would appear to be consonant with Freud's thinking about early childhood memories, as noted in Chapter 1, that perhaps we do not have "memories at all *from* our childhood," but only "memories *relating to* our childhood" (Freud, 1899, cited in Gay, 1995, p. 126, emphasis in original).

From a contemporary perspective, memory is important not as an account of history, but as a means of communicating the nature of internal representations of self–other relationships. Representational models are the invisible psychic structures that organize behavior and experience in the present, mediating our expectations and predictions of self–other relationships deriving from the silent past (Bowlby, 1973, 1988; Fonagy, 1999b; Fonagy & Target, 1997, 1998; Fosshage, 2011; Stern, 2004; Wachtel, 2008). Indeed, neuroscience has found that the brain organizes interpersonal interactions in accordance with implicit predictions rather than actual events (Pally, 2005). This being so, it is these structures themselves that need to be the focus of psychoanalytic work and not the events that might have contributed to their development. In the light of these findings, therapeutic work needs to focus on helping the patient to identify, and thus make visible, repetitive patterns of behavior for which explicit memory can provide no explanation. Therefore, a key aspect of therapeutic action consists of the modification of implicit memories and the expression of dissociated emotions that motivate the procedures underpinning habitual ways of experiencing self with other (Fonagy, 1999b; Fonagy & Target, 1998; Wachtel, 2008). Many of these procedures may be highly dysfunctional but based on powerful, yet outdated and largely nonconscious expectations generated by past experience of a cumulatively traumatic nature (Knox, 2003; Renn, 2003, 2006, 2008b; Wachtel, 2008; Wilkinson, 2010). Given that such emotional procedures are not readily accessible for verbal report, they may only become explicitly knowable when enacted in the experiential realm (Fonagy, 1999b; Lyons-Ruth et al., 1998; Pally, 2005; Reis, 2009a, 2009b; Ringstrom, 2008; Shimmerlik 2008; Stern et al., 1998b; Teicholz, 2009). The modification of implicit/procedural memories encoded and stored within representational models would seem to have certain features in common with Freud's description of *Nachträglichkeit*, which, as observed in Chapter 1, is a process by which memory traces are revised and rearranged in the light of new experience.

As noted in Chapter 2, explicit memory is not a static archive, but rather an open, dynamic and interactive system undergoing continuous recategorization (Mancia, 2006; Rose, 2005). In the light of such findings, Mancia (2006) argues that the transformational processes that occur in the therapeutic encounter indicate that the implicit memory system may be stimulated by the transference and can undergo dynamic interactions with the explicit memory system. This, in turn, leads to a recategorization of memories during the therapeutic process. Indeed, although contemporary psychoanalysis, informed by the ideas of the BCPSG (2008), emphasizes the role of implicit, nonverbal factors in the process of change, it is argued that learning new ways of experiencing self with other in the implicit/enactive domain needs to be elaborated in the explicit, verbal-reflective, and conscious domain. Thus, therapeutic change consists of a dual process, one implicit and one explicit, and needs to proceed in both of these modes (Beebe & Lachmann, 2002; Fonagy, 1999b; Fosshage, 2011; Pally, 2005; Wachtel, 2008). Becoming consciously aware of new procedural ways of interacting is crucial if these are to be available as an inner resource in other relationships or in contexts that are particularly stressful; for example, when experiencing separation and loss.

From a clinical perspective, engaging focal attention and bringing the consciousness system to bear on implicit/procedural expectations and patterns of interaction is a vital therapeutic tool. Consciousness of previously nonconscious procedures, expectations, emotions, and predictions facilitates choice, enhances behavioral and emotional regulation, and promotes therapeutic change (Fonagy, 1999b; Fonagy & Target, 1998; Fosshage, 2011; Pally, 2005; Schore, 1994; Shimmerlik 2008; Wachtel, 2008). In time, consciousness of the beliefs and expectations generated by emotional memories leads to changes in procedural rules and to the creation of a second-order representational model of the patient's inner experience (Eagle, 2003; Fonagy, 1999b; Sandler & Sandler, 1997). From a contemporary perspective, then, psychoanalysis works by modifying procedural mental models and the accompanying emotions that are generated and enacted in particular self-other relationships (Bowlby, 1988). Therefore, bringing implicit/procedural structures into conscious focus in an emotionally meaningful way is a critical component of therapeutic action (Eagle, 2003; Fonagy, 1999b; Fosshage, 2011; Orange, 1995; Pally, 2005; Schore, 1994; Sandler & Sandler, 1997; Shimmerlik, 2008; Wachtel, 2008).

Given the implicit and explicit dimensions of therapeutic action, it is, of course, important that the therapist becomes aware of the implicit/procedural aspects of his or her own affect and behavior, as well as that of the patient, so that implicit/enactive aspects of the exchange can be spoken about and reflected on. The dual aspect of therapeutic action suggests that the therapist functions both to enact and reflect on the interaction (Fosshage, 2011; Pally, 2005; Reis, 2009a, 2009b; Wallin, 2007). From a neuroscience perspective, utilizing the explicit, declarative system of the hippocampus allows optimal implicit/procedural interactions between patient and therapist to become more strongly encoded in the patient's amygdala and basal ganglia of the implicit memory system with the outcome that these more optimal procedures are activated automatically and habitually (Pally, 2005). As previously noted, this process links the nonverbal and verbal representational domains of the brain, thereby facilitating the transfer of implicit/procedural information in the right hemisphere to explicit or declarative systems in the left. Thus, body-based visceral-somatic experience is symbolically transformed into emotional and intentional states of mind that then become available for reflection and regulation (Damasio, 1999; Schore, 1994). Optimally, these new forms of agency and shared experiences become encoded and stored in the systems of implicit/procedural memory as second-order representational models (Fonagy, 1999b).

From the foregoing, it will be seen that a felt sense of safety and security needs to be established in the clinical setting before focal attention and the consciousness system can be employed to explore and reflect on habitual, nonoptimal implicit/procedural ways of experiencing and relating. The basis of a sense of felt security is the establishment of emotional connectedness or intersubjective relatedness. In the therapeutic encounter as in everyday life, such relatedness is not a given, but has to be established on each reunion and thus after every separation. In the main, this process occurs in the nonverbal, implicit/enactive domain and takes the form of interactive regulation and the moment-to-moment micro-repair of misaligned interaction, an intersubjective process operating at the level of implicit relational knowing (Beebe & Lachmann, 2002; Beebe et al., 2005; Lyons-Ruth et al., 1998; Teicholz, 2009; Tronick et al., 1978; Stern et al., 1998b). On a point of technique, I would argue that this aspect of the change process is enhanced by working face-to-face.

Although these features of the therapeutic process are fundamental prerequisites for change, in my view they are not sufficient in and of themselves to modify deeply entrenched, archaic representational models that organize relational experience. This is because such mental models and the accompanying expectations, predictions, and characteristic ways of regulating emotion are activated in contexts that generate stress, anxiety, and insecurity, leaving the self feeling threatened and endangered. Typically, in such contexts there is an excessive reaction to what, on the surface, may be seen as a relatively minor threat or injury to the self. The disproportionate quality of the reaction is itself an indication that a powerful, trauma-related representational model, which in nonstressful contexts lies dormant and quiescent, has been activated. For example, the patient may react to a break in the therapy either in an overly compliant way or by angrily disparaging the therapy and missing sessions, or, indeed, by expressing fear that the therapist will not return. Similarly, should the therapist become unwell for any reason, the patient may feel responsible, fearing that he or she is too much for the therapist to cope with and may even cause his or her death (Bowlby, 1988).

Awareness of the activation of an archaic representational model, together with an open acknowledgement and reflective exploration of what the analyst may have contributed to any consequent mutual enactment, functions to repair the disruption to the therapeutic relationship. In this context, an important aspect of therapeutic action consists in recognizing the connection between emotion and behavior. Unexpressed or dissociated emotion is seen as being largely due to nonconscious fearful predictions that the behavior, of which the emotion is a part, will lead to a dreaded outcome. Such fears are likely to be based on lived experience—repeated patterns of interaction encoded in implicit memory.

For example, the patient may carry a generalized expectation that the expression of anger will lead to hostility and punishment or that a tearful appeal for comfort and understanding will result in being rejected and humiliated (Bowlby, 1988). Responding in ways that disconfirm the patient's implicit expectations may, over time, help to generate a sense of felt security and facilitate an exploration and elaboration of the emotional procedural aspects of the enactment in the explicit, verbal, and conscious domain. With respect to emotionally detached, dissociated, or alexithymic patients, the therapist may initially need to tentatively name and express the feelings that the patient would reasonably be expected to experience in situations involving fear, anger, guilt, sadness, shame, and the like (Bowlby, 1988; Krystal, 1988; Schore, 1994). An additional salient clinical factor to consider is the finding that stress compromises our capacity for affect regulation and reflective functioning or mentalization. Thus, the stress-induced activation of an archaic representational model constricts our ability to self-regulate feelings and reflect upon and appraise our own and the other's emotional and intentional states of mind (Fonagy, 2008; Fonagy et al., 2004; Slade, 2008). This may often be an underlying factor in the emergence of a mutual enactment between therapist and patient.

With regard to related aspects of therapeutic action, I think it important to emphasize that the modification of representational models is not a function solely of enactments or reenactments in the transference/countertransference matrix, but may also occur as a result of exploring the patient's accounts of his or her intimate relationships outside the analysis (Renn, 2003, 2006, 2008b; Wachtel, 2008). Not infrequently a patient will attend a session in a heightened emotional state as a result of a distressing interpersonal encounter with a partner, child, parent, close friend, or work colleague, or, indeed, enter such a state while recounting such an encounter. Distress of this nature may also occur as a result of a chance encounter with a stranger whose actions and behavior are interpreted through the distorting lens of implicitly encoded predictions and expectations.

For example, the patient becomes involved in a road rage incident because an unwitting motorist got too close to his or her vehicle; a serious, and sometimes violent, argument ensues because the patient's partner was momentarily inattentive; a violent incident develops in a bar because the patient appraises a fellow drinker's gaze as invasive and shaming; the emotional distress of the patient's partner or child habitually activates a dismissing, avoidant response instead of an empathic, emotionally engaged interaction; the slightly late arrival home of the patient's partner engenders catastrophic fears of death and disaster and an angry, clingy, ambivalent reaction on reunion; the patient expects to enjoy some time to himself when his wife and young son leave to stay with her parents for a week, but instead experiences a sense of intense and unaccountable dread and emptiness; the patient is plunged into a highly distressed, semi-paranoid state and plagued by agonizing doubts about his or her lovability because a friend did not respond to a message with sufficient alacrity; the patient experiences an acute sense of injustice and angrily threatens to end a friendship because the friend declined an invitation to a social event; the patient becomes enraged, chronically sexually jealous and makes a public scene because his or her partner danced with the host at a party; feeling unfulfilled, empty, and alone, the patient pursues a potential partner but withdraws, feeling anxious, trapped, and colonized, when the person responds; the patient offers emotional support and financial assistance to a work colleague in need, but then complains bitterly and endlessly about being used, abused, and manipulated.

Again, the stress involved in such interpersonal encounters together with the excessive, disproportionate emotional reaction indicates that a trauma-related representational model has been activated. Such interactions are often precipitated by expectations of separation, loss, rejection, abandonment, and a shaming negation of self, on the one hand, and by fear of closeness, intimacy, attachment, and engulfment or loss of self, on the other hand. In my clinical experience, exploring, elaborating, and contextualizing such extra-analytic interpersonal encounters in micro-detail can help the patient to begin to recognize repetitive, maladaptive procedural patterns, distorted predictions, habitual roles, and self-destructive ways of experiencing self in relation to others (Renn, 2003, 2008b; Wachtel, 2008). Typically, the patient has no conscious understanding or explanation for repeatedly behaving in such ways and is confused and distressed by his or her emotional reactions and seeming inability to control them. Bringing focal attention to bear on such encounters, and on the emotional states that accompany them, in the "real" relationship with the therapist can help to access invisible, archaic representational models and lead to the gradual development of second-order mental models without necessarily requiring a direct enactment between patient and therapist in the transference/countertransference matrix. I would emphasize again, though, that working with the patient's extra-analytic implicit/procedural enactments occurs within the nonverbal, intersubjective domain characterized by ongoing interactive regulations between patient and therapist at the local level, and thus will be mediated by the patient's implicit expectations of the therapist's responsiveness to his or her distress and attachment needs (Beebe et al., 2005; Beebe & Lachmann, 2002; Bruschweiler-Stern et al. 2002, 2007; Lyons-Ruth et al., 1998; Stern et al., 1998a, 1998b). This aspect of the therapeutic process may, in part, constitute the "witnessing" feature of therapeutic action which is held to transform the patient's own relation to his or her implicitly encoded traumatic experience (Reis, 2009a).

CONCLUDING COMMENTS

In this book, I have tried to show the way in which the silent relational past lives on in invisible ways in the interpersonal present, powerfully influencing our thoughts, feelings, and behavior in our most intimate relationships. In doing so, I have stressed the significance of implicit/procedural memory in the development of personality and as a bridge between childhood and adulthood. I have argued that a neuroscientific understanding of the dynamic nature of memories and of the way in which the implicit and explicit memory systems operate and interact is salient to an understanding of the pernicious impact of trauma and of the therapeutic process of change. I have compared earlier clinical models that emphasize a verbal, interpretative technique in the explicit domain to newer models that focus on a nonverbal, affective understanding of communication in the implicit/enactive domain. In recognition of this paradigmatic shift, I have suggested that there is a need to modify certain techniques, such as working face-to-face and acknowledging the "real relationship" and our own contributions to disruptions to the therapeutic alliance. In a similar way to Wachtel (2008), I have advocated working not only with the transference relationship that develops between the therapist and patient, but also with the patient's wider relational system as experienced in his or her everyday life. I am not, however, suggesting that the new model should simply supersede the older model. Rather, I am advocating a clinical model that integrates the explicit, verbal mode of communication and the implicit, nonverbal mode of communication, and expands a two-person psychology into a multi-person psychology. In my view, these therapeutic developments will both facilitate and enhance the process of change.

Although I have emphasized the clinical usefulness of integrating the findings of cognitive and developmental psychology, neuroscience, and attachment theory into an overarching relational/intersubjective model, I hope that I have been able to illustrate that this need not detract from engaging with the patient's subjective, phenomenological experience; that an empirical, interdisciplinary dimension to our clinical work, as advocated by, among others, Aron (2010), the BCPSG (2008), Mitchell (2000), and Schore (1994, 2011), does not necessarily preclude a hermeneutic sensibility that recognizes the salience of individual meaning and subjective experience. In this context, I would stress the importance of holding theory lightly (Orange, 1995), and that integration is best accomplished at an individual practitioner level as a reflection of the therapist's personal idiom, rather than in terms of an all-encompassing grand theory. While I advocate theories that recognize the mutual, relational, and nonlinear aspects of the therapeutic process, I do not think there is an essentially right or wrong way to practice psychotherapy—what emerges in the therapeutic encounter will inevitably be unpredictable and unique, influencing and changing both the patient and the therapist.

On the specific topic of therapeutic action, it is, of course, enormously heart-warming and gratifying when our patients change, finding new ways of experiencing themselves and relating to others, seemingly as a result of their work with us. But I think that we need to be realistic, too, and acknowledge the limits of therapeutic action and accept that psychotherapy cannot bring about a complete cure. Thus, while the findings from neuroscience have revealed the ongoing plasticity of the brain, with new neural connections being made in response to novel environmental challenges and demands, such data also indicate that the traumas we have experienced do not disappear as a result of treatment, but live on within us and may, therefore, reemerge in certain stressful contexts that cue the retrieval of trauma-related implicit memories (Pally, 2005; Schacter, 1996). At such times, silent representational models from the past may be activated and old implicit/procedural ways of functioning become dominant once again in the present. In this more limited sense, therapeutic action consists in helping patients to have meaning for their traumatic experience and to enhance certain capacities, specifically affect regulation and mentalization. The goal here is to provide the patient with the resilience, self-agency, and inner resources to recognize the activation of nonoptimal representational models and the ability to transition out of a traumatic psychobiological self-state into a more coherent, organized, and reflective self-state. To this end, I have argued that an intersubjective, psychodynamic model can use the power of an emotionally meaningful therapeutic relationship to gradually facilitate both relational and neurological changes in patients with trauma histories.

Thinking about the way ahead, it is encouraging that relational psychoanalysis in particular is showing an eagerness to engage with the ideas that I present in this book. This may be seen in the number of conferences and workshops devoted to explicating the links between affect regulation, implicit processes in neuroscience, the neurobiology of attachment trauma, and nonverbal affective communication. As I noted in the introduction to this book, relational psychoanalysis is well placed to incorporate the findings emerging from related disciplines into an evolving clinical model that integrates such data with the current emphasis on intersubjectivity, trauma, dissociation, mentalization, nonlinear dynamic systems theory, and mutual enactments. However, a significant lacuna that I think it is important to fill in order to enhance the effectiveness of our clinical work is a greater understanding of the way in which the explicit and implicit memory systems operate and interact.

Although an increasing number of conferences and continuing professional development workshops and short courses are disseminating the implications of the findings that I set out in this book, it would appear that the majority of clinical training organizations have yet to develop curricula that incorporate such research data. A notable exception is the course devised and taught by Cynthia Divino and Mary Sue Moore in Boulder, Colorado, as set out in their paper in *Psychoanalytic Dialogues* (Divino & Moore, 2010). I would encourage those responsible for clinical training to peruse this article and use it as a model to develop a training module on their own courses. After all, it is the new generation of psychoanalytic psychotherapists who will have the responsibility for carrying forward the process of interdisciplinary integration so as to develop ever more effective clinical models to use in the service of relieving our patients' mental suffering.

References

Ainsworth, M. D. S., Blehar, M. C., Waters, E., & Wall, S. (1978). *Patterns of attachment: A psychological study of the Strange Situation*. Hillsdale, NJ: Lawrence Erlbaum Associates.

Alexander, F., & French, T. M. (1946). *Psychoanalytic therapy: Principles and applications*. New York: Ronald Press.

Archer, J. (2000). Sex differences in aggression between heterosexual partners: A meta-analytic review. *Psychological Bulletin, 126*(5), 651–680.

Arlow, J. A., & Brenner, C. (1964). *Psychoanalytic concepts and the structural theory*. New York: International Universities Press.

Aron, L. (1990). One-person and two-person psychologies and the method of psychoanalysis. *Psychoanalytic Psychology, 7,* 475–485.

Aron, L. (1996). *A meeting of minds: Mutuality in psychoanalysis*. Hillsdale, NJ: Analytic Press.

Aron, L. (1998). The clinical body and the reflexive mind. In L. Aron & F. S. Anderson (Eds.), *Relational perspectives on the body* (pp. 591–597). Hillsdale, NJ: Analytic Press.

Aron, L. (2000). Self-reflexivity and the therapeutic action of psychoanalysis. *Psychoanalytic Psychology, 17,* 667–689.

Aron, L. (2008). Analytic impasse and the third: Clinical implication of intersubjectivity. *International Journal of Psychoanalysis, 87*(2), 349–368.

Aron, L. (2010, January 4). Message posted to D. Wallin online colloquium: The Clinical Implications of Attachment Theory Research.

Aron, L., & Hirsch, I. (1992). Money matters in psychoanalysis. In N. J. Skolnick & S. C. Warshaw (Eds.), *Relational perspectives in psychoanalysis* (pp. 239–256). Hillsdale, NJ: Analytic Press.

Bakermans-Kranenberg, M. J., & van Ijzendoorn, M. H. (2009). The first 10,000 Adult Attachment Interviews: Distributions of adult attachment representations in clinical and non-clinical groups. *Attachment & Human Development, 11,* 223–263.

Balbernie, R. (2007). The move to intersubjectivity: A clinical and conceptual shift of perspective. *Journal of Child Psychotherapy, 33,* 308–324.

Balint, M. (1968). *The basic fault: Therapeutic aspects of regression*. London: Routledge.

Balint, M. (1972). *Focal psychotherapy: An example of applied psychoanalysis* (P. H. Ornstein & E. Balint, Eds.). London: Tavistock.

Bartholomew, K., Henderson, A., & Dutton, D. (2001a). Insecure attachment and abusive intimate relationships. In C. Clulow (Ed.), *Adult attachment and couple psychotherapy: The "secure base" in practice and research* (pp. 43–61). London: Routledge.

Bartholomew, K., Kwong, M. J., & Hart, S. D. (2001b). Attachment. In W. J. Livesley (Ed.), *Handbook of personality disorders: Theory, research, and treatment* (pp. 196–230). New York: Guilford Press.

Bateman, A., & Fonagy, P. (2004). *Psychotherapy for borderline personality disorder: Mentalization-based treatment.* Oxford: Oxford University Press.

Beebe, B., Jaffe, J., Feldstein, S., Mays, K., & Alson, D. (1985). Interpersonal timing: The application of an adult dialogue model to mother–infant vocal and kinesic interactions. In T. Field & N. Fox (Eds.), *Social perception in infants* (pp. 217–247). Norwood, NJ: Ablex.

Beebe, B., Jaffe, J. & Lachmann, F. M. (1992). A dyadic systems view of communication. In N. J. Skolnick & S. C. Warshaw (Eds.), *Relational perspectives in psychoanalysis* (pp. 61–81). Hillsdale, NJ: Analytic Press.

Beebe, B., Jaffe, J., Lachmann, F. M., Feldstein, S., Crown, C., & Jasnow, M. (2000). Systems models in development and psychoanalysis: The case of vocal rhythm coordination and attachment. *Infant Mental Health Journal, 21,* 99–122.

Beebe, B., Knoblauch, S., Rustin, J., & Sorter, D. (2005). *Forms of intersubjectivity in infant research and adult treatment: A systems view.* New York: Other Press.

Beebe, B., & Lachmann, F. M. (1992). The contribution of mother–infant mutual influence to the origins of self- and object representations. In N. J. Skolnick & S. C. Warshaw (Eds.), *Relational perspectives in psychoanalysis* (pp. 83–117). Hillsdale, NJ: Analytic Press.

Beebe, B., & Lachmann, F. M. (1994). Representation and internalization in infancy: Three principles of saliency. *Psychoanalytic Psychology, 11,* 127–165.

Beebe, B., & Lachmann, F. M. (2002). *Infant research and adult treatment: Co-constructing interactions.* Hillsdale, NJ: Analytic Press.

Benjamin, J. (1992). Psychoanalysis as a vocation. *Psychoanalytic Dialogues, 7*(6), 781–802.

Benjamin, J. (1995). Recognition and destruction: An outline of intersubjectivity. In *Like subjects, love objects: Essays on recognition and sexual difference* (pp. 27–48). New Haven, CT: Yale University Press.

Benjamin, J. (2004). Beyond doer and done to: An intersubjective view of thirdness. *Psychoanalytic Quarterly, 73,* 5–46.

Benjamin, L. S., & Pugh, C. (2001). Using interpersonal theory to select effective treatment interventions. In W. J. Livesley (Ed.), *Handbook of personality disorders: Theory, research, and treatment* (pp. 414–436). New York: Guilford Press.

Bion, W. R. (1984). *Elements of psycho-analysis.* London: Routledge.

Bion, W. R. (1990). *Second thoughts.* London: Routledge.

Black, D. M. (2001). Mapping a detour: Why did Freud speak of a death drive? *British Journal of Psychotherapy, 18*(2), 185–198.

Blum, H. P. (1994). *Reconstruction in psychoanalysis: Childhood revisited and recreated.* Madison, CT: International Universities Press.

Bograd, M., & Mederos, F. (1999). Battering and couples therapy: Universal screening and selection of treatment modality. *Journal of Marital and Family Therapy*, *25*(3), 291–312.

Bollas, C. (1987). *The shadow of the object: Psychoanalysis of the unthought known*. London: Free Association Books.

Bollas, C. (1994). *Forces of destiny*. London: Free Association Books.

Bond, S. B., & Bond, M. (2004). Attachment styles and violence within couples. *Journal of Nervous and Mental Disease, 192*(12), 857–863.

Bookwala, J., & Zdaniuk, B. (1998). Adult attachment styles and aggressive behavior within dating relationships. *Journal of Social and Personal Relationships, 15*(2), 175–190.

Boon, S., & Draijer, N. (1993). *Multiple personality disorder in the Netherlands: A study of reliability and validity of the diagnosis*. Lisse, Netherlands: Swets & Zeitlinger.

Boston Change Process Study Group. (2008). Forms of relational meaning: Issues in the relations between the implicit and reflective-verbal domains. *Psychoanalytic Dialogues, 18*, 125–148.

Boswell, G. (1996). *Young and dangerous: The backgrounds and careers of Section 53 offenders*. Aldershot: Avebury.

Boswell, G. (1998). Research-minded practice with young offenders who commit grave crimes. *Probation Journal, 45*, 202–207.

Boulanger, G. (2007). *Wounded by reality: Understanding and treating adult onset trauma*. New York: Analytic Press.

Bowlby, J. (1944). Forty-four juvenile thieves: Their characters and home-life. *International Journal of Psychoanalysis, 25*, 1–57 and 207–228.

Bowlby, J. (1958). The nature of a child's tie to his mother. *International Journal of Psychoanalysis, 39*, 350–371.

Bowlby, J. (1960). Grief and mourning in infancy and early childhood. *Psychoanalytic Study of the Child, 15*, 9–52.

Bowlby, J. (1969). *Attachment and loss, vol. 1: Attachment*. London: Pimlico.

Bowlby, J. (1973). *Attachment and loss, vol. 2: Separation, anger and anxiety*. London: Pimlico.

Bowlby, J. (1979). *The making and breaking of affectional bonds*. London: Routledge.

Bowlby, J. (1980). *Attachment and loss, vol. 3: Loss, sadness and depression*. London: Penguin.

Bowlby, J. (1984). Violence in the family as a disorder of the attachment and caregiving systems. *American Journal of Psychoanalysis, 44*, 9–27.

Bowlby, J. (1988). *A secure base: Clinical applications of attachment theory*. Bristol: Arrowsmith.

Bradley, S. J. (2003). *Affect regulation and the development of psychopathology*. New York: Guilford Press.

Brazelton, T. B., & Cramer, B. G. (1991). *The earliest relationship: Parents, infants and the drama of early attachment*. London: Karnac Books.

Bromberg, P. M. (1998). *Standing in the spaces: Essays on clinical process, trauma and dissociation*. Hillsdale, NJ: Analytic Press.

Brown, P., & van der Hart, O. (1998). Memories of sexual abuse: Janet's critique of Freud, a balanced approach. *Psychological Reports, 82*, 1027–1043.

Bruschweiler-Stern, N., Harrison, A. M., Lyons-Ruth, K., Morgan, A. C., Nahum, J. P., Sander, L. W., Stern, D. N., & Tronick, E. Z. (2002). Explicating the implicit: The local level and the microprocess of change in the analytic situation. *International Journal of Psychoanalysis, 83*, 1051–1062.

Bruschweiler-Stern, N., Harrison, A. M., Lyons-Ruth, K., Morgan, A. C., Nahum, J. P., Sander, L. W., Stern, D. N., & Tronick, E. Z. (2007). The foundational level of psychodynamic meaning: Implicit process in relation to conflict, defense and the dynamic unconscious. *International Journal of Psychoanalysis, 88*, 843–860.

Bucci, W. (1997). *Psychoanalysis and cognitive science.* New York: Guilford Press.

Bucci, W. (2011). The interplay of subsymbolic and symbolic processes in psychoanalytic treatment: It takes two to tango – but who knows the steps, who's the leader? The choreography of the psychoanalytic interchange. *Psychoanalytic Dialogues, 21*, 45–54.

Byng-Hall, J. (1999). Family and couple therapy: Toward greater security. In J. Cassidy & P. R. Shaver (Eds.), *Handbook of attachment: Theory, research and clinical applications* (pp. 625–648). New York: Guilford Press.

Cain, A. C., & Fast, I. (1972). Children's disturbed reactions to parent suicide. In A. C. Cain, (Ed.), *Survivors of suicide* (pp. 93–111). Springfield, IL: C. C. Thomas.

Carnelley, K. B., Hepper, E. G., Hicks, C., & Turner, W. (2011). Perceived parental reactions to coming out, attachment, and romantic relationships views. *Attachment & Human Development, 13*(3), 227–236.

Cartwright, D. (2002). *Psychoanalysis, violence and rage-type murder: Murdering minds.* London: Routledge.

Casement, P. (1990). *On learning from the patient.* London: Routledge.

Cassidy J., & Kobak, R. R. (1988). Avoidance and its relationship with other defensive processes. In J. Belsky & T. Nezworski (Eds.), *Clinical implications of attachments* (pp. 300–323). Hillsdale, NJ: Lawrence Erlbaum Associates.

Cawson, P., Watton, C., Brooker, S., & Kelly, G. (2000). *Child maltreatment in the United Kingdom.* London: NSPCC Publications.

Celenza, A. (2010). The analyst's need and desire. *Psychoanalytic Dialogues, 20*, 60–69.

Chused, J. F. (1991). The evocative power of enactments. *Journal of the American Psychoanalytical Association, 39*, 615–639.

Chused, J. F. (1996). The therapeutic action of psychoanalysis: Abstinence and informative experiences. *Journal of American Psychoanalytic Association, 44*(4), 1047–1071.

Clulow, C. (2001). Attachment theory and the therapeutic frame. In C. Clulow (Ed.), *Adult attachment and the therapeutic frame: The "secure base" in practice and research* (pp. 85–104). London: Routledge.

Clyman, R. (1991). The procedural organization of emotions: A contribution from cognitive science to the psychoanalytic theory of therapeutic action. *Journal of the American Psychoanalytic Association, 39*, 349–381.

Cohn, D. A., Silver, D. H., Cowan, C. P., Cowan, P. A., & Pearson, J. L. (1992). Working models of childhood attachment and couple relationships. *Journal of Family Issues, 13*, 432–449.

Copleston, F. (1979). *A history of philosophy, vol. 9.* New York: Doubleday.

Cordess, C. (1997). Discussion. In J. Sandler & P. Fonagy (Eds.), *Recovered memories of abuse: True or false?* (pp. 64–69). London: Karnac Books.

Cortina, M., & Liotti, G. (2007). New approaches to understanding unconscious processes: Implicit and explicit memory systems. *International Forum of Psychoanalysis, 16,* 204–212.

Cowan, P. A., Cowan, C. P., & Mehta, N. (2009). Adult attachment, couple attachment and children's adaptation to school: An integrated attachment template and family risk model. *Attachment & Human Development, 11,* 29–46.

Cozolino, L. J. (2002). *The neuroscience of psychotherapy: Building and rebuilding the human brain.* New York: Norton.

Cozolino, L. J. (2006). *The neuroscience of human relationships: Attachment and the developing social brain.* New York: Norton.

Craik, K. J. W. (1943). *The nature of explanation.* Cambridge: Cambridge University Press.

Crawford, T. N., Cohen, P. R., Chen, H., Anglin, D. M., & Ehrensaft, M. (2009). Early maternal separation and the trajectory of borderline personality disorder symptoms. *Development and Psychopathology, 21,* 1013–1030.

Crews, F. (1995). *The memory wars: Freud's legacy in dispute.* New York: New York Review Books.

Crittenden, P. M. (1990). Internal representational models of attachment relationships. *Journal of Infant Mental Health, 11,* 259–277.

Crittenden, P. M., & Ainsworth, M. D. S. (1989). Child maltreatment and attachment theory. In D. Ciccetti & V. Carlson (Eds.), *Child maltreatment: Theory and research on the causes and consequences of child abuse and neglect* (pp. 432–463). New York: Cambridge University Press.

Crowell, J. A., Waters, E., Treboux, D., O'Connor, E., Colon-Downs, C., & Fieder, O. (1996). Discriminant validity of the Adult Attachment Interview. *Child Development, 67,* 2584–2599.

Cummins, R. (1989). *Meaning and mental representation.* Cambridge, MA: MIT Press.

Damasio, A. (1999). *The feeling of what happens: Body, emotion and the making of consciousness.* London: Vintage.

Damasio, A. (2003). *Looking for Spinoza: Joy, sorrow and the feeling brain.* London: Heinemann.

Davies, J. M. (2004). Reply to commentaries. *Psychoanalytic Dialogues, 14,* 755–767.

Davies, J. M., & Frawley M. G. (1994). *Treating the adult survivor of childhood sexual abuse.* New York: Basic Books.

De Zulueta, F. (1993). *From pain to violence: The traumatic roots of destructiveness.* London: Whurr.

De Zulueta, F. (2007). The perversion of the professional caring relationship. *Attachment: New Directions in Psychotherapy and Relational Psychoanalysis, 1*(3), vii–xii.

Diamond, D., & Kernberg, O. (2008). Discussion. In F. N. Busch (Ed.), *Mentalization: Theoretical considerations, research findings, and clinical implication* (pp. 235–260). New York: Analytic Press.

Dicks, H. V. (1993). *Marital tensions: Clinical studies towards a psychological theory of interaction.* London: Karnac Books.

Divino, C. L., & Moore, M. S. (2010). Integrating neurobiological findings into psychodynamic psychotherapy training and practice. *Psychoanalytic Dialogues, 20*, 337–355.

Downey, G., & Feldman, S. I. (1996). Implications of rejection sensitivity for intimate relationships. *Journal of Personality and Social Psychology, 70*, 1327–1343.

Downey, G., Khoun, H., & Feldman, S. (1997). Early interpersonal trauma and later adjustment: The mediational role of rejection sensitivity. In D. Cicchetti & S. L. Toth (Eds.), *Developmental perspectives on trauma: Theory, research and intervention* (pp. 85–114). New York: University of Rochester Press.

Dozier, M., Lomax, L., Tyrrell, C. L., & Lee, S. W. (2001). The challenge of treatment for clients with dismissing states of mind. *Attachment and Human Development, 3*(1), 31–61.

Dutton, D. (1995). *The domestic assault of women.* Vancouver: University of British Columbia Press.

Dutton, D., & Painter, S. (1981). Traumatic bonding: The development of emotional attachments in battered women and other relationships of intermittent abuse. *Journal of Victimology, 6*, 139–155.

Dutton, D., Saunders, K., Starzomski, A., & Bartholomew, K. (1994). Intimacy-anger and insecure attachment as precursors of abuse in intimate relationships. *Journal of Applied Social Psychology, 24*, 1367–1386.

Eagle, M. N. (2003). Clinical implications of attachment theory. *Psychoanalytic Inquiry, 23*, 27–53.

Edcumbe, R. (2000). *Anna Freud: A view of development, disturbance and therapeutic techniques.* London: Routledge.

Edelman, G. (1987). *Neural Darwinism.* London: Basic Books.

Edelman, G. (1989). *The remembered present.* London: Basic Books.

Emde, R. N. (1980). Ways of thinking about new knowledge and further research from a developmental orientation. *Psychoanalysis and Contemporary Thought, 3*, 213–235.

Emde, R. N. (1990). Mobilizing fundamental modes of development: Empathic availability and therapeutic action. *Journal of American Psychoanalytic Association, 79*, 9903–9921.

Erdelyi, M. H. (1994). Dissociation, defense, and the unconscious. In D. Spiegel (Ed.), *Dissociation: Culture, mind, and body* (pp. 3–20). Washington, DC: American Psychiatric Association Press.

Fairbairn, W. R. D. (1946). Object-relations and dynamic structure. In D. E. Scharff & E. Fairbairn Birtles (Eds.), *Psychoanalytic studies of the personality* (pp. 137–151). London: Routledge.

Fairbairn, W. R. D. (1996). *Psychoanalytic studies of the personality.* London: Routledge.

Farhi, N. (2010). The hands of the living God: "Finding the familiar in the unfamiliar." *Psychoanalytic Dialogues, 20*, 478–503.

Fazel, S., & Baillargeon, J. (2010). The health of prisoners. *The Lancet, 377*, 956–965.

Feeney, J. A., Noller, P., & Hanrahan, M. (1994). Assessing adult attachment. In M. B. Sperling & W. H. Berman (Eds.), *Attachment in adults: Clinical and developmental perspectives* (pp. 128–152). New York: Guilford Press.

Feltham, C. (2007). Ethical agonizing. *Therapy Today, 18*(7), 4–6.

Ferenczi, S. (1933). Confusion of tongues between adults and the child. In M. Balint (Ed.) & E. Mosbacher (Trans.), *Final contributions to the problems and methods of psycho-analysis* (pp. 156–167). London: Karnac Books.

Ferro, A. (2011). *Avoiding emotions, living emotions*. Hove: Routledge.

Follette, V. M., Polusny, M. A., Bechtle, A. E., & Naugle, A.E. (1996). Cumulative trauma: The impact of child sexual abuse, adult sexual assault, and spouse trauma. *Journal of Traumatic Stress, 9*, 25–35.

Fonagy, P. (1998). Moments of change in psychoanalytic theory: Discussion of a new theory of psychic change. *Infant Mental Health Journal, 19*(3), 346–353.

Fonagy, P. (1999a). The transgenerational transmission of holocaust trauma: Lessons learned from the analysis of an adolescent with obsessive-compulsive disorder. *Attachment & Human Development, 1*(1), 92–114.

Fonagy, P. (1999b). Memory and therapeutic action. *International Journal of Psychoanalysis, 80*, 215–223.

Fonagy, P. (1999c, February). *The male perpetrator: The role of trauma and failures of mentalization in aggression against women – An attachment theory perspective*. Paper presented at the 6th John Bowlby Memorial Lecture, London.

Fonagy, P. (1999d). Psychoanalytic theory from the viewpoint of attachment theory and research. In J. Cassidy & P. R. Shaver (Eds.), *Handbook of attachment: Theory, research and clinical applications* (pp. 595–624). New York: Guilford Press.

Fonagy, P. (2008). The mentalization-focused approach to social development. In F. N. Busch (Ed.), *Mentalization: Theoretical considerations, research findings, and clinical implications* (pp. 3–56). New York: Analytic Press.

Fonagy, P., Gergely, G., Jurist, E. L., & Target, M. (2004). *Affect regulation, mentalization, and the development of the self*. New York: Other Press.

Fonagy, P., Leigh, T., Steele, M., Steele, H., Kennedy, G., Mattoon, M., et al. (1996). The relation of attachment status, psychiatric classification and response to psychotherapy. *Journal of Consulting and Clinical Psychology, 64*, 22–31.

Fonagy, P., & Target, M. (1996). Playing with reality: I. Theory of mind and the normal development of psychic reality. *International Journal of Psychoanalysis, 77*, 217–233.

Fonagy, P., & Target, M. (1997). Perspectives on the recovered memory debate. In J. Sandler & P. Fonagy (Eds.), *Recovered memories of abuse: True or false?* (pp. 183–216). London: Karnac Books.

Fonagy, P., & Target, M. (1998). An interpersonal view of the infant. In A. Hurry (Ed.), *Psychoanalysis and developmental therapy* (pp. 3–31). London: Karnac Books.

Fonagy, P., & Target, M. (1999). Towards understanding violence: The use of the body and the role of the father. In R. S. Perelberg (Ed.), *Psychoanalytic understanding of violence and suicide* (pp. 53–72). London: Routledge.

Fonagy, P., Target, M., Steele, H., & Steele, M. (1998). *Reflective-functioning manual, version 5.0, for application to Adult Attachment Interviews*. London: University College London.

Fonagy, P., Target, M., Steele, M., Steele, H., Leigh, T., Levinson, A., & Kennedy, R. (1997). Morality, disruptive behavior, borderline personality disorder, crime, and their relationships to security of attachment. In L. Atkinson & K. J. Zucker (Eds.), *Attachment and psychopathology* (pp. 223–274). New York: Guilford Press.

Fosshage, J. L. (1992). The self and its vicissitudes within a relational matrix. In N. Skolnick & S. C. Warshaw (Eds.), *Relational perspectives in psychoanalysis* (pp. 21–42). Hillsdale, NJ: Analytic Press.

Fosshage, J. L. (2011). How do we "know" what we "know"? And change what we "know"? *Psychoanalytic Dialogues, 21*, 55–74.

Frankel, J. (2002). Exploring Ferenczi's concept of identification with the aggressor: Its role in trauma, everyday life, and the therapeutic relationship. *Psychoanalytic Dialogues, 12*, 101–140.

Frankel, J. (2006). Diagnosis-of-the-moment and what kind of good object the patient needs the analyst to be: Commentary on paper by Neil Skolnick. *Psychoanalytic Dialogues, 16*(1), 29–37.

Freud, A. (1968). *The ego and the mechanisms of defense*. London: Karnac Books.

Freud, A., & Burlingham, D. (1944). *Infants without families*. New York: International Universities Press.

Freud, S. (1894). The neuro-psychoses of defense. In J. Strachey (Ed. & Trans.), *The standard edition of the complete psychological works of Sigmund Freud* (Vol. 3, pp. 43–61). London: Hogarth Press.

Freud, S. (1896). The aetiology of hysteria. In J. Strachey (Ed. & Trans.), *The standard edition of the complete psychological works of Sigmund Freud* (Vol. 3, pp. 189–221). London: Hogarth Press.

Freud, S. (1899). Screen memories. In J. Strachey (Ed. & Trans.), *The standard edition of the complete psychological works of Sigmund Freud* (Vol. 3, pp. 301–322). London: Hogarth Press.

Freud, S. (1900). The interpretation of dreams. In J. Strachey (Ed. & Trans.), *The standard edition of the complete psychological works of Sigmund Freud* (Vol. 4–5). London: Hogarth Press.

Freud, S. (1905a). Three essays on the theory of sexuality. In J. Strachey (Ed. & Trans.), *The standard edition of the complete psychological works of Sigmund Freud* (Vol. 7, pp. 125–245). London: Hogarth Press.

Freud, S. (1905b). Fragment of an analysis of a case of hysteria. In J. Strachey (Ed. & Trans.), *The standard edition of the complete psychological works of Sigmund Freud* (Vol. 7). London: Hogarth Press.

Freud, S. (1911). Formulations on the two principles of mental functioning. In J. Strachey (Ed. & Trans.), *The standard edition of the complete psychological works of Sigmund Freud* (Vol. 12, pp. 213–216). London: Hogarth Press.

Freud, S. (1914). Remembering, repeating and working-through. In J. Strachey (Ed. & Trans.), *The standard edition of the complete psychological works of Sigmund Freud* (Vol. 12). London: Hogarth Press.

Freud, S. (1915). Instincts and their vicissitudes. In J. Strachey (Ed. & Trans.), *The standard edition of the complete psychological works of Sigmund Freud* (Vol. 14, pp. 111–140). London: Hogarth Press.

Freud, S. (1920). Beyond the pleasure principle. In J. Strachey (Ed. & Trans.), *The standard edition of the complete psychological works of Sigmund Freud* (Vol. 18, pp. 1–64). London: Hogarth Press.

Freud, S. (1923). The ego and the id. In J. Strachey (Ed. & Trans.), *The standard edition of the complete psychological works of Sigmund Freud* (Vol. 19, pp. 3–36). London: Hogarth Press.

Freud, S. (1925). An autobiographical study. In J. Strachey (Ed. & Trans.), *The standard edition of the complete psychological works of Sigmund Freud* (Vol. 20, pp. 3–70). London: Hogarth Press.

Freud, S. (1926). Inhibitions, symptoms and anxiety. In J. Strachey (Ed. & Trans.), *The standard edition of the complete psychological works of Sigmund Freud* (Vol. 20, pp. 77–174). London: Hogarth Press.

Freud, S. (1937). Analysis terminable and interminable. In J. Strachey (Ed. & Trans.), *The standard edition of the complete psychological works of Sigmund Freud* (Vol. 23, pp. 211–253). London: Hogarth Press.

Freud, S., & Breuer, J. (1895). *Studies in hysteria* (N. Luckhurst, Trans.). London: Penguin Books, 2004.

Gabbard, G. O. (1996). *Love and hate in the analytic setting*. Northvale, NJ: Jason Aronson.

Gadamer, H-G. (2007). *The Gadamer reader: A bouquet of the later writings* (R. E. Palmer, Ed. & Trans.). Evanston, IL: Northwestern University Press.

Gallese, V. (2009). Mirror neurons, embodied simulation, and the neural basis of social identification. *Psychoanalytic Dialogues, 19*, 519–536.

Gay, P. (Ed.) (1995). *The Freud reader*. London: Vintage.

George, C., Kaplan, N., & Main, M. (1985). *Adult Attachment Interview* (2nd ed.). Unpublished manuscript, University of California, Berkeley.

Gilligan J. (2000). *Violence: Reflections on our deadliest epidemic*. London: Jessica Kingsley.

Ginot, E. (2007). Intersubjectivity and neuroscience. Understanding enactments and their therapeutic significance within emerging paradigms. *Psychoanalytic Psychology, 24*, 317–332.

Goldwyn, R., & Hugh-Jones, S. (2011). Using the Adult Attachment Interview to understand Reactive Attachment Disorder: Findings from a 10-case adolescent sample. *Attachment & Human Development, 13*(2), 169–191.

Gottman, J. (1981). *Time series analysis*. Cambridge: Cambridge University Press.

Green, V. (2003). Emotional development—biological and clinical approaches—towards an integration. In V. Green (Ed.), *Emotional development in psychoanalysis, attachment theory and neuroscience* (pp. 1–20). London: Brunner-Routledge.

Greenberg, J. R., & Mitchell, S. A. (1988). *Object relations in psychoanalytic theory*. Cambridge, MA: Harvard University Press.

Greenberg, M. T., Speltz, M. L., & DeKlyen, M. (1993). The role of attachment in the early development of disruptive behavior problems. *Development and Psychopathology, 5*, 191–213.

Grice, P. (1975). Logic and conversation. In P. Cole & J. L. Moran (Eds.), *Syntax and semantics, Vol. 3: Speech acts* (pp. 41–58). New York: Academic Press.

Grice, P. (1989). *Studies in the way of words*. Cambridge, MA: Harvard University Press.

Grienenberger, J., Kelly, K., & Slade, A. (2005). Maternal reflective functioning, mother–infant affective communication, and infant attachment: Exploring the link between mental states and observed caregiving behavior in the intergenerational transmission of attachment. *Attachment & Human Development*, 7(3), 299–311.

Grigsby, J., & Hartlaub, G. H. (1994). Procedural learning and the development and stability of character. *Perceptual and Motor Skills*, 79, 355–370.

Grosskurth, P. (1986). *Melanie Klein: Her world and work*. London: Hodder & Stoughton.

Grossman, K. E., & Grossman, K. (1991). Attachment quality as an organizer of emotional and behavioral responses in a longitudinal perspective. In C. M. Parkes, J. Stevenson-Hinde, & P. Marris (Eds.), *Attachment across the life cycle* (pp. 93–114). London: Routledge.

Habermas, J. (1972). *Knowledge and human interests* (J. Shapiro, Trans.). London: Heinemann.

Hamel, J., & Nicholls, T. L. (Eds.) (2006). *Family interventions in domestic violence: A handbook of gender-inclusiveness*. New York: Springer.

Harré, R., & Lamb, R. (Eds.) (1986). *The dictionary of personality and social psychology*. Oxford: Basil Blackwell.

Hasher, L., Goldstein, D., & Toppino, T. (1977). Frequency and the conference of referential validity. *Journal of Verbal Learning and Verbal Behavior*, 16, 107–112.

Hazan, C., & Shaver, P. (1987). Romantic love conceptualized as an attachment process. *Journal of Personality and Social Psychology*, 52(3), 511–524.

Heidegger, M. (1962). *Being and time*. Oxford: Basil Blackwell.

Herman, J. L. (1981). *Father–daughter incest*. Cambridge, MA: Harvard University Press.

Herman, J. L. (1992). *Trauma and recovery*. New York: Basic Books.

Herman, J. L., & van der Kolk, B. A. (1987). Traumatic antecedents of borderline personality disorder. In B. A. van der Kolk (Ed.), *Psychological trauma* (pp. 111–126). Washington, DC: American Psychiatric Press.

Hesse, E. (1999). The Adult Attachment Interview: Historical and current perspectives. In J. Cassidy & P. R. Shaver (Eds.), *Handbook of attachment: Theory, research and clinical applications* (pp. 395–433). New York: Guilford Press.

Hinshelwood, R. D. (1991). *A dictionary of Kleinian thought*. London: Free Association Books.

Hinshelwood, R. D. (1994). *Clinical Klein*. London: Free Association Books.

Hinshelwood, R. D. (1997). The elusive concept of "internal objects" (1934–1943). *International Journal of Psychoanalysis*, 78, 877–897.

Hoare, J., & Povey, D. (2008). *Violent and sexual crime: British Crime Survey 2006/07*. London: Home Office.

Holmes, J. (1993). *John Bowlby and attachment theory*. London: Routledge.

Holmes, J. (1996). *Attachment, intimacy, autonomy*. New York: Jason Aronson.

Holmes, J. (1999a). Ghosts in the consulting room: An attachment perspective on intergenerational transmission. *Attachment & Human Development*, 1(1), 115–131.

Holmes, J. (1999b). Defensive and creative uses of narrative in psychotherapy: An attachment theory perspective. In G. Roberts & J. Holmes (Eds.), *Healing stories: Narrative in psychiatry and psychotherapy* (pp. 49–66). Oxford: Oxford University Press.

Holmes, J. (2010). *Exploring in security: Towards an attachment informed psychoanalytic psychotherapy*. London: Routledge.

Holtzworth-Munroe, A., Stuart, G. L., & Hutchinson, G. (1997). Violent versus non-violent husbands: Differences in attachment patterns, dependency, and jealousy. *Journal of Family Psychology, 11*(3), 314–331.

Home Office Statistical Bulletin. (2006/07). *Homicides, firearm offences and intimate violence 2006/07*. London: Home Office.

Hurry, A. (1998). Psychoanalysis and developmental therapy. In A. Hurry (Ed.), *Psychoanalysis and developmental therapy* (pp. 32–73). London: Karnac Books.

Israels, H., & Schatzman, M. (1993). The seduction theory. *History of Psychiatry, 4*, 23–59.

Jacobs, T. J. (1986). On countertransference enactments. *Journal of the American Psychoanalytical Association, 34*, 289–307.

Jacobs, T. J. (2005). Discussion of forms of intersubjectivity in infant research and adult treatment. In B. Beebe, S. Knoblauch, J. Rustin, & D. Sorter (Eds.), *Forms of intersubjectivity in infant research and adult treatment: A systems view* (pp. 165–189). New York: Other Press.

Jaffe, J., Feldstein, S., Beebe, B., Crown, C. L., Jasnow, M., Fox, H., Anderson, S. W., & Gordon, S. (1991). *Interpersonal training and infant social development: Final report for NIMH* Grant No. MH41675.

Janet, P. (1913). *Psycho-analysis. Report to the Section of Psychiatry, XV11th International Congress of Medicine, London, 1913*. London: Oxford University Press/Hodder & Stoughton.

Johnson, S. M. (2004). *The practice of emotionally focused couple therapy: Creating connection*. New York: Routledge.

Joseph, B. (1994). *Psychic equilibrium and psychic change*. London: Routledge.

Kahr, B. (1996). *D. W. Winnicott: A biographical portrait*. London: Karnac Books.

Kalmuss, D. (1984). The intergenerational transmission of marital aggression. *Journal of Marriage and the Family, 46*, 11–19.

Kantrowitz, J. (1995). Outcome research in psychoanalysis: review and recognitions. In T. Shapiro & R. Emde (Eds.), *Research in psychoanalysis: Process, development, outcome* (pp. 313–328). Madison, CT: International Universities Press.

Kernberg, O. F. (1995). *Love relations: Normality and pathology*. New Haven, CT: Yale University Press.

Khan, M. (1979). *Alienation in perversions*. London: Karnac Books.

Kihlstrom, J. (1995). The trauma-memory argument. *Consciousness and Cognition, 4*, 65–67.

King, P. H. M., & Steiner, R. (1991). *The Freud-Klein controversies 1941–1945*. London: Routledge.

Klein, M. (1933). The early development of conscience in the child. In S. Lorand (Ed.), *Psycho-analysis today* (pp. 149–162). New York: Covici-Friede.

Klein, M. (1940). Mourning and its relation to manic-depressive states. *International Journal of Psychoanalysis, 21*, 125–153.

Klein, M. (1945). The Oedipus complex in the light of early anxieties. In J. Steiner (Ed.), *The Oedipus complex today* (pp. 11–82). London: Karnac Books, 1989.

Knox, J. (1999). The relevance of attachment theory to a contemporary Jungian view of the internal world: Internal working models, implicit memory and internal objects. *Journal of Analytical Psychology, 44*(4), 511–530.

Knox, J. (2001). Memories, fantasies, archetypes: An exploration of some connections between cognitive science and analytical science. *Journal of Analytical Psychology, 46*(4), 613–635.

Knox, J. (2003). *Archetype, attachment, analysis: Jungian psychology and the emergent mind.* London: Routledge.

Kohut, H. (1971). *The analysis of the self: A systematic approach to the psychoanalytic treatment of narcissistic personality disorders.* New York: International Universities Press.

Krystal, H. (1988). *Integration and self healing: Affect, trauma, alexithymia.* Hillsdale, NJ: Analytic Press.

Lacan, J. (1993). *The seminar of Jacques Lacan, book 3: The psychoses 1955–1956* (J. A. Miller, Ed., & J. Forrester, Trans.). New York: Norton.

Laing, R. D. (1961). *The self and others.* London: Tavistock.

Laing, R. D., & Esterson, A. (1964). *Sanity, madness and the family.* London: Penguin.

Langs, R. (1988). *A primer of psychotherapy.* New York: Gardner Press.

Laplanche, J., & Pontalis, J. B. (1988). *The language of psychoanalysis.* London: Karnac Books.

LeDoux, J. E., Romanski, L. M., & Xagoraris, A. E. (1989). Indelibility of subcortical emotional memories. *Journal of Cognitive Neuroscience, 1,* 238–243.

LeDoux, J. (1994). Emotion, memory and the brain. *Scientific American, 270,* 32–39.

LeDoux, J. (1996). *The emotional brain: The mysterious underpinnings of emotional life.* New York: Touchstone.

Lemma, A. (2000). *Humor on the couch.* London: Whurr.

Levy, K. N., Kelly, K. M. Meehan, K. B., Reynoso, J. S., Clarkin, J. F., Lenzenweger, M. F., et al. (2006). Change in attachment and reflective function in the treatment of borderline personality disorder with transference focused psychotherapy. *Journal of Consulting and Clinical Psychology, 74,* 1027–1040.

Lichtenberg, J. D. (2007). A discussion of eight essays that propel attachment and sexual theories into the 21st century. In D. Diamond, S. J. Blatt, & J. D. Lichtenberg (Eds.), *Attachment and sexuality* (pp. 237–261). New York: Analytic Press.

Lichtenberg, J. D. (2008). *Sensuality and sexuality across the divide of shame.* New York: Analytic Press.

Linington, M. (2007). Being disabled: Psychotherapy with a man with cerebral palsy and a learning disability. *Attachment: New Directions in Psychotherapy and Relational Psychoanalysis, 1*(3), 259–268.

Liotti, G. (1992). Disorganized/disoriented attachment in the etiology of the dissociative disorders. *Dissociation, 4,* 196–204.

Liotti, G. (1999). Understanding the dissociative processes: The contribution of attachment theory. *Psychoanalytic Inquiry, 9*(5), 757–783.

Lopez, F. G., & Brennan, K. A. (2000). Dynamic processes underlying adult attachment organization: Toward an attachment perspective on the healthy and effective self. *Journal of Counseling Psychology, 47*(3), 283–300.

Lyons-Ruth, K. (1991). Rapprochement or approchement: Mahler's theory reconsidered from the vantage point of recent research on early attachment relationships. *Psychoanalytic Psychology, 8*, 1–23.

Lyons-Ruth, K., & Block, D. (1996). The disturbed caregiving system: Relations among childhood trauma, maternal caregiving, and infant affect and attachment. *Infant Mental Health Journal, 17*(3), 257–275.

Lyons-Ruth, K., Bronfman, E., & Atwood, G. (1999). A relational diathesis model of hostile-helpless states of mind: Expressions in mother–infant interaction. In J. Solomon & C. George (Eds.), *Attachment disorganization* (pp. 33–70). New York: Guilford Press.

Lyons-Ruth, K., Bruschweiler-Stern, N., Harrison, A. M., Morgan, A. C., Nahum, J. P., Sander, L.W., Stern, D. N., & Tronick, E. Z. (1998). Implicit relational knowing: Its role in development and psychoanalytic treatment. *Infant Mental Health Journal, 19*(3), 282–289.

Lyons-Ruth, K. & Jacobvitz, D. (1999). Attachment disorganization: Unresolved loss, relational violence and lapses in behavioral and attentional strategies. In J. Cassidy & P. R. Shaver (Eds.), *Handbook of attachment: Theory, research and clinical applications* (pp. 520–554). New York: Guilford Press.

Lyons-Ruth, K. & Jacobvitz, D. (2008). Attachment disorganization: Genetic factors, parenting contexts, and developmental transformation from infancy to adulthood. In J. Cassidy & P. R. Shaver (Eds.), *Handbook of attachment: Theory, research and clinical applications* (2nd ed.) (pp. 666–697). New York: Guilford Press.

Lyons-Ruth, K., Yellin, C., Melnick, S., & Atwood, G. (2005). Expanding the concept of unresolved mental states: Hostile/helpless states of mind on the Adult Attachment Interview are associated with disrupted mother–infant communication and infant disorganization. *Development and Psychopathology, 17*, 1–23.

Magdol, L., Moffitt, T. E., Caspi, A., Newman, D. L., Fagan, J., & Silva, P. A. (1997). Gender differences in partner violence in a birth cohort of 21-year-olds: Bridging the gap between clinical and epidemiological approaches. *Journal of Consulting and Clinical Psychology, 65*, 68–78.

Mahler, M. S. (1969). *On human symbiosis and the vicissitudes of individuation: Infantile psychosis, vol. 1.* New York: International Universities Press.

Mahler, M. S., Pine, F., & Bergman, A. (1985). *The psychological birth of the human infant: Symbiosis and individuation.* London: Karnac Books.

Main, M. (1991). Metacognitive knowledge, metacognitive monitoring, and singular (coherent) vs. multiple (incoherent) models of attachment: Findings and directions for future research. In C. M. Parkes, J. Stevenson-Hinde, & P. Marris (Eds.), *Attachment across the life cycle* (pp. 127–159). London: Routledge.

Main, M., & Goldwyn, S. (1995). Interview-based adult attachment classifications: Related to infant-mother and infant-father attachment. *Developmental Psychology, 19*, 227–239.

Main, M., & Hesse, E. (1990). Parents' unresolved traumatic experiences are related to infant disorganized attachment status: Is frightening and/or frightened parental behavior the linking mechanism? In M. Greenberg, D. Cicchetti, & E. M. Cummings (Eds.), *Attachment in the preschool years: Theory, research and intervention* (pp. 161–182). Chicago: University of Chicago Press.

Main, M., Kaplan, N., & Cassidy, J. (1985). Security in infancy, childhood, and adulthood: A move to the level of representation. In I. Bretherton & E. Waters (Eds.), *Growing points in attachment: Theory and research* (pp. 66–104). Chicago: University of Chicago Press.

Main, M., & Weston, D. (1982). Avoidance of the attachment figure in infancy. In C. M. Parkes & J. Stevenson-Hinde (Eds.), *The place of attachment in human behavior* (pp. 31–59). London: Tavistock.

Mancia, M. (1993). *In the gaze of Narcissus: Memory, affects and creativity*. London: Karnac Books.

Mancia, M. (2006). Introduction. In M. Mancia (Ed.), *Psychoanalysis and neuroscience* (pp. 1–32). New York: Springer.

Mancia, M. (2007). *Feeling the words: Neuropsychoanalytic understanding of memory and the unconscious*. London: Routledge.

Mander, G. (2000). *A psychodynamic approach to brief therapy*. London: Sage.

Mann, D. (1997). *Psychotherapy: An erotic relationship*. London: Routledge.

Marks-Tarlow, T. (2011). Merging and emerging: A nonlinear portrait of intersubjectivity during psychotherapy. *Psychoanalytic Dialogues, 21,* 110–127.

Maroda, K. J. (1991). *The power of countertransference: Innovations in analytic technique*. New York: John Wiley & Sons.

Maroda, K. J. (2010). *Psychodynamic techniques: Working with emotion in the therapeutic relationship*. New York: Guilford Press.

Marrone, M. (1998). *Attachment and interaction*. London: Jessica Kingsley.

Mayseless, O., & Scharf, M. (2007). Adolescents' attachment representations and their capacity for intimacy in close relationships. *Journal of Research on Adolescence, 17,* 23–50.

McCarthy, G., & Taylor, A. (1999). Avoidant/ambivalent attachment style as a mediator between abusive childhood experiences and adult relationship difficulties. *Journal of Child Psychology and Psychiatry, 40,* 465–477.

McDougall, J. (1985). *Theatres of the mind: Illusion and truth on the psychoanalytic stage*. London: Free Association Books.

McDougall, J. (1989). *Theatres of the body: A psychoanalytical approach to psychosomatic illness*. London: Free Association Books.

McDougall, J. (1990). *Plea for a measure of abnormality*. London: Free Association Books.

Meloy, J. R. (1992). *Violent attachments*. London: Jason Aronson.

Miga, E. M., Hare, A., Allen, J. P., & Manning, N. (2010). The relation of insecure attachment state of mind and romantic attachment styles to adolescent aggression in romantic relationships. *Attachment & Human Development, 12*(5), 463–481.

Mikulincer, M., Florian, V., Cowan, P. A., & Cowan, C. P. (2002a). Attachment security in couple relationships: A systemic model and its implications for family dynamics. *Family Process, 41*(3), 405–434.

Mikulincer, M., Gallath, O., & Shaver, P. R. (2002b). Activation of the attachment system in adulthood: Threat-related primes increase the accessibility of mental representations of attachment figures. *Journal of Personality and Social Psychology, 83,* 881–895.

Mikulincer, M., & Shaver, P. R. (2007). *Attachment in adulthood: Structure, dynamics, and change*. New York: Guilford Press.

Milgram, S. (1974). *Obedience to authority*. London: Tavistock.

Miller, A. (1991). *Banished knowledge: Facing childhood injuries* (L. Vennewitz, Trans.). London: Virago Press.

Mills, J. (2003). A phenomenology of becoming. In R. Frie (Ed.), *Understanding experience: Psychotherapy and postmodernism* (pp. 116–136). London: Routledge.

Milner, M. (1969). *The hands of the living God: An account of a psycho-analytic treatment*. London: Hogarth Press.

Minuchin, S. (1974). *Families and family therapy*. Cambridge, MA: Harvard University Press.

Mirrlees-Black, C. (1999). *Domestic violence: Findings from a new British Crime Survey self-completion questionnaire*. London: Home Office.

Mitchell, S. A. (1988). *Relational concepts in psychoanalysis: An integration*. Cambridge, MA: Harvard University Press.

Mitchell, S. A. (1993). *Hope and dread in psychoanalysis*. New York: Basic Books.

Mitchell, S. A. (1997). *Influence and autonomy in psychoanalysis*. Hillsdale, NJ: Analytic Press.

Mitchell, S. A. (2000). *Relationality: From attachment to intersubjectivity*. Hillsdale, NJ: Analytic Press.

Modell, A. H. (2008). Implicit or unconscious? Commentary on paper by the Boston Change Process Study Group. *Psychoanalytic Dialogues, 18*, 162–167.

Mohr, J. J. (2008). Same-sex romantic attachment. In J. Cassidy & P. R. Shaver (Eds.), *Handbook of attachment: Theory, research and clinical applications* (2nd ed.) (pp. 482–502). New York: Guilford Press.

Mohr, J. J., & Fassinger, R. E. (2003). Self-acceptance and self-disclosure of sexual orientation in lesbians, gay, and bisexual adults: An attachment perspective. *Journal of Counseling Psychology, 50*, 482–495.

Mollon, P. (1996). *Multiple selves, multiple voices: Working with trauma, violation and dissociation*. Chichester: John Wiley & Sons.

Motz, A. (2001). *The psychology of female violence: Crimes against the body*. London: Routledge.

Natterson, J. (1991). *Beyond countertransference: The therapist's subjectivity in the therapeutic process*. Northvale, NJ: Jason Aronson.

Nemiah, J. C. (1978). Alexithymia and psychosomatic illness. *Journal of Continuing Education in Psychiatry, 39*, 25–37.

NSPCC. (2007). *Key child protection statistics bulletin*. NSPCC Publications.

Ogden, P., Minton, K., & Pain, C. (2006). *Trauma and the body: A sensorimotor approach to psychotherapy*. New York: Norton.

Ogden, T. H. (1986). *The matrix of the mind: Object relations and the psychoanalytic dialogue*. Northvale, NJ: Jason Aronson.

Ogden, T. H. (1994). *Subjects of analysis*. London: Karnac Books.

Ogden, T. H. (2004). The analytic third: Implications for psychoanalytic theory and technique. *Psychoanalytic Quarterly, 73*, 167–195.

Ogden, T. H. (2009). *Rediscovering psychoanalysis: Thinking and dreaming, learning and forgetting*. London: Routledge.

Orange, D. M. (1995). *Emotional understanding: Studies in psychoanalytic epistemology*. New York: Guilford Press.

Orbach, S. (1995). *Countertransference and the false body*. London: Karnac Books.

Orbach, S. (1999). *The impossibility of sex*. Harmondsworth: Allen Lane.

Orbach, S. (2004). The body in clinical practice. In K. White (Ed.), *Touch, attachment and the body* (pp. 17–48). London: Karnac Books.

Pally, R. (2000). *The mind–brain relationship*. London: Karnac Books.

Pally, R. (2005). A neuroscience perspective on forms of intersubjectivity in infant research and adult treatment. In B. Beebe, S. Knoblauch, J. Rustin, & D. Sorter (Eds.), *Forms of intersubjectivity in infant research and adult treatment: A systems view* (pp. 191–241). New York: Other Press.

Panksepp, J. (1999). Emotion as viewed by psychoanalysis and neuroscience: An exercise in consilience. *Neuro-Psychoanalysis, 1*(1), 15–39.

Panksepp, J. (2001). The long-term psychobiological consequences of infant emotions: Prescriptions for the twenty-first century. *Infant Mental Health Journal, 22*, 132–173.

Peck, S. D. (2003). Measuring sensitivity moment-by-moment: A microanalytic look at the transmission of affect. *Attachment & Human Development, 5*(1), 38–63.

Perelberg, R. J. (1999). Psychoanalytic understanding of violence and suicide: A review of the literature and some new findings. In R. J. Perelberg (Ed.), *Psychoanalytic understanding of violence and suicide* (pp. 19–50). London: Routledge.

Perry, B. D., Pollard, R. A., Blakely, T. L., Baker, W. L., & Vigilante, D. (1995). Childhood trauma, the neurobiology of adaptation, and "use-dependent" development of the brain: How "states" become "traits." *Infant Mental Health Journal, 16*, 271–291.

Peterfreund, E. (1983). *The process of psychoanalytic therapy*. Hillsdale, NJ: Analytic Press.

Pincus, L., & Dare, C. (1990). *Secrets in the family*. London: Faber & Faber.

Povey, D. & Allen, J. (2003). Violent crime in England and Wales. In J. Simmons & T. Dodd (Eds.), *Violent crime in England and Wales 2002/2003* (pp. 75–90). London: Home Office.

Quinodoz, J-M. (1993). *The taming of solitude: Separation anxiety in psychoanalysis* (P. Slotkin, Trans.). London: Routledge.

Racker, H. (1991). *Transference and countertransference*. London: Karnac Books.

Ramachandran, V. S. (2011). *The tell-tale brain: Unlocking the mystery of human nature*. London: Heinemann.

Read, J., Goodman, L., Morrison, A. P., Ross, C. A., & Aderhold, V. (2004). Childhood trauma, loss and stress. In J. Read, L. R. Mosher, & R. P. Bentall (Eds.), *Models of madness: Psychological, social and biological approaches to schizophrenia* (pp. 222–252). London: Routledge.

Reis, B. (2009a). Performative and enactive features of psychoanalytic witnessing: The transference as the scene of address. *International Journal of Psychoanalysis, 90*, 1359–1372.

Reis, B. (2009b). We: Commentary on papers by Trevarthan, Ammaniti & Trentini, and Gallese. *Psychoanalytic Dialogues, 19*, 565–579.

Renik, O. (1993). Analytic interaction: Conceptualizing technique in light of the analyst's irreducible subjectivity. *Psychoanalytic Quarterly, 62*, 553–571.

Renn, P. (2003). The link between childhood trauma and later violent offending: The application of attachment theory in a probation setting. In F. Pfäfflin & G. Adshead (Eds.), *A matter of security: The application of attachment theory to forensic psychiatry and psychotherapy* (pp. 109–144). London: Jessica Kingsley.

Renn, P. (2006). Attachment, trauma and violence: Understanding destructiveness from an attachment theory perspective. In C. Harding (Ed.), *Aggression and destructiveness: Psychoanalytic perspectives* (pp. 57–78). London: Routledge.

Renn, P. (2007). Stop thief! But what has been stolen and by whom? Discussion of paper by John Bowlby. *Attachment: New Directions in Psychotherapy and Relational Psychoanalysis, 1*(1), 71–77.

Renn, P. (2008a). Attachment, affect regulation and trauma: The transmission of patterns across generations. In E. Arnold & B. Hawkes (Eds.), *Internalizing the historical past: Issues for separation and moving on* (pp. 24–33). Newcastle: Cambridge Scholars Press.

Renn, P. (2008b). The relational past as lived in the interpersonal present: Using attachment theory to understand early trauma and later troubled relationships. In E. Arnold & B. Hawkes (Eds.), *Internalizing the historical past: Issues for separation and moving on* (pp. 59–69). Newcastle: Cambridge Scholars Press.

Renn, P. (2010). Psychoanalysis, attachment theory and the inner world: How different theories understand the concept of mind and the implications for clinical work. *Attachment: New Directions in Psychotherapy and Relational Psychoanalysis, 4*(2), 146–168.

Ringstrom, P. A. (2008). Improvisation and mutual inductive identification in couples therapy. *Psychoanalytic Dialogues, 18*, 390–402.

Rizzolatti, G., Fogassi, L., & Gallese, V. (2006, November). Mirrors in the mind. *Scientific American*, 54–69.

Roberts, G. (1999). The rehabilitation of rehabilitation: A narrative approach to psychosis. In G. Roberts & J. Holmes (Eds.), *Healing stories: Narrative in psychiatry and psychotherapy* (pp. 152–180). Oxford: Oxford University Press.

Roberts, N., & Noller, P. (1998). The associations between adult attachment and couple violence: The role of communication patterns and relationship satisfaction. In J. Simpson & S. Rholes (Eds.), *Attachment and close relationships* (pp. 331–350). New York: Guilford Press.

Robertson, J., & Robertson, J. (1989). *Separation and the very young*. London: Free Association Books.

Roisman, G. I., Clausell, E., Holland, A., Fortuna, K., & Elieff, C. (2008). Adult romantic relationships as contexts of human development: A multimethod comparison of same-sex couples with opposite-sex dating, engaged, and married dyads. *Developmental Psychology, 44*, 91–101.

Rose, S. (2003). *The making of memory: From molecules to mind*. London: Vintage.

Rose, S. (2005). *The 21st century brain: Explaining, mending and manipulating the mind*. London: Jonathan Cape.

Roth, A., & Fonagy, P. (1996). *What works for whom: Limitations and implications of the research literature*. New York: Guilford Press.

Rutter, M. (1981). *Maternal deprivation reassessed* (2nd ed.). Harmondsworth: Penguin.

Rutter, M. (1997). Clinical implications of attachment concepts: Retrospective and prospective. In L. Atkinson & K. J. Zucker (Eds.), *Attachment psychopathology* (pp. 17–46). New York: Guilford Press.

Sandler, J. (1976). Countertransference and role-responsiveness. *International Review of Psychoanalysis, 3*, 43–47.

Sandler, J., & Sandler, A-M. (1997). A psychoanalytic theory of repression and the unconscious. In J. Sandler & P. Fonagy (Eds.), *Recovered memories of abuse: True or false?* (pp. 163–181). London: Karnac Books.

Sandler, J., & Sandler, A-M. (1998). *Internal objects revisited*. London: Karnac Books.

Sartre, J-P. (1966). *Being and nothingness* (H. Barnes, Trans.). New York: Basic Books.

Schacter, D. L. (1987). Implicit memory: History and current status. *Journal of Experimental Psychology: Learning, Memory, and Cognition, 3*, 501–518.

Schacter, D. L. (1996). *Searching for memory: The brain, the mind, and the past*. New York: Basic Books.

Schore, A. N. (1991). Early superego development: The emergence of shame and narcissistic affect regulation in the practicing period. *Psychoanalysis and Contemporary Thought, 14*, 187–250.

Schore, A. N. (1994). *Affect regulation and the origin of the self: The neurobiology of emotional development*. Hillsdale, NJ: Lawrence Erlbaum Associates.

Schore, A. N. (2001). The effects of early relational trauma on right brain development, affect regulation, and infant mental health. *Infant Mental Health Journal, 22*, 201–269.

Schore, A. N. (2011). The right brain implicit self lies at the core of psychoanalysis. *Psychoanalytic Dialogues, 21*, 75–100.

Schwartz, J. (1999). *Cassandra's daughter: A history of psychoanalysis in Europe and America*. London: Penguin.

Schwartz, J. (2001). Commentary on David Black: Beyond the death drive detour – How can we deepen our understanding of cruelty, malice, hatred, envy and violence? *British Journal of Psychotherapy, 18*(2), 199–204.

Searles, H. F. (1965). Oedipal love in the countertransference. In *Collected papers on schizophrenia and related subjects* (pp. 284–303). Madison, CT: International Universities Press.

Searles, H. F. (1979). The patient as therapist to his analyst. In *Countertransference and related subjects: Selected papers* (pp. 380–459). Madison, CT: International Universities Press.

Segal, H. (1988). *Introduction to the work of Melanie Klein*. London: Karnac Books.

Seligman, S. (2009). Anchoring intersubjective models in recent advances in developmental psychology, cognitive neuroscience and parenting studies: Introduction to papers by Trevarthan, Gallese, and Ammantini & Trentini. *Psychoanalytic Dialogues, 19*, 503–506.

Settlage, C. F., Rosenthal, J., Spielman, P. M., Gassner, S., Afterman, J., Bemesderfer, S., & Kolodny, S. (1990). An exploratory study of mother–child interaction during the second year of life. *Journal of the American Psychoanalytic Association, 38*, 705–731.

Shaver, P. R., & Mikulincer, M. (2004). What do self-report attachment measures assess? In W. S. Rholes & J. A. Simpson (Eds.), *Adult attachment: Theory, research, and clinical implications*. New York: Guilford Press.

Shimmerlik, S. M. (2008). The implicit domain in couples and couple therapy. *Psychoanalytic Dialogues, 18*, 371–389.

Siegal, A., Roeling, T. A. P., Gregg, T. R., & Kruk, M. R. (1999). Neuropharmacology of brain-stimulation-evoked aggression. *Neuroscience and Biobehavioral Reviews, 23*, 359–389.

Siegel, D. J. (2001). Toward an interpersonal neurology of the developing mind: Attachment relationships, "mindsight" and neural integration. *Infant Mental Health Journal, 22*, 67–94.

Sifneos, P. E. (1973). The prevalence of "alexithymic" characteristics in psychosomatic patients. *Psychotherapy and Psychosomatics, 22*, 255–262.

Simpson, J. A. (1990). Influence of attachment styles on romantic relationships. *Journal of Personality and Social Psychology, 59*, 971–980.

Simpson, J. A., Rholes, W. S., & Nelligan, J. S. (1992). Support seeking and support giving within couples in an anxiety-provoking situation: The role of attachment styles. *Journal of Personality and Social Psychology, 62*, 434–446.

Simpson, J. A., Rholes, W. S., & Phillips, D. (1996). Conflict in close relationships: An attachment perspective. *Journal of Personality and Social Psychology, 71*, 899–914.

Slade, A. (1999). Attachment theory and research: Implications for the theory and practice of individual psychotherapy with adults. In J. Cassidy & P. R. Shaver (Eds.), *Handbook of attachment: Theory, research and clinical applications* (pp. 575–594). New York: Guildford Press.

Slade, A. (2004). The move from categories to process: Attachment phenomena and clinical evaluation. *Infant Mental Health Journal, 25*(4), 269–283.

Slade, A. (2008). Working with parents in child psychotherapy: Engaging the reflective function. In F. N. Busch (Ed.), *Mentalization: Theoretical considerations, research findings, and clinical implications* (pp. 207–234). New York: Analytic Press.

Solms, M. (2000). Foreword. In R. Pally, *The mind-brain relationship* (pp. iii–iv). London: Karnac Books.

Solomon, J., & George, C. (1996). Defining the caregiving system: Toward a theory of caregiving. *Infant Mental Health Journal, 17*, 183–197.

Solomon, J., George, C., & De Jong, A. (1995). Children classified as controlling at age six: Evidence of disorganized representational strategies and aggression at home and at school. *Development and Psychopathology, 7*, 447–463.

Spezzano, C. (1993). *Affect in psychoanalysis: A clinical synthesis.* Hillsdale, NJ: Analytic Press.

Spillius, E. B. (Ed). (1988a). *Melanie Klein today, Vol. 1, Mainly theory.* London: Routledge.

Spillius, E. B. (Ed). (1988b). *Melanie Klein today, Vol. 2, Mainly practice.* London: Routledge.

Spitz, R. A. (1959). *A genetic field theory of ego formation: Its implications for pathology.* New York: International Universities Press.

Sroufe, L. A. (1996). *Emotional development: The organization of emotional life in the early years.* New York: Cambridge University Press.

Sroufe, L. A., & Waters, E. (1977). Attachment as an organizational construct. *Child Development, 48*, 1184–1199.

Steele, H., & Steele, M. (2008). On the origins of reflective functioning. In F. N. Busch (Ed.), *Mentalization: Theoretical considerations, research findings, and clinical implications* (pp. 133–158). New York: Analytic Press.

Stein, A. (2007). *Prologue to violence: Child abuse, dissociation, and crime*. Mahwah, NJ: Analytic Press.

Steiner, J. (1989). *The Oedipus complex today*. London: Karnac Books.

Stern, D. B. (1997). *Unformulated experience: From dissociation to imagination in psychoanalysis*. Hillsdale, NJ: Analytic Press.

Stern, D. B. (2010). *Partners in thought: Working with unformulated experience, dissociation, and enactment*. New York: Routledge.

Stern, D. N. (1985). *The interpersonal world of the infant: A view from psychoanalysis and developmental psychology*. New York: Basic Books.

Stern, D. N. (1998). *The motherhood constellation: A unified view of parent–infant psychotherapy*. London: Karnac Books.

Stern, D. N. (2004). *The present moment in psychotherapy and everyday life*. New York: Norton.

Stern, D. N., Sander, L.W., Nahum, J. P., Harrison, A. M., Lyons-Ruth, K., Morgan, A. C., Bruschweiler-Stern, N., & Tronick, E. Z. (1998a). The process of therapeutic change involving implicit knowledge: Some implications of developmental observations for adult psychotherapy. *Infant Mental Health Journal, 19*(3), 300–308.

Stern, D. N., Sander, L. W., Nahum, J. P., Harrison, A. M., Lyons-Ruth, K., Morgan, A. C., Bruschweiler-Stern, N., & Tronick, E. Z. (1998b). Non-interpretive mechanisms in psychoanalytic therapy: The "something more" than interpretation. *International Journal of Psychoanalysis, 79*, 903–921.

Stets, J., & Straus, M. (1990). Gender differences in reporting marital violence and its medical and psychological consequences. In M. Straus & R. Gelles (Eds.), *Physical violence in the American family* (pp. 151–190). New Brunswick, NJ: Transaction.

Stoller, R. J. (1986). *Perversion: The erotic form of hatred*. London: Karnac Books.

Stolorow, R. D., Brandschaft, B. & Atwood, G. E. (1995). *Psychoanalytic treatment: An intersubjective approach*. Hillsdale, NJ: Analytic Press.

Straus, M. A., & Gelles R. J. (1986). Societal change in family violence from 1975 to 1985 as revealed by two national surveys. *Journal of Marriage and the Family, 48*, 465–479.

Stubrin, J. P. (1994). *Sexualities and homosexualities* (E. Reneboldi, Trans.). London: Karnac Books.

Symington, N. (1996). Mental pain and moral courage. In *The making of a psychotherapist* (pp. 50–60). London: Karnac Books.

Tähkä, V. (1993). *Mind and its treatment*. Madison, CT: International Universities Press.

Target, M. (2008). Commentary. In F. N. Busch (Ed.), *Mentalization: Theoretical considerations, research findings, and clinical implications* (pp. 261–280). New York: Analytic Press.

Teicholz, J. G. (2009). A strange convergence: Postmodern theory, infant research, and psychoanalysis. In R. Frie & D. Orange (Eds.), *Beyond postmodernism: New dimensions in clinical theory and practice* (pp. 69–91). London: Routledge.

Terr, L. C. (1981). Psychic trauma in children: Observations following the Chowchilla school-bus kidnapping. *American Journal of Psychiatry, 138*, 14–19.

Thelen, E., & Smith, L. B. (1994). *A dynamic systems approach to the development of cognition and action.* Cambridge, MA: MIT Press.

Trevarthan, C. (1979). Communication and cooperation in early infancy. In M. Bullowa (Ed.), *Before speech* (pp. 321–347). New York: Cambridge University Press.

Trevarthen, C. (2001). Intrinsic motives for companionship in understanding: Their origin, development, and significance for infant mental health. *Infant Mental Health Journal, 22*, 95–131.

Trevarthan, C. (2009). The intersubjective psychobiology of human meaning: Learning of culture depends on interest for cooperative practical work and affect for the joyful art of good company. *Psychoanalytic Dialogues, 19*, 507–518.

Trevarthan, C., & Hubley, P. (1978). Secondary intersubjectivity: Confidence, confiders and acts of meaning in the first year. In A. Lock (Ed.), *Action, gesture and symbol* (pp. 183–229). New York: Academic Press.

Tronick, E., Als, H., Adams, L., Wise, S., & Brazelton, T. B. (1978). The infant's response to entrapment between contradictory messages in face-to-face interaction. *Journal of American Child Psychiatry, 17*, 1–13.

Tulving, E. (1983). *Episodic and semantic memory.* Oxford: Clarendon Press.

Turnbull, O. & Solms, M. (2003). Memory, amnesia and intuition: A neuro-psychoanalytic perspective. In V. Green (Ed.), *Emotional development in psychoanalysis, attachment theory and neuroscience: Creating connections* (pp. 55–85). London: Routledge.

Tyson, P. (2002). The challenges of psychoanalytic developmental theory. *Journal of the American Psychoanalytic Association, 50*(1), 19–52.

Tyson, P., & Tyson, R. L. (1990). *Psychoanalytic theories of development: An integration.* New Haven, CT: Yale University Press.

van der Kolk, B. A. (1989). The compulsion to repeat the trauma. *Psychiatric Clinics of North America, 12*(2), 389–411.

van der Kolk, B. A. (1994). The body keeps the score: Memory and the evolving psychobiology of post-traumatic stress. *Harvard Review of Psychiatry, 1*, 253–265.

van der Kolk, B. A., & Fisler, R. (1995). Dissociation and the fragmentary nature of traumatic memories: Overview and exploratory study. *Journal of Traumatic Stress, 8*(4), 505–521.

van der Kolk B. A., & van der Hart, O. (1989). Pierre Janet and the breakdown of adaptation in psychological trauma. *American Journal of Psychiatry, 146*, 1530–1540.

van Ijzendoorn, M. (1995). Adult attachment representations, parental responsiveness, and infant attachment: A meta-analysis on the predictive validity of the Adult Attachment Interview. *Psychological Bulletin, 117*(3), 387–403.

Wachtel, P. L. (2008). *Relational theory and the practice of psychotherapy.* New York: Guilford Press.

Wallin, D. J. (2007). *Attachment in psychotherapy.* New York: Guilford Press.

Webster, R. (1995). *Why Freud was wrong: Sin, science and psychoanalysis.* New York: Basic Books.

Weiss, J., Lamberti, J., & Blackman, N. (1960). The sudden murderer: A comparative analysis. *Archives of General Psychiatry, 2*, 669–678.

Wekerle, C., & Wolfe, D. (1999). Dating violence in mid-adolescence: Theory, significance, and emerging prevention initiatives. *Clinical Psychological Review, 19*, 435–456.

Welldon, E. V. (1988). *Mother, Madonna, whore: The idealization and denigration of motherhood*. London: Free Association Books.

West, M., & George, C. (1999). Abuse and violence in intimate adult relationships: New perspectives from attachment theory. *Journal of Attachment and Human Development, 1*(2), 137–156.

Westen, D., & Gabbard, O. G. (2002). Cognitive neuroscience, conflict and compromise. *Journal of the American Psychoanalytic Association, 50*(1), 53–98.

Wilkinson, M. (2010). *Changing minds in therapy: Emotion, attachment, trauma and neurobiology*. London: Norton.

Winnicott, D. W. (1949). Hate in the countertransference. *International Journal of Psychoanalysis, 30*, 69–74.

Winnicott, D. W. (1958). The capacity to be alone. *International Journal of Psychoanalysis, 39*, 416–420.

Winnicott, D. W. (1960). Ego distortion in terms of true and false self. In *Maturational processes and the facilitating environment: Studies in the theory of emotional development* (pp. 140–152). London: The Hogarth Press.

Winnicott, D. W. (1967). Mirror-role of the mother and family in child development. In P. Lomas (Ed.), *The predicament of the family: A psycho-analytical symposium* (pp. 26–33). London: Hogarth Press.

Winnicott, D. W. (1969). The use of an object. *International Journal of Psychoanalysis, 50*, 711–716.

Winnicott, D. W. (1974). Fear of breakdown. *International Journal of Psychoanalysis, 1*, 103–107.

Winnicott, D. W. (1987). *The spontaneous gesture: Selected letters of D. W. Winnicott* (F. R. Rodman, Ed.). Cambridge, MA: Harvard University Press.

Winnicott, D. W. (1988). *Playing and reality*. London: Penguin.

Index